TO LIVE AN ANTISLAVERY LIFE

RACE IN THE ATLANTIC WORLD, 1700–1900

Published in Cooperation with the Library Company of Philadelphia's Program in African American History

---

SERIES EDITORS

Richard S. Newman
Rochester Institute of Technology

Manisha Sinha
University of Massachusetts, Amherst

Patrick Rael
Bowdoin College

ADVISORY BOARD

Edward Baptist
Cornell University

Leslie Harris
Emory University

Christopher Brown
Columbia University

Joanne Pope Melish
University of Kentucky

Vincent Carretta
University of Maryland

Sue Peabody
Washington State University, Vancouver

Laurent Dubois
Duke University

Erik Seeman
State University of New York, Buffalo

Erica Armstrong Dunbar
University of Delaware and the Library Company of Philadelphia

John Stauffer
Harvard University

Douglas Egerton
LeMoyne College

TO LIVE AN ANTISLAVERY LIFE

Personal Politics and the Antebellum Black Middle Class

ERICA L. BALL

The University of Georgia Press
Athens and London

A Sarah Mills Hodge Fund Publication
This publication is made possible, in part, through a grant from the
Hodge Foundation in memory of its founder, Sarah Mills Hodge, who devoted her life to
the relief and education of African Americans in Savannah, Georgia.

An earlier version of chapter 2 was published as "To Train Them for the Work:
Manhood, Morality, and Free Black Conduct Discourse in Antebellum New York," in
Fathers, Preachers, Rebels, Men: Black Masculinity in U.S. History and Literature, 1820–1945,
ed. Timothy R. Buckner and Peter Caster (Columbus: Ohio State University Press, 2011).

© 2012 by the University of Georgia Press
Athens, Georgia 30602
www.ugapress.org
All rights reserved
Set in Minion Pro by Graphic Composition, Inc.

Printed digitally in the United States of America

Library of Congress Cataloging-in-Publication Data
Ball, Erica.
To live an antislavery life : personal politics and the antebellum Black middle class / Erica L. Ball.
   p. cm. — (Race in the Atlantic world, 1700–1900)
Includes bibliographical references and index.
ISBN-13: 978-0-8203-2976-5 (hardcover : alk. paper)
ISBN-10: 0-8203-2976-2 (hardcover : alk. paper)
ISBN-13: 978-0-8203-4350-1 (pbk. : alk. paper)
ISBN-10: 0-8203-4350-1 (pbk. : alk. paper)
1. Free African Americans—History—19th century.
2. Free African Americans—Social conditions—19th century.
3. Free African Americans—Attitudes—History—19th century.
4. Citizenship—United States—History—19th century.
5. Antislavery movements—United States—History—19th century.
6. United States—Race relations—History—19th century.
I. Title.
E185.18.B35 2012
323.1196'073—dc23   2012006351

British Library Cataloging-in-Publication Data available

Cover image: William Matthew Prior, American, 1806–1873. *Three Sisters of the Copeland Family*,
1854. Oil on canvas. 68.26 × 92.71 cm (26⅞ × 36½ in.). Museum of Fine Arts, Boston. Bequest of
Martha C. Karolik for the M. and M. Karolik Collection of American Paintings, 1815–1865, 48.467.
Photograph © 2012 Museum of Fine Arts, Boston.

For my Grandparents,
Benjamin Sealy Sr. and Rita Speed Sealy
and
Eugene Ball Sr. and Nadine Smith Ball

They had for more than a century before been regarded as beings of an inferior order and altogether unfit to associate with the white race, either in social or political relations; and so far inferior that they had no rights which the white man was bound to respect; and that the Negro might justly and lawfully be reduced to slavery for his benefit.

—Justice Roger Taney, Majority Opinion, *Dred Scott v. Sanford* (1857)

God helping me wherever I shall be, at home, abroad, on land or sea, in public or private walks, as a man, a Christian, especially as a *black man*, my labours must be anti-slavery labours, because mine must be an anti-slavery life.

—Samuel Ringgold Ward, *Autobiography of a Fugitive Negro* (1855)

CONTENTS

Acknowledgments *xiii*

Introduction 1

CHAPTER ONE
African American Advice Literature and Black Middle-Class Self-Fashioning 10

CHAPTER TWO
Slave Narratives and the Black Self-Made Man 37

CHAPTER THREE
Antislavery Discourse and the African American Family 62

CHAPTER FOUR
Domestic Literature and the Antislavery Household 81

CHAPTER FIVE
Transnationalism, Revolution, and the *Anglo-African Magazine* on the Eve of the Civil War 109

EPILOGUE 132

Notes 137

Index 171

ACKNOWLEDGMENTS

I have had the good fortune to receive assistance from a number of institutions and individuals over the many years that I have worked on this project. Although it is impossible to fully convey just how much their support has meant to me, I am thrilled to have this opportunity to finally thank them properly.

At the Graduate Center of the City University of New York, I received the best possible introduction to academic culture. Carol Berkin, Ann Fabian, Kathleen McCarthy, David Nasaw, and my wonderful advisor, Colin Palmer, all offered thoughtful and constructive advice on the dissertation, helped me to secure generous fellowships, including a Minority Access/Graduate Networking President's Dissertation Year Fellowship, and served as model mentors as I progressed through the various phases of graduate study. Members of my CUNY cohort, meanwhile, made the process a genuine pleasure. Collegial, generous, filled with boundless intellectual zeal and good humor, and always ready for late-night bowling and karaoke, Megan Elias, Kathleen Feeley, Terence Kissack, Cindy Lobel, Delia Mellis, and Peter Vellon all read portions of this manuscript in its various forms, invariably offering unselfish advice and candid criticism.

During my time as a faculty member in the history department at Union College I had the privilege of enjoying the fellowship and camaraderie of some terrific colleagues. I am especially grateful for the friendship and encouragement of Ed Pavlic and Stacey Barnum, Charles Batson, Deidre Hill Butler, Lorraine Morales Cox, John Cramsie, Andy Feffer, Richard Fox, Melinda Lawson, Joyce Madancy, Teresa Meade, and Andy Morris.

Librarians and staff at the New York Public Library's Schomburg Center for Research in Black Culture, the Schaffer Library, and the Pollak Library assisted with the research for this project, going out of their way to oblige my numerous ILL requests and to track down documents. California State University, Fullerton, facilitated the completion of this project by providing me with several H&SS Faculty Summer Research and Writing Grants, a Junior Faculty Summer Stipend, and a Faculty Development Center Track Grant. CSUF American Studies Department administrators Carole Angus and Karla Arellano made book orders and travel a breeze.

The editors at the University of Georgia press have been fantastic. Project editor John Joerschke and copyeditor Ellen D. Goldlust-Gingrich have been a pleasure to work with. They whipped the book into shape and saved me from making some embarrassing errors. Acquisitions editor Derek Krissoff, in particular, remained enthusiastic about the project over the years and exhibited extraordinary patience as I slowly moved toward the finish line. I am also grateful to the two anonymous readers who reviewed the book in manuscript form, offering detailed notes and suggestions on how to tighten and pull together the threads of the narrative. Their input has improved the book immeasurably.

The book also benefitted greatly from the thoughtful questions I received from chairs, commentators, and audience members at several academic conferences. I would especially like to thank Elsa Barkley Brown, John Bezís-Selfa, Darlene Clark Hine, Graham Hodges, Kate Masur, W. Caleb McDaniel, Richard Newman, Manisha Sinha, James Brewer Stewart, and Julie Winch. Although they did not all necessarily agree with my interpretations, their insightful observations helped me to refine my ideas and sharpen my arguments and take into account possibilities I otherwise might not have considered.

It is impossible to say what a delight it is to be a part of the extraordinary Cal State Fullerton community, where I now make my home. I am daily inspired by our students and filled with admiration for our faculty: men and women who approach scholarship and teaching with extraordinary passion and enthusiasm, even in the face of staggering budget cuts and uncertainty about what the future holds for public education. My colleagues in the CSUF American Studies Department—Allan Axelrad, Jesse Battan, Adam Golub, Wayne Hobson, John Ibson, Carrie Lane, Elaine Lewinnek, Karen Lystra, Mike Steiner, Terri Snyder, and Pam Steinle—have created an environment that feels more like a family than a place of employment. I continue to be amazed that I have had the good fortune to find myself in such an intellectually vibrant and warm community. I would especially like to thank Leila "Scissors" Zenderland and my colleagues Stephen J. Mexal and Benjamin Cawthra for helping me to get "unstuck" at critical moments in the writing process.

Finally, I owe a number of debts that can never be repaid. Claire Potter, my undergraduate advisor at Wesleyan University, served as my very first model for the academic life and encouraged me to pursue graduate study. My dissertation advisor, Colin Palmer, gave me the best advice: no matter how people respond to your work, always "own" your ideas. My parents, Eugene and Carolyn Ball, taught me to love history, music, and literature and to value education. They also, along with my sister Stephanie, maintained their good humor despite having to answer countless questions from friends curious about the status of "Erica's book." Ultimately, however, I owe the greatest debt to Brian Michael Norton. He has read nearly every version of this project—from drafts of the dissertation proposal to the final proofs—over the past decade. He is, and always will be, my best everything: friend, editor, collaborator, critic, partner-in-crime. Together with our dog Abby, every day feels like a joyous adventure, and I can't wait to see where we go next.

My grandparents, to whom this book is dedicated, would be surprised, I suspect, to learn that their granddaughter had written a book about many of their most cherished ideals. Although they are not here to see the final product, I hope that they would be pleased with the result.

Introduction

By the 1830s and 1840s, a small but noticeable number of free African Americans living in the North had received the education and training necessary to take up positions as teachers, ministers, and newspaper editors; a few had even achieved some measure of financial success as entrepreneurs and small-business owners.[1] Aware of their anomalous and precarious status as free blacks in a slaveholding republic, they created a print culture to promote a spirit of racial consciousness, to provide their communities with information on the news of the day, and to offer African American readers advice on a range of personal and domestic concerns.[2]

Because much of this discourse centered on middle-class personal and domestic conduct and consisted of calls for education, morality, temperance, and economy, historians have generally characterized these efforts as evidence of "racial uplift ideology," the discursive part of a larger campaign to redirect a phenomenon historian Patrick Rael defines as "racial synecdoche": the white American tendency to highlight the "misdeeds of the few" African Americans who "were thought to have affronted public morality" and then to characterize those behaviors as innate racial traits and thus justification for continued antiblack discrimination and enslavement.[3] Scholars argue that elite African Americans hoped that this process of racial synecdoche could be redirected and that a class of "elevated"—in other words, frugal, virtuous, well-educated, and well-mannered—African Americans could engage in an antebellum version of the "politics of respectability" and serve as examples proving the worth of the entire black population, undercutting the racism of the day, and bolstering the campaign for the abolition of slavery and the acquisition of citizenship rights.[4] As scholars have also shown, the desire for "elevation" and "respectability" remained bound up in the development of northern black institutional life, political consciousness, and antislavery ideology and activism.[5]

This scholarship has done much to reveal the centrality of discourses of respectability to antebellum black protest thought and activism but has not fully explored such discourses' impact on the ethos and culture of the emerging black middle class.[6] Building on the work of scholars who see class formation as a cultural as well as economic process, this book focuses on the literature directed toward elite and "aspiring" northern African American readers in the three decades preceding the Civil War.[7] Across a variety of genres—including convention proceedings, letters, personal narratives, didactic essays, humorous stories, and sentimental vignettes—a generation of northern black writers, activists, and intellectuals crafted a set of black middle-class ideals, simultaneously respectable and subversive, that fused advice on personal and domestic conduct with antislavery and transnational revolutionary themes. Repeatedly insisting that northern free blacks internalize their political principles and interpret all their personal ambitions, private familial roles, and domestic responsibilities in light of the freedom struggle, African Americans such as Susan Paul, Frederick Douglass, and Martin Delany offered virtuous political models and exemplary figures for elite and aspiring northern black readers to emulate. This rhetoric amounted to far more than endorsements of the "politics of respectability." Rather, African American writers urged elite and aspiring African Americans to engage in a deeply personal politics by fashioning themselves into ideal husbands and wives, mothers and fathers, self-made men and transnational freedom fighters and by committing themselves to living what former slave turned Congregationalist minister Samuel Ringgold Ward would call "an anti-slavery life."[8] In the process, they began crafting a form of personal politics especially for elite and aspiring African American readers that ultimately defined the worldview of the emerging black middle class.[9]

The first chapter of *To Live an Antislavery Life* begins by exploring the various arguments that linked key forms of middle-class self-fashioning with the charge to live an antislavery life. By analyzing black conduct discourse—advice specifically directed to the courting sons and daughters and the young husbands and wives of the emerging northern black middle class—we will see that black conduct writers framed popular middle-class arguments about self-improvement as integral to a larger process of personal transformation. For these men and women, the personal conduct and behavior associated with middle-class forms of respectability constituted far more than a narrow political strategy or a public political performance. Rather, the processes of self-fashioning associated with respectability were deemed crucial to the personal transformations required to become independent, virtuous, ideal men and women and therefore embodiments of antislavery sensibilities.

Keeping in mind recent literary analysis that pairs readings of slave narratives with other generic forms, *To Live an Antislavery Life* also places African American conduct literature in conversation with black-authored antislavery texts.[10] Chapter 2 finds that in both classic slave narratives and advice literature, African American writers characterized self-improvement, self-advancement, and the independence increasingly associated with a discrete set of middle-class occupations as a duty—a racial imperative for young African American men. Slave narratives by men such as Ward, James W. C. Pennington, and Frederick Douglass provided personal examples of the positive rewards of temperance, education, and morality and narrativized a path of upward mobility and antislavery commitment for aspiring African American readers. In other words, slave narratives worked hand in hand with black conduct discourse to create a model of ideal black manhood for young, aspiring free black men. By placing slave narratives in dialogue with African American advice literature, we can see the various ways that the central themes of antislavery and self-improvement worked in concert, linking the personal with the political.

The third chapter continues to analyze slave narratives, building on the work of scholars who have argued that classic slave narratives have much to say about African American families.[11] The narratives of Henry Bibb, Harriet Jacobs, and others, when read alongside African American personal conduct and domestic discourse, reflected many of the anxieties felt by aspiring African Americans living in the North. In particular, I explore the many ways that slave narratives sharpened specific concerns about slavery's impact on black male independence and female virtue while reminding northern black readers of the literal and figurative family bonds they shared with southern slaves. These texts dramatized precisely why it was so important for aspiring black readers to live antislavery lives, making the works a vital backdrop for reading northern black domestic discourse.

The fourth chapter turns to this domestic discourse, arguing that it infused middle-class ideals about home and marriage with extraordinary political significance, placing the free black family on the front lines of the antislavery campaign.[12] African American writers such as Sarah Mapps Douglass and Martin Delany celebrated a distinct vision of domestic life for free African Americans and argued that African American families and domestic relations, when properly organized, played an essential role in the freedom struggle. Believing that the family would serve as the cells or building blocks of the race—that is, the primary training ground for the virtue and morality necessary to maintain black men's independence—black conduct writers characterized the free black husband-wife relationship as a bond essential for shoring up male political capacity, the family itself as the engine for the expansion of black antislavery and race consciousness, and the female-centered domestic sphere as a bulwark against the racism of the outside world and as the space to nurture appreciation for the personal politics involved in living an antislavery life. Consequently, throughout the antebellum era, contributors to black print culture urged African American wives and husbands, mothers and fathers, to make their homes personal sites of resistance to slavery, appropriately to execute their familial duties as spouses and parents, and to attend to the health of the domestic sphere.

The final chapter returns to the theme of individual conduct, assessing how Ward's charge that free blacks should fully embody resistance to slavery and become living refutations of proslavery arguments ultimately offered the possibility for aspiring and elite African Americans to imagine themselves living radical, revolutionary antislavery lives. I analyze how northern black contributors to the *Anglo-African Magazine*—"arguably one of the most important African American publications before the Civil War"—reframed history and contemporary politics, fiction, and theology to articulate a more radical vision of antislavery living and put forward a model revolutionary identity for emulation on the eve of the Civil War.[13] By calling for a personal investment in the battle to vanquish the peculiar institution, African American writers characterized those men and women who fought and died for freedom as exemplary antislavery figures, models of virtue and sacrifice for northern free blacks. And in addition to praising the activities of revolutionaries in locations throughout the African diaspora, including Toussaint-Louverture, Jean-Jacques Dessalines, and Joseph Cinque, African American writers and activists often likened these black founding fathers to contemporary European nationalists such as Italian Giuseppe Mazzini and Hungarian Louis Kossuth. In the process, these authors helped to create a transnational discourse of revolution that drew on gender-specific republican notions of virtue and sacrifice.[14] The fiction and history published in the *Anglo-African Magazine* ultimately offered these militant models to elite and aspiring African American readers, characterizing them as figures to be embraced in the days immediately preceding disunion and the Civil War.

By examining the various ways northern black writers defined "an antislavery life" for elite and aspiring black readers, *To Live an Antislavery Life* ultimately challenges three long-standing assumptions about the personal politics of the antebellum black middle class. First, scholars generally limit discussions of black middle-class personal politics to the politics of respectability and, given its embrace of bourgeois culture and its seeming elevation of individual behavior over collective activism, generally place discourses of respectability on the conservative end of a spectrum of black political ideology. When measured against the exponential growth of racism in the antebellum era, elite and middle-class African American faith in the persuasive power of a bourgeois form of personal politics appears at best to be a failure of imagination, an inability to comprehend the depths of white American racism, and an unwillingness to chart a more radical course of political action. In fact, scholars argue that once prominent free blacks understood the intransigence of white racism, they abandoned the politics of respectability in favor of more radical, aggressive forms of abolitionist activism, independent institutions, black nationalist ideology, and ultimately emigration efforts.[15]

The tendency to insist on dichotomies such as respectability versus activism or elevation versus black nationalism may stem from the practice of characterizing the supporters of the American Moral Reform Society (AMRS) as the typical advocates of African American respectability. The leaders of the AMRS, which was organized at the end of the National Convention of 1835 and remained active until 1841, believed that attention to the moral reform of whites and blacks would inevitably lead to the eradication of all vices, including those of slavery and racism. The most vocal African American proponents of this moral reform approach were elite black Philadelphians such as William Whipper and Robert Purvis, who opposed race-specific organizations on the principle that all forms of racial segregation, whether forced or voluntary, were sinful; supporters of this view insisted that by working with white reformers to facilitate the moral improvement of the masses of African Americans, northern free blacks would ultimately defeat slavery and gain their rightful civil and political rights. With the AMRS's agenda in mind, scholars, already inclined to view black separatism as more radical than interracial abolitionist activism, characterize all reform and uplift efforts as the conservative precursor to more substantive forms of radical political engagement.

However, even the most ardent champions of reform conceptualized the personal politics of respectability as but one weapon in a much larger antislavery arsenal. Black New Yorkers, for example, continued to offer advice on respectability even as they pushed for separate African American conventions over the objections of some prominent black Philadelphians.[16] And even among AMRS members such as Whipper and Purvis, commitment to moral reform never superseded their devotion to antislavery activism. In fact, these men remained active in radical abolitionist organizations throughout their lives. Moreover, even though the majority of African American activists increasingly endorsed self-defense, nationalist enterprises, emigration, and violent efforts to overthrow slavery by the eve of the Civil War, they also continued to praise and offer advice on the path to respectability. Like their late-nineteenth- and early-twentieth-century counterparts, a range of men and women including Martin Delany, "the father of black nationalism"; Mary Ann Shadd Cary, the fiery Canadian émigré and newspaper publisher; and fugitive abolitionist Frederick Douglass continued to endorse the principles of respectability through the 1850s and beyond even while they championed forms of black nationalism.[17] Consequently, *To Live an Antislavery Life* shifts the discussion away from charting the path from the politics of respectability to the rise of black nationalism, instead considering additional ways elite and aspiring free blacks conceptualized their personal politics, framing them as an essential part of their collective middle-class identity.[18]

Second, in addition to characterizing respectability as a conservative and misguided form of personal politics, scholars have assumed that the advice on middle-class respectability appearing in antebellum black print culture was directed primarily downward—that is, issued by a small population of prominent African American writers, editors, and activists and intended for the poor and working-class African Americans who made up the bulk of free black communities. And with this idea in mind, admonishments about self-improvement and respectable conduct appear to be remarkably ineffective methods of social control. As historians Graham Russell Hodges and Shane White and Graham White have shown, the masses of free African American men and women often claimed their freedom by participating in the raucous street culture of the urban North, by challenging former slaveholders on a physical level, by drinking alcohol, by attending the theater, by wearing vibrant clothing, and by dancing and parading in the streets—forms of behavior that black conduct writers regularly discouraged.[19] Moreover, scholars also see this didactic discourse—particularly its critique of popular leisure activities and cultural practices—as complicit in the development of northeastern racial ideologies.[20] By accepting and promoting the idea that African Americans needed to be "elevated" and made respectable, scholars suggest that elite free blacks merely strengthened white arguments about black inferiority and thus undercut precisely the arguments for freedom they hoped to embody. Examples of respectable African Americans, in other words, simply became the exceptions proving the rule.

But elite and aspiring African Americans were hardly as naive as scholars often assume, and African American discourses of respectability were not solely directed downward at those lower on the socioeconomic ladder. Studies of the emergence of the middle class in the early nineteenth century have found that those who sought to "assume a new and better social identity" or at the very least who were anxious about maintaining their character and reputation were most likely to pore over the vast array of conduct manuals published in the 1830s and 1840s.[21] Similarly, in her study of late-nineteenth- and early-twentieth-century African American reformers, Michele Mitchell has suggested that advice literature appealed to African Americans who were already eager to master the rules of proper behavior and was "therefore most likely consumed by aspiring women and men."[22] Much like the mainstream conduct discourse meant for white middle-class readers in the early nineteenth century and the prescriptive literature consumed by aspiring African Americans in the decades after Reconstruction, antebellum black personal and domestic advice literature was largely oriented toward members of what can loosely be called the black middle classes—aspiring men and women looking for more ways to ensure that their behavior matched their sense of themselves as virtuous and respectable.

Finally, scholars consistently assume that antebellum black ministers, writers, and convention delegates urged African Americans to exhibit respectable, middle-class forms of behavior primarily as a public strategy, focusing entirely on its potential positive impact on white audiences. In this view, African Americans sought to become respectable to demonstrate or prove their fitness for citizenship to whites. But the sources suggest that elite and aspiring African Americans appeared to value respectability for a host of reasons that had little to do with the white gaze. Indeed, what we know about the private lives of aspiring and elite African Americans in the North suggests that they, like their elite and middle-class white counterparts, sought to act in a respectable manner in private as well as in public. Erica Armstrong Dunbar's recent analysis of the genteel and sentimental friendship albums shared by middle-class and elite black Philadelphians suggests that respectability remained a central concern of elite and aspiring free blacks, even in the company of friends.[23] And so does Joseph Willson's 1841 *Sketches of the Higher Classes of Colored Society in Philadelphia*, a description of the social mores of antebellum Philadelphia's community of aspiring and wealthy free blacks. According to Willson, a member of the city's black elite, "the better" classes of black Philadelphians remained respectable in private, domestic, and intraracial spaces in addition to public interracial ones. Dinner parties, for example, were not extravagant or decadent affairs but were tasteful and modest, ending at an early hour so that attendees could rise early the next morning and start about their business. The guests were as respectable and virtuous as the hosts, exhibiting the manners and conversational skills appropriate for such settings. According to Willson, "In this way," elite black Philadelphians "collect[ed] a very agreeable company, all perhaps on terms of perfect agreement and intimacy."[24] Of course, Willson wrote this book because whites never saw the private manifestations of African American respectability: according to Willson, "The ease and grace of the manner with which [African Americans] are capable of bearing themselves in company—their strict observance of all the nicer etiquettes, proprieties and observances that are characteristic of the well-bred . . . speak loudly against the injustice that is done them."[25] But the approval of the white reader did not legitimize the respectable behavior of Philadelphia's black elite in their own eyes: as far as they were concerned, they were already legitimate.

Elite and aspiring African Americans never framed their personal politics in limited terms. As Ward's comments suggest, these free blacks understood their personal politics, including their respectable personal conduct, as much deeper than an act to be performed before the gaze of white observers. Rather, respectability is better understood as something valued for itself, irrespective of the presence or absence of whites, and as continuing to shape the conduct of elite and aspiring African Americans in spite of a hostile white public. Consequently, respectability is best understood as a value at the heart of the culture of the emerging black middle class: essential to the self-conception and personal identity of its members, their idealization of family life, their belief in the importance of gender-specific notions of virtue and independence, and ultimately their determination to live and die in a way that was utterly antithetical to the life deemed appropriate for them by slavery's supporters. Indeed, as Ward put it, respectability lay at the core of his being, indistinguishable from his antislavery politics and his identity as "a man," a "Christian," and a "*black* man."[26] Living in such a way required more than deploying the politics of respectability in public, interracial settings. It required a willingness to embody one's total commitment to the freedom struggle at all times, to conceptualize oneself as a freedom fighter, and to fully integrate one's radical antislavery principles with the many other facets of one's identity—from one's gender, class status, and occupation to one's familial role as a mother or father, wife or husband.

Finally, it is important to point out that elite and aspiring African Americans did not necessarily speak for the majority of free African Americans living in the North before the Civil War, but they are not automatically, therefore, unworthy subjects of study. Given the frequency with which African American leaders would call for racial uplift at the turn of the twentieth century and the long-standing relationships among gendered notions of respectability, antiracist activism, and black middle-class identity, it is important to understand both the origins of these concepts and the ways they have changed over time. In other words, if we are to fully understand the dynamics of black middle-class formation and political consciousness, we must explore the print culture of the black middle class at its inception—the early nineteenth century. By examining this concept of antislavery living, we see how completely this first generation of elite and aspiring African Americans were willing to put their bodies in the service of the freedom struggle and to interpret their personal successes and failures, their homes and families, their identity and collective sense of history in that context. In so doing, they would inaugurate a form of personal politics that would continue to shape the political consciousness and cultural identity of the black middle class well into the twentieth century.

CHAPTER ONE

African American Advice Literature and Black Middle-Class Self-Fashioning

> But why should I repine; are we not to sacrifice rather than indulge self? Born as we are to the stern *performance* of *duty* rather than the *pursuit of happiness*.
> —Charlotte Forten (1855)

In the decades after the American Revolution and the founding of the new nation, northern states began abolishing the practice of racial slavery. Beginning with the state of Vermont, which outlawed slavery in its 1777 constitution; Pennsylvania, which enacted gradual emancipation legislation in 1780; and Massachusetts, whose supreme court ruled in 1783 that slavery violated the state constitution, the institution slowly disappeared from the North, becoming instead a sectional phenomenon exclusive to the states of the Upper and Deep South.[1]

In the midst of this transition, free northern African Americans set about creating a vibrant set of community institutions—establishing churches and schools; founding literary, temperance, and mutual aid societies; and organizing to combat the spread of slavery, promote the welfare of their brothers and sisters, and fight for civil and political rights. They also began fostering and increasingly relying on a black public sphere and print culture to discuss and deliberate the political issues of the day. In forums such as all–African American conventions, black-edited newspapers, and black-authored pamphlets, roughly 230,000 northern African Americans created community, nurtured abolitionist ideals, debated whether to leave the United States for distant shores, and attempted to unify a population of free blacks—a mere 500,000 free black men, women and children in the North and South combined—and facilitate the liberation of the four million African Americans who remained enslaved on the eve of the Civil War.[2]

In this context, the Reverend John Berry Meachum, a clergyman living in St. Louis, Missouri, published a brief pamphlet, *Address to All the Colored Citizens of the United States*. Equal parts personal narrative, scriptural exegesis, black history lesson, assessment of the current state of the race, and discussion of the political choices and strategies available to antebellum free blacks, Meachum's short 1846 *Address* tackled an astonishing array of subjects that the author believed would be of interest to his African American readers. He called for free African Americans to promote a spirit of racial unity by holding regular political conventions and building a stratum of leaders who would be capable of guiding their brothers and sisters forward into a better, truly free world. Sounding surprisingly like some twentieth- and twenty-first-century critics of black culture, Meachum also admonished free blacks to stop using the "term Negro" as one of reproof. Pointing out that "it is now used as a term of reproach by both black and white," Meachum argued that "we must therefore stop it, for unless we do, others will use and apply those terms to us with impunity." And throughout the pamphlet, Meachum insisted that his readers cultivate an air of respectability. Proclaiming, "If you do not respect yourself others will not respect you," Meachum urged his readers to fashion themselves into respectable men and women through education, temperance, industry, and morality. He advised them to remain industrious throughout the week rather than "work a great deal one or two days and then loiter three or four days." He insisted that a "good education" was the "principal way of advancing in life" for those who hoped to rise in status and fashion themselves into truly free men and women. Reminding his readers to attend to matters of character and conduct, as he had, Meachum wrote, "We must cultivate all the christian graces which the apostle Peter recommends—'add to your faith virtue, and to virtue knowledge, and to knowledge temperance, and to temperance patience, and to patience godliness, and to godliness brotherly kindness, and to brotherly kindness charity.' Upon the exercise of these graces and christian qualities depend our elevation in this life, and our eternal happiness in the world to come." Finally, he underscored the prescriptive nature of his pamphlet by closing his preface with an admonishment: "Do not look at this little book with a careless eye, but receive instruction and advice."[3]

Meachum's *Address*, with its interest in fostering black unity and improving the social and political condition of Americans of African descent, is a classic example of early-nineteenth-century free African American political discourse. Given its emphasis on manners and morals, education, temperance, and self-improvement, however, Meachum's tract must also be considered as part of a much larger wave of American conduct discourse and advice literature articulating the goals, conventions, and anxieties of an emerging middle class in the early years of the republic. By the 1820s, as the last of the northern states outlawed slavery, they also experienced a market revolution that not only saw the rise and expansion of the factory system but also spurred a dramatic shift in class structure and social relations in the towns and cities of border states from Missouri and Maryland to New England and Upstate New York. By the time Meachum's *Address* appeared in print, the static "middling sort" of the eighteenth century had broadened into an amorphous new "middle class" composed of independent farmers and educated, largely urban, and native-born white men and women who "imagined themselves on a social escalator to greater wealth and prestige" and "lived suspended between the facts of their present social position" and great expectations for "their economic future."[4] Because theirs was a new, difficult to define, and liminal status, aspiring men and women had to engage in a self-conscious project of class self-identification, claiming virtue, morality, and respectability as the cultural markers that would distinguish them from those above and below them on the social and economic scale. To help with this anxiety-ridden process, white middle-class men and women turned to conduct manuals and advice literature for much-needed direction. Conduct literature, they hoped, would teach them how to acquire and maintain the precise manners, moral habits, and restrained, virtuous character that would help them to rise in status, mark them as members of a higher station, and enable them to safeguard the virtue and moral integrity necessary to navigate the vicissitudes of a dangerous, often dishonest new market-oriented culture.[5]

Northern African Americans who sought to rise from their former condition as enslaved men and women and to transform themselves into "ideal" free men and women also turned to conduct literature for guidance and support. Indeed, works written by Meachum and others offered aspiring African Americans discussions of conduct tailored to their specific circumstances. Throughout the antebellum era, African American ministers, newspaper editors, convention delegates, and community leaders created a brand of prescriptive discourse especially for this audience. Consequently, an array of printed materials provided young free black men and women with advice on how to behave: didactic essays and letters, humorous stories, sentimental vignettes and poems, and personal memoirs and narratives. Such advice could also be gleaned from sermons issued from pulpits of black churches and speeches at local, state, and national black conventions. Across these genres, African American writers and public figures repeatedly sketched out the various ways they thought northern free blacks should conduct themselves and admonished listeners and readers to follow a specific set of behavioral guidelines in their daily lives.[6]

This chapter analyzes this discourse and assesses its role in defining the identity of a newly emerging free black middle class in the antebellum North. Unlike the mainstream conduct discourse so important for the Northeast's elite and aspiring white Americans, black conduct discourse maintained a persistent political sensibility that correlated the acquisition of the traits and habits of the period's middle-class ideals with the transition from slavery to freedom. During this period, African American conduct writers implicitly and explicitly associated middle-class ideals about respectable conduct with antislavery politics and race consciousness, characterizing certain forms of behavior as the means through which African Americans could transform themselves into living refutations of proslavery doctrine. By linking racial politics and personal behavior so tightly and by tying each man's, woman's, and child's personal character to the collective salvation of the entire race, African American conduct writers endowed the individual behaviors, habits, and social graces associated with the northeastern middle class with extraordinary political significance, making such conventions a grave responsibility for elite and aspiring free black Americans. In the process, these African American writers and public figures helped to place a distinct brand of antislavery consciousness at the center of an emerging black middle-class culture.

CONDUCT DISCOURSE AND FREE BLACK LIMINALITY

Antebellum African Americans living in cities like Boston, New York, Philadelphia, Rochester, Pittsburgh, and Albany would have been hard-pressed to find an African American institution or publication that did not offer advice on matters of personal conduct. *Freedom's Journal* (1827–29), the *Colored American* (1837–41), the *Provincial Freeman* (1853–57), the *Weekly Anglo-African* (1859–61), and other African American newspapers, along with such key abolitionist newspapers as William Lloyd Garrison's *Liberator* (1831–66), Samuel Ringgold

Ward's *Impartial Citizen* (1849–56), and Frederick Douglass's *North Star* (1847–51), circulated widely across the northern United States and Canada, offering a first wave of conduct literature to a generation of young, free African Americans. In the pages of these publications, African American writers, ministers, and editors offered a mixture of original African American–authored and reprinted white-authored essays, stories, poems, editorials, letters, and advice on all forms of personal conduct.[7]

Like the conduct discourse designed by and for aspiring white Americans in the early republic, black conduct discourse identified the "appropriate" paths to economic upward mobility and financial independence and detailed the manners and social graces increasingly associated with respectable middle-class status. Within this prescriptive literature, African American writers regularly praised education, thrift, hard work, temperance, and Christian morality as key routes to upward mobility while offering advice on how to speak, what to eat and wear, how to court potential spouses, and how to govern and raise families. Original columns in the black press repeatedly reminded readers to "eat sound and wholesome food," to drink pure water, and to avoid "rum, or any kind of intoxicating liquors; for they are ruinous to health and productive of the greatest miseries." Contributors to the black press also prompted African Americans to be "clothed in clean and neat" garments, to "be prudent, as well as industrious," and to "never forget, that if you are filthy in your person, or your family, that you give evidence of a low and degraded mind."[8] Editors also routinely reprinted advice from white authors, as in 1839, when the *Colored American* ran an excerpt from Mrs. John Farrar's popular book, *The Young Ladies' Friend*, that instructed young women on how to behave while being examined by a physician.[9]

In addition to publishing original and reprinted articles outlining ideal habits and mores, African American newspapers also advertised conduct manuals for those who hoped to spend even more time and money on self-improvement. Much like the guides that would be advertised in the black press in the decades after the end of the Civil War, these antebellum advice manuals instructed a class of individuals "anxious over their own mastery of ostensibly proper behavior" on how to improve themselves and on what key traits and habits to nurture.[10] For example, an advertisement headed "Hand Books for Home Improvement" that appeared regularly in the classified section of the *Weekly Anglo-African* in 1860 hawked conduct manuals on composition, public speaking, manners, and business practices that could either be purchased individually or "bound in one large, handsome gilt volume" for $1.50. Rather than offering rudimentary lessons for the less accomplished reader, the manuals appear to have been designed to polish the manners and social graces of those in higher social circles, guiding those who aspired to rise still further. The book on "composition and letter writing" was described as "just the thing for everybody who writes business letters, family letters, friendly letters, love letters, notes and cards." For its part, *How to Behave* was "a new guide to correct personal habits," directed toward young men who wished to acquit themselves admirably "at home, at a party, at church, at table, in conversation, in traveling, in the company of ladies," and "in courtship"—in other words, in all the public and private spaces of respectable society.[11]

Northern free blacks could avail themselves of this literature in a variety of ways. Newspapers and conduct manuals were made accessible in African American literary societies and antislavery reading rooms where patrons could borrow books and attend lectures and debates on topics such as "Which would be the most expedient, an immediate or a gradual emancipation of the American slaves?" and "Which has been the greatest evil in the world, human slavery, or intemperance?"[12] Those who aspired to acquire respectability by improving their literary character but perhaps lacked the basic literacy skills required to read a newspaper could attend literary societies where designated readers would recite excerpts from a publication. Those with solid literacy skills who aspired to further improve themselves could peruse the pages of the *Colored American*, the *North Star*, or *Frederick Douglass's Paper* to glean advice on the maintenance of the era's middle-class sensibilities. And African Americans who hoped to cultivate an even more refined literary character might subscribe to the *Anglo-African Magazine* or carry copies of the *Repository of Religion and Literature, and of Science and Art* in their pockets as they went about their daily business. In these ways, African Americans could partake of the sort of instruction that helped to define the boundaries as well as the cultural mores of an emerging black middle class.[13]

Although this literature targeted African Americans who aspired to improve their manners, morals, and literacy skills, the African American readers who were most likely to borrow or purchase these sorts of manuals for home improvement or peruse the pages of the black press for advice on how to behave occupied a very different social status than the middle-class white Americans who also sought guidance on respectable behavior. While they might exhibit the manners and morals that made one "respectable" in the first half of the nineteenth century, few free blacks had the financial means generally associated with middle-class status. Education and training did not automatically translate into economic security: as one scholar has noted, "Skilled blacks found it difficult to obtain work, and, once they did to be paid a fair wage" above the Mason-Dixon Line.[14] Frederick Douglass, for example, found that the skills as a caulker that had served him so well on the wharves of Baltimore meant little when he applied for jobs on the segregated docks of Massachusetts.[15] And while middle-class white Americans established neighborhoods some distance away from their poor and working-class white counterparts, aspiring and elite African Americans lived in close proximity with their less wealthy African American neighbors and attended the same churches and community associations. Thus, as historian Peter Hinks has noted of black pamphleteer David Walker's Boston neighborhood, "Differences in income were never enough to create glaring dissimilarities in condition among segments of the black population."[16]

Moreover, if aspiring whites were a liminal group in the early years of the republic, as scholars have argued, aspiring African Americans—free blacks who hoped to rise in rank and standing while living in the midst of a slaveholding nation—occupied a far more precarious position in northern society. First, unlike aspiring white Americans, northern free blacks contended with a rapidly proliferating body of proslavery political discourse and racist scientific theory that claimed that the "degraded" character of people of African descent—African immorality, criminality, and intellectual inferiority—made African Americans unsuitable for freedom and incorporation into the body politic. These popular arguments about innate African American depravity were invariably invoked in the rhetoric used to justify the expansion of slavery, the extension of antiblack legislation, and the de facto exclusion of African Americans throughout the early nineteenth century. These beliefs would become the law of the land with the 1857 *Dred Scott* decision, in which Justice Roger B. Taney's powerful majority opinion held that African Americans had never had and never could have any "rights which the white man was bound to respect."[17]

Second, while respectability secured access for white Americans, all African Americans, irrespective of their education, manners, morals, or financial resources, found themselves regularly excluded from the public spaces and private establishments of northern cities—the ice cream gardens, reading rooms, lecture halls, and galleries that had by the 1830s become respectable places of leisure for members of the emerging middle classes. African Americans were also habitually refused passage on public transportation or forced to ride on the outside platforms of streetcars and stagecoaches and on the uncomfortable and unhealthful deck levels of steamboats. In 1838, one African American recalled that after finally finding a captain who was willing to allow his aged and respectable mother, who was "out of health and desirous to get home," to board a packet canal boat and shorten their long overland journey to forty miles along a waterway, the agent for the vessel refused to allow the captain to make an exception for them. "I went with him to the agent's office," the man wrote in a letter published in the *Colored American*, where "the captain told the agent . . . that he would be very glad to take her, as she was 'as nice and respectable a woman as anybody.' But he could not get the agent's consent."[18] Friends of a black Presbyterian minister, Theodore S. Wright, experienced similar difficulties as they traveled from Princeton, New Jersey, to Schenectady, New York, for a visit. Instead of sailing up the Hudson in a comfortable stateroom, they spent a chilly fall evening huddled on the deck of their steamboat. Attempting to transfer to a stagecoach for the final leg of their journey, the "light complexioned" woman was "interrogated very promptly whether she wished a passage," but "when she spoke to her husband, and they discovered he was a dark man, the baggage was taken off the stage, and they refused a passage in it." According to Rev. Wright, the exhausted young woman then "sat down upon the baggage, with her babe in her arms, and wept."[19]

These indignities were more than personal slights to the sensibilities of elite and aspiring free blacks. Indeed, they could have dire consequences. Wright was certain that the exclusion of promising young Philadelphia minister Jeremiah Gloucester from a steamboat cabin on a cold New England evening hastened the young man's death from consumption. And he told an 1837 audience at a meeting of the New York State Antislavery Society of "Mrs. Smith," a "pious woman" from Newburgh, New York, who "plead for a place, where with her dear babe she might be comfortable, and its life and health not be jeopard[iz]ed" during a journey to New York City. But "such a place she was refused." After they arrived in the city, "her child died, and after a short period, she died herself, from the cold she then caught." Wright's wife, too, fell ill after being forced to sit on the deck of a steamboat traveling up the icy Hudson. Although the captain ultimately allowed her "to sleep with the cook, in a dirty apartment near the machinery," the damage had been done. "My wife had received the fatal shaft," he said, "and she died after a few months, in consequence of the cold she then caught." After recounting a number of such tales, Wright concluded, "The sufferings of the colored man are fully known only to him who experiences them."[20]

Northern African Americans interpreted these forms of discrimination as an extension of proslavery sentiment and characterized these barriers to access as the northern manifestation of slavery, a dispiriting burden for aspiring African Americans to bear. In his 1841 portrait of the mores of Philadelphia's black upper classes, *Sketches of the Higher Classes of Colored Society in Philadelphia*, Joseph Willson, a member of that community, noted, "The educated man of color, in the United States, is by no means, so far as he may be affected by exterior circumstances, the *happiest* man. He finds himself in possession of abilities and acquirements which fit him for most of the useful and honorable stations in life, where such qualities are requisite; but does he find—can he even with reason anticipate—their ever being in like manner appreciated and rewarded?"[21] And in his 1837 *Treatise on the Intellectual Character and Civil and Political Condition of the Colored People of the U. States*, black Connecticut minister Hosea Easton asked his readers to "contemplate the numerous free people of color under the despotic reign of prejudice—contemplate a young man in the ardor of youth, blessed with a mind as prolific as the air, aspiring to eminence and worth—contemplate his first early hopes blasted by the frost of prejudice." He continued,

> Let the oppressed assume the character of capable men in business, either mercantile, mechanical, or agricultural,—let them assume the right of exercising themselves in the use of the common privileges of the country—let them claim the right of enjoying liberty, in the general acceptation of the term—let them exercise the right of speech and of thought—let them presume to enjoy the privileges of the sanctuary and the Bible, let their souls be filled with glory and of God, and wish to bow their knee at the sacred altar, and commemorate the dying love of Christ the Lord—let them seek a decent burial for their departed friend in the church yard—and they are immediately made to feel that they are as a carcass destined to be preyed upon by the eagles of persecution. Thus they are followed from life's dawn to death's-doom.[22]

Easton found that "the effect of these discouragements are every where manifest among the colored people. I will venture to say, from my own experience and observation, that hundreds of them come to an untimely grave, by no other disease than that occasioned by oppression." As far as Easton was concerned, "Slavery, in the form and character of prejudice, is as fatal, yea, more fatal than the pestilence."[23]

The northern free blacks who found themselves and members of their families refused entry into an array of northern spaces undoubtedly agreed with Willson's and Easton's assessments. Although African Americans fought verbally and physically against these forms of discrimination whenever they could—Elizabeth Jennings, for example, won a suit against a streetcar company that refused to allow her passage on the way to Sunday services at her New York City church—the inability to gain access to the respectable spaces of urban life provided daily reminders of the constant battle with northern racism as well as southern slavery.[24] Growing antiblack sentiment and de jure and de facto forms of discrimination made plain to middle-class African Americans that they, unlike aspiring white Americans, faced limits on how far they could rise. Meanwhile, their sorrow at slavery's continued cruelty to their brothers and sisters just across the southern borders of Ohio, Illinois, Pennsylvania, and New Jersey and their ever-present awareness of the institution's northern agents—slave catchers, kidnappers, and sympathetic politicians—provided northern free blacks with horrifying examples of how far from their present position they might easily fall. In other words, irrespective of their occupation or income, manners or morals, all northern free blacks occupied an unstable and unenviable position, perched between slavery and the full privileges of freedom.

A DUTY TO RECEIVE INSTRUCTION AND ADVICE

Given free blacks' peculiar position as outsiders within the nation of their birth, "presumed in the white imagination to be in every way inferior and incapable of rational thought," African American conduct literature and discussions of respectability must "be seen as both polite and political gesture."[25] Indeed, African American conduct writers consistently linked individual personal conduct and behavior with a specific set of racial, political aims. Newspaper editors did so pointedly, by making it their mission to offer advice on respectable personal conduct while simultaneously providing forums to discuss the political issues of the day. *Freedom's Journal*, for example, had two major goals: creating a sense of community, common identity, and political unity for the free black populace, and imparting advice on self-improvement. "It is our earnest wish," editor John Russworm wrote in the inaugural issue, "to make our Journal a medium of intercourse between our brethren in the different states of this great confederacy." And because "no publication, as yet, has been devoted exclusively" to the "improvement" of those "FIVE HUNDRED THOUSAND free persons of colour, one half of whom might peruse, and on the whole be benefitted by the publication of the Journal," *Freedom's Journal* would devote itself to that endeavor.[26] Frederick Douglass described his *North Star* as a newspaper that would "attack SLAVERY in all its forms and aspects, advocate UNIVERSAL EMANCIPATION; exalt the standard of PUBLIC MORALITY; promote the moral and intellectual improvement of the colored people; and hasten the day of FREEDOM to the THREE MILLION of our ENSLAVED FELLOW COUNTRYMEN."[27] And Canadian émigré Mary Ann Shadd Cary advertised her *Provincial Freeman* as "devoted to Anti-Slavery" and "Emigration" as well as "Temperance and General Literature."[28] In this way, African American editors used the press to group together conduct literature, opposition to slavery, and civil rights activism under the same masthead. Readers appear to have responded well to this mix. A letter from a reader in Troy, New York, praised the *Weekly Anglo-African* precisely for this range of subject matter: "What I admire more particularly about your paper is that it seems to be peculiarly adapted to the family circle, its pleasant sketches, its humorous anecdotes, its column of personalities all seeming designed for those whose minds lead them to desire such light matter, while those who have a taste for heavy and solid material find it there also."[29]

While editorials and advertisements demonstrated that these journals provided their readers with information on the personal as well as the political, the placement of advice literature suggests just how closely discussions of overtly political questions and forms of private conduct were intertwined. Essays on respectable conduct frequently appeared next to articles about pressing political concerns and events that would have been of particular interest to African American readers. For example, in the *Colored American*, an essay with advice directed "To Young Men" appeared adjacent to an article on the arrest of a notorious slave smuggler.[30] Likewise, *Freedom's Journal* published an article discussing the history of slavery in the West Indies alongside a humorous piece warning young women to be mindful that the inevitable fate of a "lively female wit of eighteen" was devolvement into "a most venomous backbiting old maid of forty-five."[31] In a similar vein, when Frederick Douglass reprinted Jane Grey Swisshelm's "Letters to Country Girls" in an 1849 issue of the *North Star*, a newspaper devoted to abolitionism, he provided young female readers with advice on how to avoid "ruin[ing] their complexions" and thereby repelling potential suitors. Thus, in addition to hearing about the most pressing abolitionist issues of the week, young female readers would have learned that "the woman who roasts her head by the fire" is a woman who "disorders her blood, brings on head-aches, injures her health, and makes her face look like a piece of leather." They also would have been taught that the woman who "swallows hot coffee, hot bread, greasy victuals and strong pickles" always "destroys her stomach, rots her teeth, shortens her life, and makes herself too ugly for any use, except scaring the crows off the corn."[32]

Other black public figures often more directly linked discussions of personal conduct, political topics, and denunciations of slavery and racism. Didactic writers such as Meachum often wove advice on private conduct into explicitly political pamphlets and essays. Similarly, the delegates attending the local, state, and national African American political conventions that began in the 1830s and met with some frequency in the late 1840s and 1850s spent a considerable amount of time discussing the value of respectable personal conduct. In these forums, where elected community representatives met to discuss the best methods for eradicating northern prejudice and advancing the antislavery cause, delegates passed resolutions and made speeches that dictated the guidelines for what they deemed "appropriate" and "inappropriate" forms of behavior for free African Americans, emphasizing education, temperance, and economy while proclaiming their devotion to the quest for universal liberty.[33] For example, after discussing the political rights owed to African Americans by the Declaration of Independence and the Constitution, which "guarantees in letter and spirit to every freeman born in this country, all the rights and immunities of citizenship," a report on the "Condition of the Free People of Colour of the United States" issued during the first national black convention of 1831 quickly shifted to a discussion of respectable personal conduct and individual self-improvement: in the delegates' "opinion, *Education, Temperance* and *Economy*, are best calculated to promote the elevation of mankind" and "enable him to discharge all those duties enjoined on him by his Creator." They concluded, "We would therefore respectfully request an early attention to those virtues among our brethren, who have a desire to be useful."[34]

In addition to linking personal behavior directly and indirectly with political discussions, black public figures drew on Christian teachings to remind aspiring free blacks of their racial responsibilities. Throughout the first half of the nineteenth century, Meachum and other free black ministers regularly urged the men and women of the North to understand that with freedom came the charge to take up the fight for the emancipation of southern slaves. In his 1827 Emancipation Day "Address" to the black citizens of Albany, New York, for example, the Reverend Nathaniel Paul exhorted his audience to action, saying that as newly liberated people, "new duties devolve upon us." Because "every act of ours is more or less connected with the general cause of the people of colour, and with the general cause of emancipation" in "every part of the world where the abomination of slavery is known," northern free blacks had a "duty" to advance God's plan.[35] Wright made a similar point in a speech given to the more than five hundred black and white delegates attending the 1836 convention of the New England Anti-Slavery Society: "I am identified with two millions and a half of men, women, and children, whose minds, as well as their bodies are chained down by slavery, and who have no power to speak for themselves. Every one of them, if their voice could reach my ears, would say 'Speak for us!—Oh, plead for us!' They would say, 'Oh, if I were in your place, how I would speak and plead for myself, and for my fellow-sufferers.'"[36] Secular public figures echoed this perspective, consistently reminding free northern African Americans that they bore a special responsibility to act in the name of their enslaved brothers and sisters. In "Responsibility of Colored People in the Free States," the editors of the *Colored American* agreed that "on our conduct, in great measure, *their* salvation depends."[37] And by 1860, elite and aspiring free blacks could agree "by common assent" that their advantages made them the vanguard of the race; therefore, "on the condition and prospects of *free* colored men ... rests in a great degree, the condition and prospects of *enslaved* colored men."[38]

The behavior of elite and aspiring free blacks suggests that they internalized this political assessment of the personal, interpreting their respectable behavior in light of their antislavery principles even in the most apolitical of social situations. With this idea in mind, aspiring African Americans also sought to live their antislavery principles in respectable, private intraracial settings as much as they sought to demonstrate them in the public interracial arena. Consequently, private intraracial gatherings offered occasions to act on antislavery principles with like-minded friends and family. Parlors, for example, served as spaces to blend antislavery politics with middle-class courtship rituals. Indeed, when William C. Nell wrote an essay on the "Elevation" of the race for the *North Star*, he placed parlor courtship rituals in the context of the struggle for racial equality. Nell instructed young African American men to "practise that deportment towards the young ladies of their acquaintance, as to inspire them with a congenial taste for *intellectual and moral* elevation"; "instead of the *small talk* so generally engaging the social circle," these men should introduce more "interesting and instructive topics."[39] And the diary of young Charlotte Forten, the granddaughter of James Forten, a wealthy black sailmaker and Revolutionary War veteran, suggests that elite and middle-class African Americans continued to discuss antislavery politics in informal home situations. On several occasions, she confided that she and her friends engaged in "a long conversation" on the "all-absorbing subject" of slavery. And if her "intelligent" callers proved "ignorant of true Anti-slavery," she "soon wearied" of them.[40]

Like Forten, black conduct writers framed antislavery consciousness as a political ideology that, when properly internalized, would suffuse readers' private interactions, choices, and behavior as fully as it directed public political activities. This concept appears clearly in "a dialogue between a mother and her children," a sketch of an idealized African American domestic scene appearing in an 1832 issue of the *Liberator*. In this short vignette by Sarah Mapps Douglass, an African American teacher from Philadelphia who often wrote under the pen name "Zillah," a mother chastises her young boy, Henry, for throwing away his uneaten bread. She then tells the story of a starving, elderly slave who, after receiving a little money, purchased a "loaf of wheat bread, which he alternately pressed to his lips and bosom, while floods of grateful tears coursed... down his furrowed cheeks." Henry and his sister, Matilda, fully comprehend the lesson in the story, and Henry apologizes, offering to "save all the money my grandmother and uncle give me, and buy some bread to send to the old man." His mother explains that the old slave had long since gone to "that place where hunger and slavery are things unknown." Instead, she advises the boy "to save your money, and when you have collected a handsome sum, uncle will put it into the funds now preparing to build a College for our youth." The story ends with Henry "clapping his hands joyfully" and saying, "O yes, mother, I will, I will!"[41]

Such stories served as lessons for African Americans of all ages. These fables linked education, economy, and self-improvement with antislavery sentiment in a manner that made the acquisition of these traits a moral and political obligation for the rising generation of aspiring African Americans. For as with the white middle class of the period, members of the northern black middle class were engaged in a self-conscious process of identity formation. But unlike their white counterparts, aspiring African Americans carried the additional challenge of placing every aspect of their lives in the service of a larger freedom struggle.

"PRAY, WHO DOES HE APE?"

If northern free blacks needed any confirmation that the type of self-fashioning black conduct writers espoused had political implications, they had only to look at the reaction examples of black respectability provoked among white observers. Elite and aspiring African Americans were made quite aware that their slightly elevated status, respectable dress, and sense of propriety made them particular targets of northern white antipathy. Indeed, participants in mainstream stage and print culture found the idea of free black respectability a fruitful source of comedy for white audiences. Between 1816 and 1828, a series of satirical "bobalition broadsides" lampooning black public activities and celebrations on July 14, the day black Bostonians set aside to commemorate the anniversary of the abolition of the slave trade, gained popularity from New England to Pennsylvania. These images and their accompanying text used humor to suggest that men and women of African descent were utterly unfit for the full privileges of citizenship and were impossible to incorporate into the body politic. To make this case, the broadsides pointedly ridiculed the community institutions, dress, and speech of middle-class African Americans. Around the same time, white performers began blacking up to play the character Zip Coon on the minstrel stage. Unlike the enslaved, southern Jim Crow character, Zip Coon was a northerner, a loquacious free black and a pretentious dandy decked out in an absurd array of finery no matter the occasion. By highlighting dialect in these representations of elite and aspiring African Americans, white American writers and performers characterized all African Americans as a people better suited to their previous condition as slaves, unable to master the lingua franca, and therefore inassimilable and permanent outsiders living within a white community.[42]

Political cartoonist Edward Clay's two popular series, *Life in Philadelphia* and *Life in New York*, reinforced these notions, portraying the African American elite and middle classes of those cities as particularly ridiculous for their attempts to take on the dress, manners, and patterns of speech of white elites. Indeed, the cartoonist invited white readers to laugh at the idea of African American respectability. Clay's figures spoke in a flurry of puns and malapropisms, insisted on formal manners at the most inappropriate moments, and dressed in an absurdly ostentatious fashion. The implication was that free blacks could do no more than "ape" white elites, taking on habits that they could never fully understand, much less master. As a group, these expressive forms popularized the belief that the elite and aspiring free African Americans of the North were absurd figures, awkwardly imitating the cultural practices of their betters and unable to adjust to the demands of freedom.[43]

The behavior of northern white Americans, however, suggested that they considered elite and middle-class African Americans to be more of a serious threat than a joke. As historian Julie Winch points out, respectable African Americans often found themselves vulnerable to physical assaults in the street precisely because the markers of respectability they so carefully cultivated challenged white observers' beliefs about the proper social order.[44] Indeed, as historian Emma Jones Lapsansky demonstrates, symbols of black social mobility and independence, "institutions that signaled increasing economic progress and 'status' in the black community," particularly churches and schools, "were especially attractive targets for destruction," regularly damaged by white mobs.[45] In 1831, a white abolitionist, the Reverend Simeon Jocelyn, joined forces with a black New York minister, Peter Williams, and proposed creating a "manual labor" college combining physical education with "classical, agricultural, and vocational study," in New Haven, Connecticut, that would enroll the best and brightest black men of the United States and the Caribbean. Within days of hearing of the plan, the city's whites gathered and voted 700 to 4 to bar the boosters from establishing the college. Rioters also attacked a black-owned hotel, an African American residence, and the home of prominent white abolitionist and college supporter Arthur Tappan. Faced with such a show of forceful opposition, the college's supporters quickly backed down. In 1833, when a white Quaker, Prudence Crandall, who ran a Canterbury, Connecticut, academy for girls, allowed an African American student to enroll, white parents pulled their children from the institution. When Crandall reacted by declaring her school expressly for "Young Ladies and Misses of Color," townspeople vandalized the building, lawmakers passed legislation curtailing the education of African Americans, and officials arrested and jailed Crandall.[46] Similarly, in 1835, when fourteen African American students (including a young Henry Highland Garnet) integrated Noyes Academy in Canaan, New Hampshire, the townspeople responded by forming a mob and using a team of oxen to pull the school building off its foundation before moving on to threaten the homes where the Afri-

Figure 1. "How you find youself dis hot weader Miss Chloe?" "Pretty well I tank you Mr. Cesar only I aspire too much!" From Edward W. Clay, *Life in Philadelphia* (Philadelphia: Hart, 1830). Courtesy of the Library Company of Philadelphia.

can American students had taken shelter.⁴⁷ Even informal educational institutions created a stir. In 1834, when Hosea Easton began raising funds to establish a literary and religious institution for black residents of Hartford, Connecticut, whites attacked his parishioners and terrorized the African American neighborhood for three days. The city saw a similar rampage the following year. And in 1836, Easton's church would mysteriously burn to the ground.⁴⁸

Elite and aspiring African Americans understood that such institutions became targets because they challenged conventional wisdom about the appropriate place for people of African descent in the United States. In an 1834 report to the American Anti-Slavery Society, African American newspaper editor Samuel E. Cornish analyzed the events at Crandall's school and concluded that the backlash against the school was so dramatic because white northerners refused to allow free African Americans to be treated with the respect they deserved: local whites destroyed the school simply "because she dared to teach them, *as if they were white*—to treat them with the same delicacy and respect which an instructress is expected to extend to young ladies in good society."⁴⁹ Douglass expanded on this observation in an 1850 issue of the *North Star*, recounting a physical assault he experienced during a visit to Manhattan. "Thousands of colored men can bear witness to the truth of this representation," he wrote. "While we are servants we are never offensive to the whites, or marks of popular displeasure."⁵⁰ And when "he is drunken, idle, ignorant and vicious . . . 'Black Bill' is a source of amusement: he is called a good-natured fellow." He "is the first to touch his hat to the stranger approaching the hotel, and offer his service in holding his horse, or blacking his boots. The white gentleman tells the landlord to give 'Bill' '*something to drink*,' and actually drinks with 'Bill' himself!—While poor black 'Bill' will minister to the pride, vanity and laziness of white American gentlemen—while he consents to play the buffoon for their sport, he will share their regard." Only by behaving in a respectable manner, Douglass argued, did African Americans attract white ire: "But let ['Bill'] cease to be what we have described him to be, let him shake off the filthy rags that cover him—let him abandon drunkenness for sobriety . . . ignorance for intelligence, and give up his menial occupation for respectable employment—let him quit the hotel and go to the church, and assume there the rights and privileges of one for whom the Son of God died, and he will be pursued with the fiercest hatred. His name will be cast out as evil; and his life will be embittered with all the venom which hate and malice can generate."⁵¹ In an 1849 editorial in the *Impartial Citizen*, the Reverend Samuel Ringgold Ward, a black New

Yorker, suggested that these forms of discrimination were as soul crushing for aspiring African Americans as the physical intimidation they might meet in the streets. While "poor whites" assaulted African Americans bodily, elite whites chose a less violent approach to emphasize their disdain for "elevated" African Americans: "If from among the mass of persons they crushed, one dares to raise his head above the common level, and take himself to books, letters, learning; determined to be a man, and by patience, industry, energy and perseverance, acquires some means of usefulness," Ward wrote, "*how piously* the pro-slavery whites . . . rush away from their own Literary Hall, or Meeting House, rather than pollute their sanctified ears, or un-starch a little of their would-be dignity, by listening to a black man! 'He is out of his place!' . . . 'Niggers can't rise here': say the learned, the religious, the refined. 'Go to Hell, you nigger!' say the less refined, less religious, and less learned, *in the very same spirit*."[52]

Elite and aspiring African Americans were susceptible not only to the insults and attacks of their enemies but also to inadvertent but deeply revealing slights by their white friends. Schoolteacher Sarah Mapps Douglass recalled the day a member of the Quaker meeting she attended approached her to ask, "Does thee go out ahouse cleaning?" In a letter to white abolitionist Sarah Grimké, Douglass wrote, "I looked at her with astonishment, my eyes filled with tears & I answered no. . . . I wept during the whole of that mtg. & for many succeeding Sabbaths & I believe they were not the tears of wounded pride alone."[53] In an 1839 letter to white abolitionist Nathaniel P. Rogers, James Forten recounted the time a white visitor to his Philadelphia home "requested my daughter to open the piano, adding that he had never heard a colored lady play." But respectable black Philadelphians regularly trained their daughters to become competent singers and performers "on the piano-forte, guitar, or some other appropriate musical instrument." Assuming the best of his acquaintance, Forten added, "he would not, I dare say, for the world have said this, had he thought it would have wounded her feelings, or that it conveyed to her mind the appearance of rudeness, of which I am sure he would have been the last to be guilty." But Forten admitted being "surprised" by the "many little incidents like this," when "our friends should wonder at our being just like other people."[54]

Aware that whites persecuted and ridiculed them no matter what they did or how they behaved, and convinced that the success of the freedom struggle rested primarily on their shoulders, aspiring African Americans wrestled with the bizarre cognitive dissonance caused by the gap between their view of themselves and the way they were perceived by others. We can catch a glimpse of the stress this might have caused in a young woman's "tart, sharp letter" published in the *North Star* in 1849. The author critiqued an unnamed but "renowned" antislavery lecturer who "laid a great many sins at the door of the Philadelphia people" during his talk on the importance of black unity. She was particularly annoyed by the accusation that black Philadelphians were "too fond of dress; ladies with curls and ribbons flying, in imitation of our oppressors; and girls who live at service spending their earnings in bedecking themselves equally in appearance with their employers." The sting of the antislavery speaker's reproach moved the writer to reply in a public forum. "I should like to know," she asked, "how the gentleman would have us dress. I suppose the old-fashioned bonnets and dresses of our grandmothers would please him. I know they would please our oppressors, for the unwelcome truth would not stare them in the face, that we are as capable of refinement and taste as they are." After pointedly noting the subversive potential of her sartorial choices, she took on the charges levied by white humorists such as Clay: "America does not originate her fashions, she receives them from France and England." Consequently, "when we follow a fashion, we consider ourselves no more imitators than our oppressors." After defending herself and the women of her circle, the author of the letter then came to the defense of black female domestics: "I think our service girls have been unjustly handled. Most of them have poor parents, and a great part of their earnings go to assist them, which leaves them little to spend upon themselves; yet a stranger, who knows nothing of the social relations of the laboring people of our city, undertakes to censure them for extravagance!" And she concluded by defending the city's respectable young men: "The gentleman speaks much against our young men wearing broadcloth; but I may say, that I see none of them dress as fashionably" as the abolitionist did. "Pray," she shot back at her community's detractor, "who does he ape?"[55]

For this young woman, respectable conduct, both public and private, was a deeply important issue. But it was not, as she forcefully pointed out, a matter of "imitating" whites, a performance for a white audience, or a style to be forced on the black masses. Issues of conduct, dress, and comportment were crucial to her personal sense of herself as an elite free black woman living in a slaveholding republic. She clearly understood that the power of dress and manners lay not in their ability to change whites' minds but rather in their status as a symbolic assertion of "the unwelcome truth" that whites refused to see: her humanity, individuality, and determination to thrive as a free woman.

ETHIOPIA SHALL STRETCH FORTH HER HANDS

Given its limited utility as a strategy to persuade whites of African Americans' worthiness for inclusion in the national community, why did writers and public figures continue to praise respectability? And why did they persist in doing so even as the prospects of free African Americans deteriorated in the decades preceding the Civil War? A full answer to these questions requires analyzing both how these writers characterized the intrinsic value of respectability and, more important, what they saw as the path to respectability: self-improvement.

First, aspiring African Americans and black public figures believed that education, morality, and industry had inherent rewards for individuals who actively pursued these goals.[56] African American conduct writers found respectability so appealing in and of itself that they continued to praise its virtue in spite of the fact that evidence of black respectability seemed to do little but enrage white Americans. As Willson explained, "If there was nothing in education to recommend *itself*, well might reason be construed against the utility of the man of color's entering its path.... But education possesses its own intrinsic worth, which it imparts to those who enter its pursuits."[57] Instead of simply insisting that respectable conduct had the power to change whites' negative opinions about African Americans, conduct discourse taught African American readers that the forms of self-improvement that placed individuals on the path to respectability were part of a larger process of self-transformation, an opportunity to become something better in the eyes of one's family, one's peers, and one's God. Therefore, when black public figures championed respectability, they advocated more than public performances of bourgeois behavior. Rather, they celebrated the human agency and processes of self-fashioning they associated with the acquisition of respectability and what they understood to be its transformative power: its ability to remake an individual into a new being elevated to a higher state. And as budding black nationalist Martin Delany pointed out in an 1849 issue of the *North Star*, whenever free African Americans claimed their ability to act in their own best interests, to "learn how to gain a living, to make our bread," they "lost the feeling common to master and servant." Unless African Americans fully took possession of their personal agency, "we are only fit for slaves."[58] By promoting reform and self-improvement, then, black conduct writers hoped to provide instruction on how individuals could transform themselves from slaves into ideal free men and women.

The belief that one could remake oneself into something new arose in part from the millennial religious movements that swept through the North during the Second Great Awakening of the late eighteenth and early nineteenth centuries. Millennial interpretations of Christianity spread by popular revival leader Charles Grandison Finney and other ministers suggested that with faith and personal effort, individuals could improve themselves and their communities in preparation for the thousand years of peace and prosperity that would herald the final judgment of God. To facilitate this process, men and women across the Northeast joined together to create a "benevolent empire" of voluntary associations and reform organizations designed to help individuals fashion themselves into educated, virtuous, temperate beings and to combat and vanquish the nation's sins.[59]

Northern African Americans participated actively in these religious and social developments. Indeed, several of the most prominent free black activists of the era had been influenced by millennial religious movements, attending services and revivals and experiencing profound conversion experiences.[60] In a personal narrative, *Twenty-Two Years a Slave and Forty Years a Freeman*, a successful Rochester grocer, Austin Steward, described 1825 as having been "rendered memorable" by the arrival of Finney, the most famous revival minister of the Second Great Awakening: Finney's "faithful preaching of the gospel" brought many people "to a saving knowledge of the truth."[61] In an autobiography written decades later, Reconstruction-era politician John Mercer Langston also made a special note of Finney's charisma and influence in recounting his education under Finney's tutelage at Oberlin College in Ohio.[62] Some black northerners, including Sojourner Truth, expressed their religious transformation by becoming itinerant ministers or joining one of the many experimental utopian religious communities of the period.[63] Most African Americans, however, focused on the fact that, as historian David Blight notes in his intellectual biography of Frederick Douglass, "millennialism was an activist faith" that "depended greatly on human action" and turned that belief toward institution-building and self-improvement efforts, readying themselves for the coming day of judgment.[64]

While evangelical impulses helped to generate extraordinary faith in the power of personal transformation, African American ministers also invoked the prediction in Psalm 68:31: "Princes shall come out of Egypt, and Ethiopia shall soon stretch out her hands to God."[65] Readings of this biblical verse often privileged personal agency, making it essential to the success of the freedom struggle. And with this idea in mind, African American ministers insisted that deliverance from slavery and racism would occur only if the members of their northern communities put their shoulders to the wheel on behalf of the race. In the three decades preceding the Civil War, ministers exhorted northern African Americans not to wait for God alone but to act to redeem themselves from all forms of bondage—psychic, economic, political, and physical. In so doing, religious leaders thus added scriptural authority to free black institutional development and self-improvement efforts, making them a religious and racial duty for free northern blacks old and young. As the Reverend Henry Highland Garnet wrote, African American attention to collective and individual self-help was "the brightest, the most glorious, and the most hopeful" sign of the coming liberation of the race. Whether regarded "in a moral, physical, or intellectual light," self-help "is to an oppressed people what Moses was to the Hebrews—what Virginius was to Rome, and what Toussaint L'Overture was to his golden Island of the ocean." Garnet then proclaimed, "My heart leaps with joy, as I behold my long-suffering and noble people laying aside their old garments of dependence, and entering upon their own work. God helps those who help themselves; and hence, if we are true to this principle, we shall have the best help that the universe can afford. If God be with us, who of all the sons of men need we fear? Let us trust in Him, and work manfully."[66]

As Garnet's comments suggest, examples of free black self-improvement, educational achievement, morality, material success, and other forms of respectability were framed as essential for the fulfillment of divine prophecy heralding the dawn of freedom. And when northern free blacks expressed their desire for the complete liberation of their people, they never failed to characterize these particular forms of activism and agency as revolutionary acts, steps they must first take to put divine prophecy into action. For this reason, an 1841 contributor to the *Colored American* insisted that the progress of the Literary and Library Union of New York served as evidence that the time for "the triumph of justice—the redemption of an oppressed people draweth nigh." As he saw it, "The organization of societies for our moral and mental improvement—public debates and lectures are sufficient evidence that there is a determination to apply the great lever—Education—to the unholy system. On every hand we find the young and the old, male and female, enlisting in the intellectual war against slavery."[67]

This tendency to imbue self-improvement with religious and even revolutionary significance was particularly apparent in the famous jeremiads of black Boston residents David Walker and Maria Stewart. Stewart, noted for her protofeminist speeches, consistently urged northern blacks to organize and work toward improving the moral, mental, and material status of the race by building institutions that supported collective efforts at education, thrift, and fidelity to the principles of Protestant Christianity. She mixed rhetoric of self-improvement with arguments that the efforts of northern blacks were instrumental for the fulfillment of God's larger plan.[68] Walker made a similar case for the power of education in his *Appeal to the Coloured Citizens of the World*, "one of the single most important works to issue from an African American in the antebellum era." As Peter Hinks has written, Walker consistently called for education and advancement in the American free labor economy alongside his notably strident denunciation of American slavery and racism. Thus, when Walker told the African American readers of his *Appeal*, "I say unto you again, you must go to work and prepare the way of the Lord," he clearly placed free black self-improvement, particularly education, alongside self-defense and slave insurrection as examples of human agency and essential forms of racial advancement and self-liberation.[69]

Men and women like Walker and Stewart believed that in a nation that equated blackness with every trait deemed incommensurate with the maintenance of a virtuous, free republic, claiming respectability allowed aspiring free blacks to transcend—if only for themselves—the proslavery ideology used to define them and instead claim a positive identity of their own choosing. Irrespective of how others might view African Americans, they considered self-improvement to be a means for individuals to transform themselves into free and independent agents. Meachum sought to make this point by describing such personal revolutions to readers of his *Address*. In his preface, he explained that by the age of twenty-one, he had bought his freedom as well as that of his father. And after marrying an enslaved woman, he obtained enough business as a carpenter and cooper to pay for his wife and his children. "Since that period," he continued, "I have purchased about twenty slaves, most of whom paid back the greatest part of the money, and some paid all. They are all doing well except one, who happened to be a drunkard," for "no drunkard can do well." Black conduct writers such as Meachum insisted that if African Americans followed the path to respectability and fashioned themselves into ideal men and women, they would never fully succumb to the many limitations placed on them. For this reason, the delegates to the African American Ohio State Convention of 1852 resolved "that self-respect is a first and an essential element, for he who does not respect himself, no one else will respect him, and what is true of one is true of a nation."[70] As Ward framed it, "The government may knock off every shackle, unrivet every fetter, sunder every chain, and declare every slave free, and clothe him with all that appertains to legal and constitutional equality, with all other men. Then the friends of the colored man might invite him to complete and perfect equality in the social circle, and in business relations. The school, the academy, the college, might be thrown open to his children, as freely as to all other youth. All this would be right, and nothing beyond simple right." But, he continued, "if, with all these advantages," African Americans "did not decree and achieve their own elevation, they never would, never *could* be elevated." He continued,

> If with such advantages as we have named, we chose not to respect ourselves, to abstain from the dram shop, the gambling hall, the house of ill-fame; if we wouldn't learn to read, and acquaint ourselves with the intelligence of the day; if we would not cultivate polished manners, and refined sensibilities; if we would not fit ourselves for the society of the upright and the elevated; why we should be just what we now are; i.e., our present position would remain, morally, what it now is. . . . On the other hand, if, in the midst of our present depressions and discouragements, we shall cultivate self-respect, dignity of demeanor, refinement of manners, intelligence, morality, and religion; if we shall be industrious, frugal, temperate, chaste, we shall be an elevated people, in spite of all the pro-slavery negro-hate this boasted, lying Republic is disgraced and degraded with.[71]

Like fugitive slaves who transformed themselves into independent free men, personal agency could be used to truly remake an individual into a new being: someone who refused to be defined by the racial ideologies of the nation. As William C. Nell concluded in an essay on "Elevation" published in Frederick Douglass's *North Star*, "A giant *is* a giant, though always in the valley."[72]

ON POLITICS AND RESPECTABILITY

Elite and aspiring African Americans living in the antebellum North created and consumed conduct discourse in the context of a very different set of circumstances than those of upwardly mobile whites. Irrespective of their education, manners, morals, or economic status, all free blacks found themselves increasingly marginalized: barred from most educational institutions and public accommodations, restricted to the lowest-paid forms of employment, disfranchised by most state constitutions, and constrained by an increasingly hostile white majority. By the 1850s, the roughly 250,000 free African Americans living in the North were hemmed in by the politically powerful slave states to the south, limited by de jure and de facto discrimination, and daily threatened by the long arm of the 1850 Fugitive Slave Law. Moreover, evidence of the respectability advocated by conduct writers made African Americans at best figures of curiosity and at worst tantalizing targets for white hostility. Therefore, while middle-class white Americans had to remain conscious of their precarious position perched between those above and below them on the economic scale, elite and aspiring African Americans also had to grapple with the instability of their position as free blacks trying to carve out a place for themselves within a slaveholding republic.

Given the ironies of their peculiar situation, African American conduct discourse could never become completely distinct from these larger political goals. Black conduct writers framed respectability as a religious duty, a racial responsibility, and a potent weapon in the antislavery arsenal. They believed that its power stemmed not, as scholars have argued, solely from its effects on whites but also, and more important, from its effects on the individuals who embraced it. The process of self-fashioning, black conduct writers argued, was transformative. And the response respectable African Americans received from white observers only served to confirm for aspiring free blacks the subversive nature of what they believed to be a revolutionary personal transformation.

Black conduct discourse ultimately redefined respectability in terms by and for elite and aspiring African Americans. At the same time, however, black conduct discourse revealed a series of implications about the high stakes of personal, private behavior that middle-class free blacks quickly internalized. Every example of black self-actualization, virtue, morality, respectability, and success, they hoped, would be a boon to the antislavery cause. They knew, however, that every failure, no matter how small, reflected not just on the individuals involved but on every African American, free and enslaved, north and south. By defining personal improvement as a racial responsibility, elite and aspiring northern free blacks were weaving their individual personal, private aspirations into their larger political, racial goals. They were creating something that was less dependent on the white gaze than on the desire to perform God's will and to fulfill one's responsibility to act on behalf of the race. In so doing, they opened the door to a variety of ways to position oneself in the freedom struggle, to transform oneself into something bigger and better than one's adversaries, to personalize one's antislavery politics, and to embody a complete and total rejection of the period's racist legal and ideological codes.

CHAPTER TWO

Slave Narratives and the Black Self-Made Man

> It is not without a feeling of pride, dear reader, that I present you with this book. The son of a self-emancipated bond-woman, I feel joy in introducing to you my brother, who has rent his own bonds, and who, in his every relation—as a public man, as a husband and as a father—is such as does honor to the land which gave him birth. I shall place this book in the hands of the only child spared me, bidding him to strive and emulate its noble example. You may do likewise.
>
> —Dr. James McCune Smith, Introduction to Frederick Douglass, *My Bondage and My Freedom* (1855)

In 1855, just weeks after emigrating from the United States to Jamaica, abolitionist activist, orator, newspaper editor, and Congregational minister Samuel Ringgold Ward published his life story, *Autobiography of a Fugitive Negro: His Anti-Slavery Labours in the United States, Canada, and England*. By putting his personal narrative before the public, Ward was participating in a long-established North American tradition and joining a fast-growing group of former slaves who used their personal experiences to reveal the human toll taken by the institution of slavery and to generate support for the international antislavery campaign. By the 1840s and 1850s, these men and women were receiving critical acclaim for their contributions to abolitionist literature and rhetoric. Their public pronouncements about the moral costs of the peculiar institution could push moderate whites into the radical antislavery camp and became the basis for a canon of antislavery literature that united abolitionists in disparate communities across the North.[1]

Although the abolitionist literature produced by African Americans was largely directed at a white audience, northern blacks were consumers of this discourse as well.² Northern free blacks, like the women of Philadelphia's Female Literary Society, read and discussed antislavery writings at weekly or monthly gatherings. In 1832, a white observer noted that the Philadelphia women read from the Bible, sat in silence, offered a prayer, and then took turns reading "affecting slave tales."³ Northern free blacks also availed themselves of black-authored abolitionist materials in less formal settings. Charlotte Forten, for example, noted in her diary that she enjoyed listening to her uncle read "some of F. Douglass' best speeches" while packing her belongings in preparation for a summer vacation.⁴ Abolitionist newspapers with sizable African American readerships, like the *Liberator*, along with newspapers edited and published by African Americans, advertised black-authored antislavery literature and reviewed slave narratives with some regularity. And authors of slave narratives such as Frederick Douglass and William Wells Brown frequently lectured before the congregations of African American churches and the members of African American voluntary associations.

Like his fugitive compatriots, Ward spoke with authority about issues that would have been of concern to both his black and white readers. His *Autobiography* offered fascinating details about his family's escape from slavery in Maryland and his upbringing in the free state of New York. But thirty-four pages into his story, Ward departed from the conventional narrative of escape from bondage to speak directly to his African American audience and make an important point about how free northern blacks could incorporate the fight against slavery and racism into their daily lives. After asking, "What is antislavery labour?" he argued that it is done "not alone by lecturing, holding anti-slavery conventions, distributing anti-slavery tracts, maintaining anti-slavery societies, and editing anti-slavery journals." Rather, he insisted that "in connection with these labours," antislavery work is "the cultivation of all the upward tendencies of the coloured man." He suggested that by simply succeeding "in his vocation from day to day, with his hoe, hammer, pen, tongue, or lancet," the "expert black cordwainer, blacksmith . . . mechanic or artisan, the teacher, the lawyer, the doctor, the farmer, or the divine," would be "living down the base calumnies of his heartless adversaries"—in other words, "demonstrating his truth and their falsity." He concluded this advice by proclaiming, "God helping me wherever I shall be, at home, abroad, on land or sea, in public or private walks, as a man, a Christian, especially as a *black man*, my labours must be anti-slavery labours, because mine must be an anti-slavery life."⁵

Brief as it is, Ward's declaration provides remarkable insight about the

Figure 2. Frontispiece to Samuel Ringgold Ward, *Autobiography of a Fugitive Negro: His Anti-Slavery Labours in the United States, Canada, and England* (London: Snow, 1855). By placing his likeness in the frontispiece of his narrative, Ward not only claimed the status of author but also offered a visual representation of the ideal of the black self-made man. Image courtesy of Documenting the American South, the University of North Carolina at Chapel Hill Libraries.

ways certain ideals about manhood shaped the personal politics embraced by members of the emerging black middle class. At a moment when mainstream conduct writers idealized respectable, virtuous, and restrained self-made men and characterized a short list of occupations as suitable for educated, upwardly mobile, young middle-class white men, northern free black newspaper editors, community leaders, ministers, and public speakers also identified and celebrated a discrete set of respectable occupations for young African American men, implicitly and explicitly equating these enterprises with the larger freedom struggle. At the same time, conduct writers warned young black men that upward mobility (along with its antislavery implications) required strict attention to personal morality. And as far as these writers were concerned, the leisure activities so popular in the urban areas where so many free African Americans resided posed a grave threat to the virtue and moral health of their most promising young men. Slave narratives served as a counterpoint to these particular anxieties, essentially narrativizing conduct writers' arguments about the power of human agency, the remarkable transformative potential of self-improvement, and the antislavery implications of upward mobility.[6] Narratives demonstrated that if formerly enslaved men such as Ward could rise to prominent stature and dedicate their life to antislavery work, it was incumbent on the free and aspiring young black men of the North to strive to do the same, to place every aspect of their lives, whether "at home" or "abroad," in "public or private walks," in the service of the larger freedom struggle.[7] In this way, slave narratives and conduct discourse worked together to create the framework for a middle-class ideal of black manhood: the black self-made man.[8]

VIRTUE, INDEPENDENCE, AND ADVICE TO YOUNG MEN

By the 1840s, the prescriptive discourse being produced in the North idealized the virtuous, respectable, independent, self-made man. This model was expected to be "manly"—that is, a paragon of virtue and high-minded self-restraint who shunned immoral spaces and activities and preferred moderation to excess. The perfect man was also expected to be self-made, someone who rather than resting on his ancestors' laurels proved himself in the public sphere and found success in the new and rapidly expanding market order. The ideal manly man was, by definition, an independent man of good character, free of debt and vice, who embraced the Protestant work ethic in his business affairs and attended to self-improvement and self-cultivation. And by remaking themselves in this image, virtuous middle-class men expected to achieve a Franklinesque rise from obscurity to greatness.⁹

Although this manly ideal was new to the early republic, it had its roots in the eighteenth century and continued to be shaped by the vestiges of eighteenth-century republican ideologies positing independence and virtue as prerequisites for the full privileges of citizenship. In the nation's early days, popular public figures insisted that only an independent citizenry could exhibit the civic virtue necessary for the success of the republic. And as several historians have found, republicanism continued to thrive into the nineteenth century, informing discussions of race, class, character, and political participation.¹⁰ White laborers in particular were defensive about their independence in the early nineteenth century, exhibiting a kind of "labor republicanism" in which they positioned themselves as members of the "producing classes," more virtuous than the corrupt elites higher in the social order and the dependent enslaved African Americans below. White male servants insisted on being called "help" rather than "servants" and refused to call their employers "master" in an effort to neutralize the implication that they lacked the independent spirit expected of those who participated in the political process.¹¹ The American tendency to define independence as a key prerequisite for the full privileges of citizenship put African American men in a particularly difficult position. As a consequence of the recent history of bondage in the northern states, the expansion of slavery in the southern states, the forms of labor to which free blacks were generally limited, and the pseudoscientific arguments of proslavery theorists, many white northerners had difficulty imagining African Americans in any position other than dependent on whites. In this view, blackness, much like womanhood, naturally signified a dependent state and served as reason enough to exclude African Americans from the body politic.¹²

As slavery came to an end in the North, African Americans fought this characterization by demonstrating their newfound freedom and independence whenever possible, refusing to defer to whites in the manner to which they, protective of the link between whiteness and citizenship, increasingly seemed to expect. Poorer free blacks claimed the streets, sidewalks, and less-than-respectable places of leisure as evidence of their free and independent status, their right to control the terms of their own leisure as well as their labor. And working-class black New Yorkers staged parades to celebrate their own holidays and worked, lounged, played, and promenaded in the streets of Lower Manhattan.¹³ Those conduct writers who offered advice for the aspiring classes of

African Americans endorsed a slightly different method of asserting freedom and independence, however. At a moment when ideal men were expected not just to restrain themselves morally but to improve and fashion themselves into more successful, more moral, more elevated individuals, black conduct writers offered advice on how to transcend the conventional wisdom about the many deficiencies of black masculinity by achieving the period's new ideal of the self-made man.

Black conduct writers insisted that training for a key set of occupations was essential for those African Americans who hoped to become self-made men and thus transform themselves into living refutations of proslavery arguments. Ward's description of how to live an antislavery life, for example, listed specific middle-class occupations that called to mind older eighteenth-century republican ideals of male virtue and independence and linked them with the fight against slavery, racism, and injustice. Throughout the first half of the nineteenth century, African Americans writers suggested that by prospering and living the frugal, industrious, and independent life associated with these "respectable" occupations, free black men could become living embodiments of their discursive refutations of the period's increasingly popular proslavery nationalism that defined African American men as naturally servile, dependent, and thoroughly degraded—unfit for freedom and incorporation into the body politic of the young republic. And other black public figures, such as the delegates to the Colored National Convention of 1848, urged parents to "try to get your sons into mechanical trades; press them into the blacksmith's shop, the machine shop, the joiner's shop, the wheelright's shop, the cooper's shop, and the tailor's shop." In this view, "Every blow of the sledge-hammer, wielded by a sable arm, is a powerful blow in support of our cause. Every colored mechanic, is by virtue of circumstances, an elevator of his race. Every house built by black men, is a strong tower against the allied hosts of prejudice." Consequently, they concluded, "it is impossible for us to attach too much importance to this aspect of the subject."[14]

Believing that individual occupations held extraordinary political significance, some black public figures also urged northern free black men to abandon all employment that might hinder the larger cause and to prevent their wives and daughters from entering into domestic service. Beginning in the 1830s, as newly freed African Americans migrated from rural to urban areas, pronouncements against settling in cities where "our people ... allow themselves to be made 'hewers of wood and drawers of water'; barbers and waiters" began appearing with some frequency in the black public sphere.[15] As Martin Delany asked in *The Condition, Elevation, Emigration, and Destiny of the Colored People*, "How do we compare with" whites? He answered, "Our fathers are their coachmen, our brothers their cookmen, and ourselves their waiting-men." Moreover, "Our mothers [are] their nurse-women, our sisters their scrub-women, our daughters their maid-women, and our wives their washer-women." In his view, "Until colored men, attain to a position above permitting their mothers, sisters, wives, and daughters, to do the drudgery and menial offices of other men's wives and daughters; it is useless, it is nonsense, it is pitiable mockery, to talk about equality and elevation in society. The world is looking upon us, with feelings of commiseration, sorrow, and contempt."[16] Concerns that these forms of labor heightened white disdain for African Americans gave rise to a heated series of debates in the state and national conventions of the 1840s. Delegates divided into two camps: those who insisted that all honest employment should be seen as respectable, and those who argued that service was degraded work that failed to challenge prevailing characterizations of African American men as servile by nature. Delany insisted during the National Convention of 1848 that "he would rather receive a telegraphic dispatch that his wife and two children had fallen victims to a loathsome disease, than to hear that they had become servants of any man." Convention delegates ultimately softened Delany's language somewhat, resolving that "the occupation of domestics and servants among our people is degrading to us as a class, and we deem it our bounden duty to discountenance such pursuits, except where necessity compels the person to resort thereto as a means of livelihood." The delegates assured their audience that they did not mean to "inculcate the doctrine that any kind of needful toil is in itself dishonorable, or that colored persons are to be exempt from what are called menial employments." Rather, because "such employments have been so long and universally filled by colored men" that they have "become a badge of degradation in that it has established the conviction that colored men are only fit for such employments." As a result, "we therefore advise you, by all means, to cease from such employments, as far as practicable, by pressing into others" with more powerful antislavery implications: those that fell within the parameters of the period's most respectable independent male ideal.[17]

The desire to build up a race of independent black men also shaped conduct writers' representations of African American landownership and rural life. Scholars have long understood this tendency as a reaction to the limited economic opportunities and racism free blacks faced in crowded northern cities, where they often, as the delegates at the 1831 National Convention lamented, "suffer for want of employment."[18] But the emphasis on property ownership also reflected the extent to which northern black leaders placed the popular ideal of the self-made man in the service of the freedom struggle.[19] Believing that landownership provided the surest road to virtue, prosperity, and independence, prominent free blacks emphasized the importance of property accumulation—particularly through agricultural pursuits—as critical for young black men. "In our large cities," spokesmen pointed out, "we are passed by as not at all incorporated in the body politic." To remedy this situation, they argued that free black men should follow the example of those who "overcame all obstacles, conquered the soil, and finally became the independent masters of it"; only then would free blacks become "respectable," with "power" and "influence."[20] Prominent African Americans repeatedly advised young men to leave behind the city's limited occupational opportunities, dirt, crime, and vice and establish new lives as independent landowners in the countryside.[21] The Reverend John Berry Meachum, for example, extolled the virtues of landownership: "I think if you would live a little more plain, and save some of your money, you might in time be able to buy yourself a good farm," he wrote. "There are very few of our people that have their own house to live in. They generally live in rented houses or on rented farms. Is there no help for this? I should work night and day, and never stop till I got a piece of land to build a house on." Meachum hoped that "you will consider that just as long as you are living in rented houses you are making yourself a slave for somebody else, and you say you do not like slavery."[22] Country life also offered a respite from the temptations of the city and was thus assumed to be more conducive to the cultivation of virtue in the young men whose "characters are forming for good and evil."[23] Many black leaders also believed that rural landownership leveled the racial playing field and that in the countryside, "a Colored farmer has just the same chance of getting along that a white one has." A contributor to the *Colored American* asserted that "in this department of industry, if in no other, he is on perfect equality. Nature has no prejudice in her heart."[24] Former slave Austin Steward made a similar point in his narrative, *Twenty-Two Years a Slave*: while he resided in Upstate New York, "I knew many colored farmers, all of whom are well respected in the neighborhood of their residence." Based on these observations, he argued that "it is a mistaken idea that there is more prejudice against color in the country. True, it exists everywhere, but I regard it less potent in the country, where a farmer can live less dependent on his oppressors."[25] Black writers' insistence that a virtuous, independent country life could be an antislavery life drew unmistakably on an eighteenth-century republican vision of civic virtue as upheld by independent men capable of representing the best interests of their families and communities. In New York state, where black male suffrage was limited to those with $250 in property, the links among property ownership, independence, and the political rights of a male adult would have been most explicit.[26] But the connection was not lost on black conduct writers across the North, and the concept continued to give gender specificity, political significance, urgency, and anxiety to discussions of personal conduct and economic mobility.

For some northern free blacks, the path to true male independence lay in emigration. Throughout the first half of the nineteenth century, African Americans used the pages of the black press, community meetings, public speeches, and political tracts to debate the possible advantages of leaving behind the United States. Proponents of emigration often insisted that young African American men had the best chance of becoming self-made men and ensuring the independence of the race outside U.S. borders.[27] Indeed, as scholars have long pointed out, African American elites became early supporters of emigration to Liberia, intrigued by the possibility of securing land and building up commercial markets. And their initial support for the white-controlled American Colonization Society was overridden only by the skepticism of poor and working-class free blacks who intended to stay in the land of their fathers.[28] As historian Bruce Dorsey demonstrates, even those few who ultimately emigrated to Liberia framed the colony as the best home for the "development" of African American "manhood and intellect."[29]

Efforts to establish new homes in Canada, Mexico, Trinidad, and Haiti proved much more appealing to northern free blacks, who continued to express their support for these ventures in terms of emigration's potential impact on the political and economic aspirations of their young men. When one African American woman expressed her support for emigration, she insisted that leaving would be the best way for African American men to express their independent, republican spirit and finally enable individuals to rise according to their merits. In an 1832 letter to the *Liberator*, she wrote, "We profess to be republicans, and such I hope we are; but wherein do we show our republican spirit, by sitting still and sighing for that liberty our white brethren tell us we never shall obtain; or in hoping that in some fifty or hundred years hence, our children's children will be made free?" She then declared,

> I think we do not evince republicanism by this conduct, but verily believe that the time has arrived, when we too ought to manifest that spirit of independence which shines so conspicuously in the character of Europeans, by leaving the land of oppression, and emigrating where we may be received and treated as brothers; where our worth will be felt and acknowledged; and where we may acquire education, wealth and respectability, together with a knowledge of the arts and sciences; all of which may be in our power—of the enjoyment of which the government of the separate states in the union is adopting means to deprive us.

Instead of remaining in the United States, blacks should emigrate to Mexico, a truly "independent nation, where indeed 'all men are born free and equal,' possessing those inalienable rights which our constitution guarantees."[30] In 1852, Delany similarly urged free blacks to emigrate to Central and South America and the West Indies: "In going, let us have but one object—to become elevated men and women, worthy of freedom—the worthy citizens of an adopted country. What to us will be adopted—to our children will be legitimate. Go not with an anxiety of political aspirations; but go with the fixed intention—as Europeans come to the United States—of cultivating the soil, entering into the mechanical operations, keeping of shops, carrying on merchandise, trading on land and water, improving property—in a word, to become the producers of the country, instead of the consumers."[31] Whether achieved inside the United States or abroad, these goals, which blurred the lines between late-eighteenth-century notions of virtue and independence and emerging middle-class ideals of respectability, were perceived as key vehicles for a larger race-building enterprise, a movement toward self-sufficiency and independence. In their "Address to the Colored People of the United States," delegates to the National Black Convention of 1848 made certain that their African American audience understood the links among landownership, "respectable" male occupations, and independence: "Independence is an essential condition of respectability." Conversely, "to be dependent, is to be degraded."[32] In other words, young African American men who sought to live truly antislavery lives would need to prepare themselves to take up new forms of labor and embody the ideal of the self-made man.

"THE PROP AND SHELTER OF MORALITY"

Given the form of personal politics favored by aspiring free blacks, the charge to live an antislavery life also heightened typical middle-class anxieties about male independence—or the lack thereof—for aspiring African Americans. These concerns became most pronounced when black conduct writers addressed the subject of young black male morality. Indeed, one of the most striking features of antebellum black conduct discourse is the urgency with which black conduct writers fretted over the moral state of young, free African American men and the comparative silence on the subject of the character of their female counterparts.[33] Writing to the editor of the *Colored American* in 1839, a man complained about this discrepancy: "While our Editors and Divines are declaiming through the press and the pulpit, on the necessity of the moral and mental elevation of our young men, lamenting, in doleful strains, the apathy and indifference of our *hopeful youth*, shedding rivers of ink and oceans of briny tears, on the prevalence of vice and immorality among our men in embryo," they failed fully to address the concerns of the young women of the free black community.[34] While warnings about intemperate, talkative, and profligate women were not unknown in the black press, antebellum African American reformers more frequently referred to women, both black and white, as innately pure.[35] In so doing, these authors joined company with white conduct writers, who celebrated what the historian Barbara Welter has called "the Cult of True Womanhood," insisting that women were inherently pious, pure, virtuous, and submissive.[36] Although women could become corrupted and fall from this exalted position, black conduct writers consistently wrote as if "respectable" African American women were largely above moral reproach. In fact, the idea that any young woman would ever need to be morally elevated seemed preposterous to one *Freedom's Journal* contributor, who noted a "society in Brazil for mending the morals and manners of young ladies! What next? Young ladies are admitted to be angelic; and really we consider them as patterns of all that is moral and mannerly. The men had better set about reforming themselves before they undertake to improve the ladies."[37] In contrast, many writers seemed to feel that young, urban, African American men were at constant risk of moral corruption and in dire need of the protection offered by various forms of moral improvement. Reprinting a short piece by S. Rose, "To Young Men," the *Colored American* hoped young male readers would understand their uniquely important and precarious situation in the world and therefore be more mindful about safeguarding their virtue and morality. For unlike "Woman," who is "sheltered by fond arms and loving counsel," the "young man" must stand "amid the temptations of the world like a self-balanced tower." Given the dangers of this position, "happy is he who seeks and gains the prop and shelter of morality."[38]

Black conduct writers agonized over the threat that key forms of urban entertainment posed to the moral state of young black men. As part of a series on "Means of Elevation," a New Yorker complained of the "numerous porterhouses and low grog-shops that . . . are more or less frequented by youth and young men, on every day of the week, but more especially upon the Sabbath." The young men "who neglect their business and desecrate God's holy day, to congregate in these vicious places" did so "to the utter ruin of their prospects and their reputation."[39] Similarly, Boston resident Maria Stewart gave an 1833 address in which she "implore[d] our men, and especially our rising youth, to flee from the gambling board and the dance-hall."[40] And when discussing the need to improve the moral fiber of the free black population in general terms, the Reverend Lewis Woodson advised young men "to cease to haunt . . . the corners of our streets" along Manhattan's Lower Broadway and instead to "crowd into the lecture room or library" and "read the newspaper" rather than "drinking grog or smoking tobacco."[41]

These persistent expressions of anxiety regarding young male behavior had more to do with the rough-and-tumble nature of masculine forms of urban leisure than any measurable moral deficiencies in the northern free black population. Within these urban locales, laboring men's free time revolved around rough, masculine spaces such as theaters, taverns, and dance halls.[42] There, observed David Ruggles, the fiery leader of New York City's Vigilance Committee, "many are in danger of being led into idle and licentious habits by the allurements of vice which surround them on every side."[43] The implication that young urban African American men were in a state of crisis annoyed at least one "poor beardless youth" who wrote to the Weekly Anglo-African in 1859 to suggest that the oft-asked question, "What are the colored young men of New York doing?" could be posed "with propriety in relation to our young women" as well. "Instead of improving their minds, are they not found perfecting themselves in the games of cards, dominoes, billiards, and Mr. Morphy's favorite game of chess?"[44] But such complaints seem to have had little effect, for antebellum conduct writers consistently characterized the most popular of entertainment venues as vice-ridden, immoral, and illicit spaces that respectable young men in particular should avoid at all costs.

Black conduct writers' explicitly gendered anxieties about urban forms of leisure became most pointed when forgetting the culture of the antebellum theater. As Lawrence Levine has demonstrated, the American theater was a far cry from a respectable space in the early nineteenth century, attracting a mix of laborers, criminals, and confidence men who routinely punctuated the evening's performances with obscenities, oaths, barrages of rotten vegetables, and running commentary on the strengths and weaknesses of the production.[45] Respectable women dared not attend the theater unaccompanied by male escorts and even then ran the risk of being mistaken for one of the scores of prostitutes who attended each performance, soliciting customers from seats upstairs in the third tier, or gallery.[46] African American spectators were also relegated to the gallery, thus reinforcing the prevailing wisdom that African Americans belonged beyond the boundaries of respectable society.[47] Consequently, black conduct writers turned their attention toward the young black men who were more likely to be tempted to attend the theater than their female counterparts, urging that men avoid these spaces precisely because "people of color" were "only allowed an entrance in the galleries, where they must mingle with the very lowest order of the white visitants."[48]

Black conduct writers also worried about how the theatrical subject matter might affect African American patrons. Just "think," wrote an 1837 contributor to the *Weekly Advocate*, of "a young man" returning from the theater "at the hour of midnight," with "his passions inflamed by every thing he has seen, and every thing he has heard." The poor, defenseless young man would then be forced to "pass through ranks of wretched creatures waiting to ensnare him and rob him of his virtue" on his way home. Resisting such an "attack" would "require extraordinary strength of principle." Respectable young African American women were seen as less susceptible to these threats. Though a few females might be drawn into "intrigue with a bold and wily adventurer," young men might become addicted to spending their earnings on popular entertainment, "one of the broadest avenues which lead to destruction."[49]

Conduct writers also believed that taverns, like theaters, posed a dire threat to aspiring young men who might be tempted to relax, unwind, and enjoy some male camaraderie in these popular and decidedly less than respectable spaces. Conduct writers insisted that in addition to reinforcing white justifications for slavery, the young black men who participated in urban theater and tavern culture derailed their prospects for becoming ideal self-made men. One writer complained about the New York City porterhouses that were "kept and patronized, almost exclusively by colored men," and reminded his audience that "when the enemies of the colored man (and these are not a few) see these places, they say, 'O, I see how it is—the slaves, if liberated, would do just the same.'"[50] The popularity of such places was especially troubling because black conduct writers also characterized the rising generation of respectable young men as the primary hope of the race, destined to lead their people from the dark present to a brighter future of freedom and opportunity. Given such great expectations, a contributor to the *Mirror of Liberty* was horrified by "the alarming increase of groggeries, which have been established within the last two or three years, and sustained by heretofore promising young men of our depressed race." One minister blamed the presence of these establishments on white pub owners: "I live near the church in which I have the honor to officiate; and in one square there are fifteen grog-shops located . . . and in the immediate neighborhood there are forty-five. When *you* set the trap, is the rabbit to blamed for being caught? The weary traveler or laborer is snared in the gins that are set by those in authority, who ought to know better." But no matter who owned the taverns or pubs, black conduct writers were convinced that these establishments could destroy young men's attempts to live virtuous antislavery lives. Therefore, authors encouraged all our "young women and old women, fathers and mothers, brothers and sisters, wives and husbands, parents and children, saints and sinners, ministers and laymen" to "'cry aloud and spare not' against this tide of intemperance, which is sweeping our young men, some of our very best men, into an inextricable gulf of destruction."[51]

Many of the expressions of anxiety about young urban black men's moral state reflected larger concerns about African American access to economic mobility and the acquisition of independence. When enumerating the many threats facing young men, conduct writers offered a series of economic and moral objections to urban forms of leisure, often blurring any distinction between the two critiques. Stewart, for example, couched her arguments in practical financial terms, suggesting that those young men who spent their earnings in taverns, dance halls, or theaters were undermining the larger attempt to raise the economic status of the northern black population. "We are poor," Stewart reminded them, "and have no money to throw away"; therefore, "it is astonishing to me that our fine young men are so blind to their own interest and the future welfare of their children as to spend their hard earnings for this frivolous amusement."[52] More often than not, black conduct writers framed the economic dangers they perceived urban leisure activities to pose in explicitly masculine economic and moral terms. Thus, when African American conduct writers discussed the importance of "morality, or purity of conduct," and the eradication of "licentiousness" and "vice," they turned their attention toward those spaces where the young men of the race might be tempted to spend their hard-earned wages—"the most fruitful sources of vice in this community . . . *the theatre, the gaming table,* and *the porter house,*" all of which were most often frequented by men.[53] Here the young men of the race could be led astray down the slippery slope of intemperance and Sabbath breaking to economic ruin, poverty, and ultimately eternal damnation.

In so easily conflating male profligacy with immorality, black conduct writers were drawing on the language used by white reformers of the period. By the 1830s, many white middle-class northerners considered poverty more of a flaw in one's moral character, a vice, and a sign of one's dependence on other people, pastimes, or substances than simply an economic state. Many of these reformers also believed that the vices that "caused" poverty—dependence on alcohol, for example—called into question a man's ability to exhibit self-control, drained his economic resources, and imperiled his ability to support his wife and children and thus to fulfill his obligations as head of the household.[54] Because of these close associations, many reformers saw male poverty in and of itself as suggesting intemperate, immoderate, and even immoral conduct. And because male poverty simultaneously signified dependence and immorality, it held far greater political implications for northerners than did the poverty of women, who were expected to be dependent on their fathers, husbands, and brothers. Thus, members of the northern middle class increasingly viewed intemperance and other displays of "vice and debauchery" as signs of laziness, dependence, and poor character, traits incompatible with political behavior and ideal middle-class manliness.[55] To black conduct writers, surveying the scene through the lens of republicanism, all of the leisure activities that urban men found so appealing threatened the independence and virtue of aspiring young black men. For middle-class African Americans who believed so fervently in the transformative power of self-improvement and respectability, black male poverty, intemperance, and other moral failings could do nothing but devastate efforts to create a generation of black men who embodied refutations of proslavery arguments.

Anxious to protect their communities from immorality and all its attendant political implications, some African American reformers argued that free blacks should focus their energies on combating vice by joining the American

Moral Reform Society. The most vocal advocates of this approach were elite Philadelphians such as William Whipper and Robert Purvis who opposed race-specific organizations and institutions on principle and insisted that evidence of immorality ultimately exacerbated the prejudices faced by all members of the race. Proponents of this view argued that by focusing solely on moral improvement and eschewing racial exclusivity, northern free blacks would ultimately defeat slavery and gain their rightful civil and political rights.[56] This approach failed to gain popularity with the majority of middle-class and aspiring African Americans, however, who made the moral improvement of young men merely one of several weapons in their antislavery arsenal. New Yorkers Lewis Woodson and Charles B. Ray and those who shared their views argued that the moral reform of young men could also be effected through separate black conventions and community institutions that fostered independence as well as morality. Keeping in mind the popular tendency to conflate immorality, poverty, and dependence and claiming the same tropes of republicanism—virtue and independence—used to write African Americans out of the body politic, black conduct writers emphasized the importance of moral improvement, education, thrift, and independence. As Woodson, a young African Methodist Episcopal minister, wrote in the first installment in his series on "Moral Work for Colored Men," "the young colored men of the United States are our present hope: and it is to them I chiefly address myself. Brethren, shall we, notwithstanding our superior advantages, do no more than our fathers have done before us?—Shall we live and shall we die, without leaving a single monument of our existence behind, to beckon our children on to further and higher moral improvement?" He called for a national convention or society to facilitate this process.[57] And when Robert Banks addressed the annual meeting of the Female Dorcas Society of Buffalo, New York, he rallied the young men in attendance: "There must, young men, there *must* be a rousing up to action if we expect to keep pace with the times." Free black men "should gird on the armor of moral improvement, and take hold of the work with spirit and energy. A united effort, with such views, would have a powerful tendency to improve our moral, intellectual and political situation." He wondered, "Shall it be said that the colored people alone are inactive? No, young men, let not this charge be brought against us; but let us be diligent, unite our efforts, and we shall eventually ascend the rugged steep to the temple of knowledge and respectability."[58]

The aspiring free black men who chose to remain in the United States sought to meet this challenge, follow the path laid out by conduct writers, and attend to matters of self-improvement. For example, to safeguard their virtue and acquire the education that would place them in ideal occupations, young African American men created literary societies offering the opportunity for self-improvement. Unlike women's literary societies, which generally taught basic literacy skills to those enrolled, young men's literary societies often functioned as valuable substitutes for a college education.[59] Young men's societies usually offered public lectures (sometimes to audiences of men and women), sponsored debates and scholarly presentations, and maintained libraries.[60] Though instruction was rarely formal, members would work together through cooperation and criticism to improve their body of knowledge and their writing, public speaking, and analytical skills.[61] In New York City, the men of the Phoenix Society maintained a reading room, while the Young Men's Society entertained the black public by demonstrating debating and public speaking skills. Black Bostonians patronized the male-controlled Adelphic Union Library Association and the Young Men's Literary Society.[62] In Philadelphia, men developed and polished these skills at the Philadelphia Library Company of Colored Persons, the Rush Library Company and Debating Society, and the Demosthenian Institute.[63]

For aspiring African Americans, such societies offered an opportunity to educate sons excluded from the American colleges of the Northeast and without the funds or sponsorship to travel and be educated abroad or at Ohio's Oberlin College, one of the few institutions that accepted African American students. These community institutions, in turn, reinforced the link between intellectual improvement and morality by limiting membership to young men who abstained from the consumption of alcohol and maintained high moral standing in their community. For example, membership in the Young Men's Union Literary Association of Philadelphia was limited to young men "of a strict moral character" between the ages of eighteen and forty.[64] And in April 1834, when Henry Highland Garnet joined other young black men in New York City to found the Garrisonian Literary and Benevolent Association for young male abolitionists, the organization sought to promote the "diffusion of knowledge" while encouraging the "moral and intellectual improvement" of its young members. Toward that end, they passed resolutions against degraded displays of behavior, including intemperance and "profane swearing."[65]

By participating in such institutions rather than spending time in the tavern or theater, young African American men protected their morality and virtue. They also enhanced their education, improved their rhetorical and public speaking skills, honed their leadership abilities, developed their political consciousness, socialized with other promising young members of black communities, and established relationships with prominent elders.[66] Altogether, they formed an active and respectable if not necessarily wealthy stratum of the northern free black population and congratulated themselves for their efforts and achievements.[67] The delegates at the 1840 New York State Convention exemplified this perspective when they wrote, "If we look into the past, we behold nothing . . . but 'chains and slavery.' . . . From this state, we have been but a few years relieved. During this time, we have been working our way up, with steady perseverance, to respectability and intelligence. Improvement and elevation, then for the future, is the universal sentiment among us."[68] In this view, attention to personal virtues, acquisition of land, and manly occupations would ensure that African Americans lived up to the respectable middle-class male ideal and thus embodied antislavery principles even as they vigorously campaigned for freedom and the full privileges of citizenship.

NARRATIVIZING AN ANTISLAVERY LIFE

If the political stakes involved in living an antislavery life heightened middle-class anxieties about young black male morality and independence, narratives written by male former slaves demonstrated the power of fusing the personal with the political. Like the conduct literature published in the black press and the discourse offered during conventions, personal narratives could link self-improvement, race consciousness, and antislavery activism in ways that would have resonated with aspiring free black readers. In fact, the narratives penned by former slaves who had achieved prominence in the free black community provided excellent examples of how to live an antislavery life. And if all nineteenth-century Americans were to learn lessons from the various types of personal narratives so popular in the period, aspiring northern blacks could see the principles of elevation in action in these particular black-authored texts and take from them a series of lessons.[69]

Indeed, slave narratives were advertised alongside more standard self-improvement texts and political speeches. For example, the February 25, 1860, "Books" section of the *Weekly Anglo-African* newspaper included reviews of a temperance book, *The Dream; or, The True History of Dea. Giles's Distillery and Dea. Jones's Brewery*; William C. Nell's history, *Colored Patriots of the American Revolution*; Frederick Douglass's narrative, *My Bondage and My Freedom*;

George Thompson's *The Palm Land; or, West Africa, Illustrated*; Solomon Northup's memoir, *Twelve Years a Slave*; Gerrit Smith's speech, "Slavery Has No Right but to Die!"; and the *Life of Jermain W. Loguen, the Great Underground Railroad King*. More important, African American editors praised and marketed slave narratives not solely for their denunciations of slavery but also for the moral lessons and example they offered readers. The advertisement for the *Life of Jermain W. Loguen*, for example, announced, "There are few men whose history is so marked with stirring incidents, instructive lessons and encouraging examples, as Mr. Loguen's."[70] Offering a model of black behavior, such a work was especially advantageous for young readers. "We sincerely thank Mr. Loguen for the appearance of this book," remarked the editors of the *Weekly Anglo-African* in their review, "and hope it will find its way into every family in the land; and especially do we hope that no colored family, and no Sabbath School library, and no colored youth, will be found without a copy."[71] And Dr. James McCune Smith concluded his introduction to the revised and expanded 1855 version of Douglass's personal narrative, *My Bondage and My Freedom*, "It is not without a feeling of pride, dear reader, that I present you with this book. The son of a self-emancipated bond-woman, I feel joy in introducing to you my brother, who has rent his own bonds, and who, in his every relation—as a public man, as a husband and as a father—is such as does honor to the land which gave him birth. I shall place this book in the hands of the only child spared me, bidding him to strive and emulate its noble example. You may do likewise."[72]

The narratives written by male former slaves dramatized the link between male self-improvement and the independence that came with freedom. In addition to critiquing the violence, inhumanity, and greed fostered by the system of slavery, the slave narrative functioned as an elevation story for the northern black reader. For example, as literary critic David Leverenz argues, Douglass's original *Narrative* and all its subsequent revisions focus on manhood, "the dignity of labor and the Protestant work ethic" as well as on "being a self-made man, a topic on which he frequently spoke."[73] But the authors of these narratives not only invoked the idea of the self-made man on the printed page but reminded readers that they physically embodied that concept. The arc of the slave narrative illustrated self-improvement principles in the most distilled fashion—a movement from the degradation of total dependence demanded by the slave power to freedom and ostensibly independence in the North. Many authors crystallized this arc of elevation in the titles of their narratives, including James W. C. Pennington's *The Fugitive Blacksmith; or, Events in the History of James W. C. Pennington, Pastor of a Presbyterian Church, New York, Formerly a Slave in the State of Maryland, United States*; Austin Steward's *Twenty-Two Years a Slave, and Forty Years a Freeman*; and, most notably, Douglass's *My Bondage and My Freedom*.

As these titles suggest, many of those who wrote about the institution of slavery were established members of the northern black community. Steward was a regular delegate to local, state, and national black conventions. Henry Bibb, who published his *Narrative of the Life and Adventures of Henry Bibb, an American Slave* in 1849, was an important leader of the fugitive slave community in Canada West, where he served as an educator and a newspaper editor. Samuel Ringgold Ward was a student of classics and theology, a Congregationalist minister, and a newspaper editor as well as a celebrated antislavery lecturer.[74] Douglass won fame for editing the *North Star* as well as for his oratorical skills. Pennington was a Presbyterian minister whose 1841 *Textbook on the Origins and History ... of the Colored People* made him a founding father of the black intellectual tradition.[75] And William Wells Brown, author of an 1847 narrative, was a prolific writer as well as antislavery lecturer, publishing plays, a novel, and works of African American history after gaining his freedom.[76]

The same qualities that threatened these men's "authenticity" for white audiences made them "representative men" for members of the northern black activist community. White abolitionists often worried that educated black lecturers would not convince hostile white audiences that they had, in fact, been enslaved. In *My Bondage and My Freedom*, Douglass wrote that white abolitionists had encouraged him to mask his oratorical abilities and asked him to keep "a *little* of the plantation manner of speech" to avoid appearing "too learned."[77] By contrast, northern blacks valued literary skill and oratorical prowess as badges of leadership. Martin Delany praised the narratives of Douglass, Brown, and Bibb as "masterly efforts, manifesting great force of talents." Delany described Bibb as "an eloquent speaker" who "with equal advantages, would equal many of those who fill high places in the country, and now assume superiority over him and his kindred." And Delany characterized Ward as "a man of great talents" whose "fame is widespread as an orator and a man of learning." Ward had "stood on nomination for two or three years, as Liberty-party candidate for Vice President of the United States," and New York governor William H. Seward said that he had "never heard true eloquence until he heard Samuel R. Ward speak." Delany was certain that Ward was "destined to be a great statesman."[78]

Through courage and ingenuity, these men had transformed themselves from chattel into the literate, eloquent, and famous. Brown pointed out that "in our own country, there are men who once held the plough, and that too without any compensation, that are now presiding at the editor's table."[79] Such men provided living proof that the ideal of the black self-made man was attainable. Force of will had transformed them from personal property owned by another into free men, even statesmen of sorts, ambassadors for the African American population. If these once-enslaved men could rise to prominence and independence and dedicate their lives to antislavery work, free black northerners had a duty to strive to do the same.

In addition to offering an elevation story, slave narratives illustrated that the process of living an antislavery life required constant work and continuous effort. Authors were particularly explicit on this point when describing their personal commitment to continuing their educational advancement and fighting slavery even after they had secured their own freedom. In the North, they received their education however they could, often combining work and studies and relying on the institutions of the free black community for support. Ward's parents enrolled their son in New York City's African Free School, where his classmates included future Shakespearean actor Ira Aldridge and future activist Henry Highland Garnet. While there, "poverty compelled" Ward "to work, but inclination led me to study." And in 1833, Ward "became a clerk of Thomas L. Jennings, Esq., one of the most worthy of the coloured race." Later Ward and his brother "served David Ruggles, Esq.," leader of New York City's Vigilance Committee.[80] Bibb obtained only three formal weeks of schooling while living in Detroit in January 1842. Yet he persevered, receiving enough instruction to pen his narrative in 1849.[81] Arriving in New York City as a fugitive in his early twenties, Pennington immediately began pursuing an education.[82] When reflecting on his experience, Pennington contrasted his former enslaved condition with his new life in New York City, where he "was earning respectable wages, and by means of evening schools and private tuition, was making encouraging progress in my studies." But self-improvement and the rise to respectability and independence still required an extraordinary effort. Pennington reflected, "It cost me two years' hard labour, after I fled, to unshackle my mind; it was three years before I had purged my language of slavery's idioms; it was four years before I had thrown off the crouching aspect of slavery."[83]

These struggles must certainly have resonated with northern blacks who scrimped, saved, and sacrificed to keep their children in school or who attended African American Sabbath schools and literary societies to learn. In fact, these authors were building on some of the lessons laid out in northern black directives to children. For example, in a piece on young women's education published in the *Emancipator* in 1833, Sarah Mapps Douglass recounted the mobbing and destruction of Prudence Crandall's Connecticut school for young ladies of color and urged "all who have *promised* to become Miss Crandall's pupils to go forward. Let not the fear of insult deter any one from embracing this glorious opportunity.—We seldom walk abroad without being wounded by 'the cruel language of the eye,' and methinks, for the sake of an education, we might be willing to bear not only scornful looks, but oppressive acts." She concluded, "Our enemies know that education will elevate us to an equality with themselves. We also know, that it is of more importance to us than gold, 'yes more to be desired than much fine gold.'"[84]

As scholars have long pointed out, Frederick Douglass placed the same lessons at the center of his narrative, characterizing his hard fight for literacy as the beginning of his transformation from bondsman to free man. Douglass recalled how he learned to read while still enslaved, gleaning knowledge from the whites around him: the mistress who made the mistake of teaching him the alphabet, the young white schoolboys who gave him lessons between errands. He learned to write by watching the carpenters at the Baltimore shipyard where he hired out his time for his master. "When a piece of timber was intended for the larboard side, it would be marked thus—'L.' When a piece was for the starboard side forward, it would be marked thus—'S.F.,'" he wrote. "I soon learned the names of these letters, and for what they were intended when placed upon a piece of timber in the ship-yard. I immediately commenced copying them." He goaded boys into giving him writing lessons by challenging them to beat his ability to write the few letters he knew. He used whatever writing implements he could find or fashion to improve his skills: "During this time," he recalled, "my copy-book was the board fence, brick wall, and pavement; my pen and ink was a lump of chalk." Finally, he wrote in the empty spaces of his young master's copybook, until "after a long, tedious effort for years, I finally succeeded in learning how to write."[85] In short, he made it clear that the process of self-elevation was not an easy one and that attempts at personal transformation could and should be inextricably bound up with one's desire to vanquish the peculiar institution.

When they arrived in the free states or newly adopted countries, these fugitives felt compelled to continue their antislavery labors by joining abolitionist organizations, traveling as antislavery lecturers, and participating in societies designed to aid the region's free black population. As Pennington explained, once he found himself "among the free people of colour in New York, where slavery was so recently abolished; and finding much to do for their elevation," he "resolved to give my strength in that direction."[86] Douglass joined Brown on the abolitionist lecture circuit before settling in Rochester and inaugurating the *North Star*. Ward also lectured extensively, traveling to Canada and Britain before moving to Jamaica, purchasing land, and becoming a gentleman farmer. And Bibb ultimately emigrated to Canada West, becoming a leader of the fugitive community established there.

As the activities of these men make apparent, narratives highlighted the ongoing quest for independence, ultimately narrativizing a uniquely African American interpretation of class mobility: a person garnered dignity, respect, and acclaim not on the basis of his or her origins but rather by success at forms of self-fashioning, at rising in society, and at working on behalf of their people. Writing in 1855, Douglass recalled that before the 1840s, "a colored man was deemed a fool who confessed himself a runaway slave, not only because of the danger to which he exposed himself of being retaken, but because it was a confession of a very *low* origin!"[87] But by the end of the decade, northern blacks praised "self-made" and "great" men such as Bibb precisely because he began life as "an ignorant slave," and "by his own powers" became "an educated free man" who "left a name that will not soon fade away."[88] Loguen's narrative was marketed both as a story that "contains the peculiarities of his childhood, his daring escape from bondage, the perils and hardships he endured in his passage to freedom" and for its depiction of "the acts of subsequent manhood, which have honorably connected his name with the moral and political causes of the last twenty years, which, to a large extent, have made the subject of African freedom the living topic of private and public circles of the press, the pulpit, and the State and National Legislatures."[89] For northern black audiences, then, famous fugitive slaves clearly served as examples of courage, resilience, perseverance, strength, and virtue, and young aspiring African Americans were expected to emulate these examples and to place personal conduct and behavior in the service of the freedom struggle. While slaveholders inevitably sank further into the depths of sin, the African American heroes of some of the most powerful abolitionist texts could maintain their dignity in the face of overwhelming odds, claim their freedom, and elevate themselves to the status of free men, model self-made men, and even statesmen. As James McCune Smith wrote, Douglass's life "shows that any man in our land, 'no matter in what battle his liberty may have been cloven down'... not only may 'stand forth redeemed and disenthralled,' but may also stand up a candidate for the highest suffrage of a great people—the tribute of their honest hearty admiration."[90]

UP FROM SLAVERY?

During the 1840s and 1850s, as memoirs and narratives by African Americans proliferated, they helped to create the archetype of the black self-made man. Slave narratives sketched out the path free black men could take up from slavery and reinforced the links northern black conduct writers forged among independence, morality, and education. Together, this discourse offered an ideal to which young black men were expected to aspire as they trained themselves to live antislavery lives; it also served as a counterpoint to the anxieties black conduct writers expressed about the many temptations and moral dangers faced by their most promising young men. Indeed, by 1859, Douglass, exemplar of the revolutionary possibilities of the processes of self-fashioning, would be lecturing on "Self-Made Men" to audiences across the North.[91]

Of course, slave narratives could not soothe all the worries plaguing northern free blacks. As Ann Fabian reminds us, slave narratives did not ultimately end in true freedom and "the narrator's incorporation into a free society." Rather, they "ended with the narrators on the lecture circuit—no longer enslaved, to be sure, but suspended somewhere between slavery and freedom."[92] Narratives, therefore, mirrored the questions northern free blacks were increasingly asking by the 1850s: Was it indeed possible to become a black self-made man and live an antislavery life within the boundaries of the United States? And was it truly possible to shake off all vestiges of dependence while living in a nation that insisted that slavery was the appropriate status for men of African descent? As the authors' varied resettlement choices make apparent, narratives ultimately could not resolve these two important questions for aspiring black readers.

More important, even as they narrated the path up from slavery and provided a model of ideal behavior, slave narratives also offered vivid details of what continued to befall those left behind in the prison house of slavery. In 1853, Solomon Northup, a free black farmer and musician from Upstate New York, published a personal narrative about his experiences with slavery. During a trip to Washington, D.C., Northup had been drugged, bound, and sold into slavery by his white traveling companions. Alone in a slave pen in the shadow of the

Capitol, he endured deep emotional distress as he came to terms with his new circumstances. Northup

> listened intently for some sign or sound of life, but nothing broke the oppressive silence, save the clinking of my chains, whenever I chanced to move. I spoke aloud, but the sound of my voice startled me. I felt of my pockets, so far as the fetters would allow—far enough, indeed, to ascertain that I had not only been robbed of liberty, but that my money and free papers were also gone! Then did the idea begin to break upon my mind, at first dim and confused, that I had been kidnapped. But that I thought was incredible. There must have been some misapprehension—some unfortunate mistake. It could not be that a free citizen of New-York, who had wronged no man, nor violated any law, should be dealt with thus inhumanly. The more I contemplated my situation, however, the more I became confirmed in my suspicions. It was a desolate thought, indeed. I felt there was no trust or mercy in unfeeling man; and commending myself to the God of the oppressed, bowed my head upon my fettered hands, and wept most bitterly.[93]

In this sudden reversal of fortune, Northup would soon find himself in the cotton fields of Louisiana, far from his friends and his home, his wife, and his three children. And twelve years would pass before Northup would find an ally to help him contact his friends and family in New York, engineer a rescue, and begin the process of reclaiming his former status as a free man.[94]

As the next chapter will show, experiences like these demonstrated that it was far easier to go from being a respectable independent citizen to a complete dependent than to reverse the process. Commenting on Northup's account, Douglass wrote, "Think of it: For thirty years a *man*, with all a man's hopes, fears and aspirations—with a wife and children to call him by the endearing names of husband and father—with a home . . . then for twelve years a *thing*, a chattel personal, classed with mules and horses."[95] Narratives, then, not only provided models for young free black men to emulate but also reinforced concerns about the dangers facing free blacks in the North and the horrors experienced by those who remained enslaved in the South.

CHAPTER THREE

Antislavery Discourse and the African American Family

And unfortunately for me, I am the father of a slave, a word too obnoxious to be spoken by a fugitive slave. It calls fresh to my mind the separation of husband and wife; of stripping, tying up and flogging; of tearing children from their parents, and selling them on the auction block. It calls to mind female virtue trampled under foot with impunity. But oh! when I remember that my daughter, my only child, is still there, destined to share the fate of all these calamities, it is too much to bear. If ever there was any one act of my life while a slave, that I have to lament over it is that of being a father and a husband of slaves. I have the satisfaction of knowing that I am only the father of one slave. She is bone of my bone, and flesh of my flesh; poor unfortunate child. She was the first and shall be the last slave that ever I will father, for chains and slavery on this earth.

—Henry Bibb, *Narrative of the Life and Adventures of Henry Bibb* (1849)

When Harriet Jacobs began writing her memoir, she must have known that her story would be difficult to believe. After all, she had spent seven years of her life hiding from her master in a crawl space in her free grandmother's attic before finally escaping from Edenton, North Carolina, and securing her freedom in New York. Still, as she put it in a letter to white abolitionist Amy Post, "I must write just what I have lived and witnessed myself."[1] Publishing under the pseudonym Linda Brent and using false names for all the people whose experiences she detailed in print, Jacobs hoped to protect the safety and reputation of her friends and family and to avoid "attract[ing] attention" to herself or "excit[ing] sympathy" for her "own sufferings." Rather, she hoped that her female perspective on the peculiar institution would help "to convince the people of the Free States what slavery really is."[2]

As scholars have noted, the narrative Jacobs ultimately published in 1861,

Incidents in the Life of a Slave Girl, Written by Herself, was not an authoritative account of a man's quest for liberty and triumph of will but instead constituted a domestic tale about family, community, and feminine virtue struggling to survive under the oppressive weight of slavery. Jacobs told her readers of her aged grandmother's deep love for her children and grandchildren and of her father's care and concern for his family. She also detailed her experiences as a fifteen-year-old girl living in the household of a lecherous middle-aged master and jealous mistress, describing her devastation when her owner, determined to make her his concubine, refused to allow her to marry the free black carpenter she loved. Certain that she would be unable to continue eluding her master's sexual advances and aware that he would surely sell any children she might bear, Jacobs entered instead into a sexual relationship with a young unmarried white attorney from a family more prominent than that of her owner. Hopeful that her lover would purchase and emancipate any children he might father, Jacobs defined this decision as a necessary self-protective measure, the first in a series of sacrifices she would make on behalf of the son and daughter she would later bear. Her love for these children ultimately kept her hiding close to them in Edenton and determined to make a home for them in the free North.

Jacobs's tale serves as the quintessential reminder that slave narratives did not limit themselves to the struggle of men throwing off their chains. Throughout the antebellum era, concerns about slavery's impact on African American domestic relationships remained a central theme in black antislavery discourse.[3] While these stories were designed to counter proslavery propaganda and increase abolitionist sentiment by revealing the true nature of the chattel principle, they also performed an additional function for African American readers. Rather than enlightening northern free blacks about the evils of slavery, antislavery discourse in general and slave narratives in particular reminded free black readers of slavery's impact on their literal and figurative families, past, present, and future. In this way, slave narratives offered a distinctly personal lens through which northern free blacks could review the horrors of slavery, crystallizing the imperative of living an antislavery life and strengthening their sense of solidarity with their enslaved brothers and sisters in distant lands.

"THE MORE TENDER RELATIONS"

White and black abolitionists alike insisted that slavery had a particularly dreadful impact on the gender dynamics and family life of the enslaved. In this view, "the slave family was the immediate victim" of the peculiar institution.[4]

Wives and husbands were separated, children were torn from their parents, and young women were sold into prostitution. To emphasize this point, the masthead of William Lloyd Garrison's *Liberator* newspaper regularly featured images of enslaved families on the auction block, waiting to be sold alongside horses and cattle. Antislavery poetry and prose, meanwhile, highlighted descriptions of families shattered simply to satisfy the greed of their masters, making them symbols of slavery's unfathomable and deeply personal cruelty.

Northern black activists agreed that slaveholders were, as Martin Delany wrote, "robbers of the dearest social ties, and ruthless despoilers of the most sacred family connection!"[5] And visual and narrative descriptions of these violations held great emotional power, as is evidenced by the reception of one of the most famous speeches of the day, the Reverend Henry Highland Garnet's "Address to the Slaves." First given in 1843 at the National Negro Convention in Buffalo, New York, this address has long been considered an important harbinger of the growing militancy of free black activists.[6] Addressing his "Brethren and Fellow Citizens," Garnet denounced slavery as "sinful" and called for the enslaved to "use every means, both moral, intellectual, and physical," to put it to an end. He urged enslaved African Americans to stop working for their masters, to "cease to toil for the heartless tyrants, who give you no other reward but stripes and abuse." Saying, "there is not much hope of Redemption without the shedding of blood," Garnet demanded they take up the motto "Resistance! Resistance! Resistance!" and make it clear to slaveholders that it was "no longer" a "debatable question, whether it is better to choose LIBERTY or DEATH!"[7] While the militancy in Garnet's speech is undeniable, an examination of how the speech was recorded in the published minutes of the 1843 convention proceedings is instructive.[8] Although the speech apparently took "nearly one hour and a half," when the recording secretary summarized Garnet's words and their reception, only two sentences were devoted to the speech's contents, focusing on Garnet's critique of slavery's impact on African American families: Garnet "reviewed the abominable system of slavery, showed its mighty workings, its deeds of darkness and of death—how it robbed parents of children, and children of parents, husbands of wives; how it prostituted the daughters of the slaves; how it murdered the colored man." These stories apparently had a powerful effect on the convention delegates and spectators, for after hearing Garnet recount these abuses, the entire convention was "literally infused with tears."[9]

Those African Americans who wrote slave narratives provided personal testimony that corroborated Garnet's descriptions of slavery's corrosive power.

Authors wrote evocatively of the misery experienced by enslaved children. Abolitionist literature consistently portrayed enslaved children as the "victims of emotional and psychic pain, ranging from separation from their families, to the denial of education and religious instruction."[10] In their narratives, Frederick Douglass and James W. C. Pennington pointed out that as enslaved children, they suffered from neglect. Douglass recalled that because his mother was hired out to a planter who lived twelve miles away, she was unable to care for him or even visit with any regularity: the "four or five times" that he did see his mother, the visits were "very short in duration, and at night."[11] And Pennington wrote that when he was around age four, he "began to feel another evil of slavery—I mean the want of parental care and attention to the children during the day." Pennington remembered enduring hunger and loneliness and being left to fend for himself while his parents labored. "To estimate the sad state of a slave child," he wrote, "you must look at it as a hopeless human being thrown into the world without a social circle to flee to for hope, shelter, comfort, or instruction."[12]

These descriptions provided a startling contrast with the sentimental version of childhood so important to the emerging middle classes in the period. By the 1830s, as household manufacturing declined and birthrates decreased, childhood began to take on a divine status in middle-class families. "Ministers, physicians, educators and other moralists from the Northeast" created a romantic image of innocent children, idealizing childhood as a precious and sentimental time meant to be free from care. Middle-class parents were expected to attend very closely to their children's spiritual, intellectual, and material needs and to discipline them gently with "maternal tenderness, patience and love."[13] As the narratives of Pennington and Douglass demonstrated, however, enslaved children enjoyed none of these considerations. Instead of receiving proper middle-class instruction from attentive parents, the "slave-boy" was allowed to run "wild," as Douglass put it, doing "whatever his boyish nature suggests; enacting, by turns, all the strange antics and freaks of horses, dogs, pigs, and barn yard fowls," rather than having "pretty little verses to learn in the nursery" or "nice little speeches to make for aunts, uncles, or cousins, to show how smart he is."[14]

Narrators also wrote of the pain they experienced as parents forced to attend to the economic and domestic needs of the master's family and thus unable to come to the aid of their young, vulnerable children. Jacobs described the miserable life of her aunt, who spent her days working in their owner's household and evenings lying on the floor by their mistress's bedroom door, on call should the mistress or her children want anything. Forced to prioritize the needs of her mistress, Jacobs's aunt's health rapidly deteriorated, and she suffered a series of miscarriages and premature deliveries. Recalling her aunt's "patient sorrow as she held the last dead baby in her arms," Jacobs blamed the woman's anguish on the mistress she had known since childhood but who still, "apparently without any compunction; and with cruel selfishness" had "rendered her poor foster-sister childless" and "ruined her health by years of incessant, unrequited toil, and broken rest."[15] Henry Bibb described his sorrow at his inability to protect his "dear little daughter" during the day. Although he and his wife, Malinda, "nurtured and caressed" the girl during the evenings, "there was no one to take care of poor little Frances, while her mother was toiling in the field." Instead, "she was left at the house to creep under the feet of an unmerciful old mistress, whom I have known to slap with her hand the face of little Frances, for crying after her mother, until her little face was left black and blue." Bibb recalled an incident in which "Malinda and myself came from the field one summer's day at noon, and poor little Frances came creeping to her mother smiling, but with large tear drops standing in her dear little eyes, sobbing and trying to tell her mother that she had been abused, but was not able to utter a word. Her little face was bruised black with the whole print of Mrs. Gatewood's hand. This print was plainly to be seen for eight days after it was done. But oh! this darling child was a slave; born of a slave mother."[16]

Northern blacks, only a generation or two removed from slavery, could hardly have remained unaffected by these stories or by Bibb's question, "Who can imagine what could be the feelings of a father and mother, when looking upon their infant child whipped and tortured with impunity, and then placed in a situation where they could afford it no protection?"[17] They not only could imagine these feelings but could remember them. Only a few decades earlier, as northern states gradually transitioned to free labor, African American families in New York, New Jersey, and New England experienced the same type of vulnerability. Consequently, antislavery discourse had the potential to raise a set of painful emotions for northern free black audiences. More than surprising revelations, they were family stories, traumatic memories, sharpened in the retelling. Sojourner Truth recalled the abuses she and others experienced as slaves in early-nineteenth-century Ulster County, New York. Even though she extolled the kindness of her final master, Mr. Dumont, she audibly groaned as she remembered "how many times I let my children go hungry, rather than take secretly the bread I liked not to ask for." Truth's interviewer noted that "she shudders, even now, as she goes back in memory" to relive her childhood and to recall the cellar in which she, her family members, and other slaves were forced to live, "sleeping on those damp boards, like the horse" and inhaling "noxious vapors" that were "chilling and fatal to health." After describing the bloody beating she received as a nine-year-old when her native Dutch language made it impossible to understand the demands of a new English-speaking master, Truth declared, when "I hear 'em tell of whipping women on the bare flesh, it makes *my* flesh crawl, and my very hair rise on my head! Oh! my God! . . . What a way is this of treating human beings?"[18]

Moreover, while white abolitionists could choose to relate to enslaved blacks as brothers and sisters, northern free blacks often were just that—intimately connected with those in bondage by ties of blood. Indeed, Garnet took this idea as the premise for his "Address to the Slaves." "Many of you," he said, "are bound to us, not only by the ties of a common humanity, but we are connected by the more tender relations of parents, wives, husbands, children, brothers, and sisters, and friends." "As such," he continued, "we most affectionately address you."[19] For an audience that had relatives still living under the yoke of slavery, slave narratives detailed the continuing reality for the wives and husbands, children, siblings, friends, and parents they expected never to see again. As William Wells Brown noted near the end of his account, awareness of the fate awaiting those they left behind caused fugitives great emotional distress. "During the last night that I served in slavery," Brown recalled, "I did not close my eyes a single moment. When not thinking of the future, my mind dwelt on the past. The love of a dear mother, a dear sister, and three dear brothers, yet living, caused me to shed many tears. If I could only have been assured of their being dead, I should have felt satisfied; but I imagined I saw my dear mother in the cotton-field, followed by a merciless taskmaster, and no one to speak a consoling word to her! I beheld my dear sister in the hands of a slave-driver, and compelled to submit to his cruelty!" Noting that such visions caused him deep pain and sorrow, Brown remarked, "None but one placed in such a situation can for a moment imagine the intense agony to which these reflections subjected me."[20] For his part, the act of writing his memoirs forced Bibb to relive the experiences of his past: "It calls fresh to my mind the separation of husband and wife; of stripping, tying up and flogging; of tearing children from their parents, and selling them on the auction block. It calls to mind female virtue trampled under foot with impunity." But these memories also compelled him to confront the memory of the child he left behind. "But oh!" he wrote, "when I remember that my daughter, my only child, is still there, destined to share the fate of all these calamities, it is too much to bear."[21] When Pennington wrote an 1844 public letter to his father, mother, brothers, and sisters remaining in bondage, he indicated that he continued to feel their pain. "Mother, dear mother," he wrote, "I know, I feel, mother, the pangs of thy bleeding heart, that thou hast endured, during so many years of vexation. Thy agonies are by a genuine son-like sympathy mine; I will, I must, I do share daily in those agonies of thine."[22] These descriptions were more than sentimental conventions designed to evoke sympathy in white audiences. The knowledge that family members remained in bondage meant that the memory of slavery was never far from these writers' minds.

Slave narratives not only raised painful past memories and sharpened concerns about trapped brothers and sisters but also narrated distinct possibilities northern free blacks might yet face. Despite their residence in the free states, they, loved ones, and friends were hardly safe from being identified as or mistaken for fugitives or simply kidnapped and sold into bondage. In 1837, Jerry Morgan's wife, Margaret, and their children were forcibly carried to Maryland on the grounds that Margaret's emancipation had never been formalized, so she and her Pennsylvania-born children belonged to her former master's heir. Before the U.S. Supreme Court affirmed the heir's right to claim Morgan's family as property in *Prigg v. Pennsylvania* (1842), Morgan traveled to Harrisburg in the hopes that the governor of Pennsylvania might assist him in locating his wife and children and regaining their freedom. But during his return trip, a boatman misplaced Morgan's free papers, and he found himself detained on suspicion of being a runaway. Morgan's frantic escape attempt ended when he lost his footing in a desperate leap off the boat and was dragged under and drowned.[23] In another 1859 instance, the members of a family known "for their industry, sobriety, and general good behavior" were kidnapped in the dead of night and carried from Cumberland County, Pennsylvania, across the state line to Maryland. According to a report published in *Douglass's Monthly*, "The next morning the family were missing, and the house was found empty. Articles of clothing were strewn around in confusion. The bread which had been put to rise for Saturday's baking stood on the hearth ready to be worked for the oven. The bed in which the little girl had been wont to sleep showed by its rumpled state that it had been robbed of its occupant."[24] These "disappearances" were traumatic events for northern African Americans, as Samuel Ringgold Ward pointed out: "Two of my father's nephews, who had escaped to New York, were taken back in the most summary manner, in 1828. I never saw a family thrown into such deep distress by the death of any two of its members, as were our family by the re-enslavement of these two young men. Seven-and-twenty years have past, but we have none of us heard a word concerning them, since their consignment to the living death, the temporal hell, of American slavery."[25] Enduring years of silence and uncertainty about his whereabouts, Solomon Northup's children "returned from school" one afternoon "weeping bitterly" to their mother. "On inquiring the cause of the children's sorrow, it was found that, while studying geography, their attention had been attracted to the picture of slaves working in the cotton-field, and an overseer following them with his whip. It reminded them of the sufferings their father might be, and as it happened, actually *was*, enduring in the South."[26] Narratives such as Northup's, then, also allowed northern black readers to imagine and mourn the fate that befell lost family members.

Such stories also tightened the figurative bonds among all northern free blacks and their enslaved brothers and sisters. In a letter to William Lloyd Garrison, James McCune Smith explained that he could not "feel free, while these, my countrymen, are stripped, and wounded, and left in the cotton fields and the rice swamps, to bleed and to die; and, among them, my own brothers and sisters, who are as dear to me as my heart's blood. . . . I am still bound with my brethren. I feel the cruel lash, and their chains."[27] Jacobs certainly thought as much. In a description that must be read as a metaphor for the race as well as a description of the love between long-lost siblings, she divulged her feelings at being reunited with her brother in New York. After spying him from an upstairs window, Jacobs "flew down stairs, opened the front door," and "in less than a minute I was clasped in my brother's arms." Jacobs noted "his old feelings of affection for me . . . were as lively as ever," for "there are no bonds so strong as those which are formed by suffering together."[28]

That suffering, slave narratives made clear, took place in the North as well as the South, for in addition to describing what happened after their friends and family members disappeared, narratives also illustrated the difficult conditions under which African Americans lived in the North. In the closing chapter of his 1837 narrative, *Slavery in the United States*, Charles Ball explained that his wife, Lucy, and their children, "all of whom had been free from their birth," had lived together in Baltimore before Ball was sold to a Georgia trader. After escaping and making his way back to Maryland, Ball learned that only a few days after his sale, his wife and children had been kidnapped "and driven into southern slavery." Overwhelmed with grief and despair, Ball rushed out of his empty house, "and returned to Pennsylvania with a broken heart." His life became a kind of half freedom, and "for the last few years, I have resided about fifty miles from Philadelphia, where I expect to pass the evening of my life, in working hard for my subsistence, without the least hope of ever again seeing my wife and children:—fearful, at this day, to let my place of residence be known, lest even yet it may be supposed, that as an article of property, I am of sufficient value to be worth pursuing in my old age."[29] In other words, slavery not only deprived his free wife and children of their liberty, shattering his family just as his father's family had been broken apart a generation earlier, but also continued to shape his life in the "free" North, where he lived more like a hunted criminal than a free man.

"UNPROTECTED BY LAW OR CUSTOM"

For aspiring African Americans, representations of slavery's impact on their brothers and sisters raised serious concerns about the moral condition of the rising generation of bondspeople. Foremost among these concerns were those involving slavery's ability to corrupt the emotional instincts of young women and men.[30] Rather than looking forward to forming chaste but romantic attachments, marrying, and establishing families, former slaves wrote about how their efforts to resist slavery led them to avoid the life steps that aspiring free blacks viewed as both natural and essential for the future prospects of the race. Brown, for example, avoided marrying a woman to whom he was deeply attached: "I was determined to make another trial to get my liberty," he wrote, "and I knew that if I should have a wife, I should not be willing to leave her behind; and if I should attempt to bring her with me, the chances would be difficult for success."[31] Rather than looking forward to bearing and raising children, Ellen Craft dreaded the idea of assuming a family role that middle-class nineteenth-century writers characterized as an exalted state. According to William Craft, "My wife was torn from her mother's embrace in childhood, and taken to a distant part of the country. She had seen so many other children separated from their parents in this cruel manner, that the mere thought of her ever becoming the mother of a child, to linger out a miserable existence under the wretched system of American slavery, appeared to fill her very soul with horror." As a result, William Craft "did not, at first, press the marriage, but agreed to assist her in trying to devise some plan by which we might escape from our unhappy condition, and then be married."[32]

Even more troubling, slave narratives repeatedly warned that slaveholders regularly forced the best young women of the race into concubinage and prostitution. Pennington noted that "it is under the mildest form of slavery, as it exists in Maryland, Virginia, and Kentucky, that the finest specimens of coloured females are reared. There are no mothers who rear, and educate in the natural graces, finer daughters than the Ethiopian women, who have the least chance to give scope to their maternal affections." But "what is generally the fate of such female slaves?" he asked. "When they are not raised for the express purpose of supplying the market of a class of economical Louisian and Mississippi gentleman, who do not wish to incur the expense of rearing legitimate families, they are nevertheless, on account of their attractions, exposed to the most shameful degradation, by the young masters in the families where it is claimed they are so well off."[33] This theme became a standard trope of antislavery discourse and a central critique of the peculiar institution. While proslavery theorists could insist that slavery was a positive good for all involved, authors of slave narratives would transgress societal norms by highlighting the sexual violence and coercion experienced by enslaved women on a daily basis.

Narrators also revealed that young women who escaped this fate and married young men of their choosing found that the marriage bond offered them no legal or personal protection. Brown explained that although "it is common for slaves to be married, there is no such thing as slaves being lawfully married. There has never yet a case occurred where a slave has been tried for bigamy. The man may have as many women as he wishes, and the women as many men; and the law takes no cognizance of such acts among slaves. And in fact some masters, when they have sold the husband from the wife, compel her to take another."[34] Bibb could barely contain his rage while discussing the vulnerability of slave marriages. After explaining that there "is no legal marriage among the slaves of the South," he declared "that every slaveholder, who is the keeper of a number of slaves of both sexes, is also the keeper of a house or houses of ill-fame." Moreover, "licentious white men, can and do, enter at night or day the lodging places of slaves; break up the bonds of affection in families; destroy all their domestic and social union for life; and the laws of the country offer them no protection."[35]

Under such circumstances, pious free blacks fretted not simply about the physical and emotional circumstances of young enslaved men and women but also about state of their souls. Despite their radical critiques of slavery and racism, some African Americans believed that even when acting under force and compulsion, men and women ultimately remained responsible for their actions and behavior. From this perspective, slavery was an abominable system that forced their brothers and especially their sisters into a life of sin and subsequently an eternity of damnation. Indeed, Rev. Garnet highlighted this rationale for rebellion in his "Address to the Slaves": "The divine commandments, you are in duty bound to reverence and obey. If you do not obey them you will surely meet with the displeasure of the almighty. He requires you to love him supremely, and your neighbor as yourself—to keep the Sabbath day holy—to search the Scriptures—and bring up your children with respect for his laws, and to worship no other God but him." Garnet explained "slavery sets all these at naught, and hurls defiance in the face of Jehovah." But still, he believed that, "God will not receive slavery, nor ignorance, nor any other state of mind," as a substitute "for love, and obedience to him. Your condition does not absolve you from your moral obligation."[36] Thus, although slavery forced people to sin, northern black abolitionists, like their white counterparts, believed that enslaved African Americans who did not follow biblical precepts would ultimately reckon with the consequences of their actions after death.[37] This religious critique of the peculiar institution was powerfully damning, but it also could make navigating the mores of the northern black middle classes rather difficult for young female fugitives. For example, when Jacobs first arrived in Philadelphia, taking refuge with the family of the Reverend Jeremiah Durham, the pastor of Bethel Church, she was disheartened by his reaction to her story. Although he was deeply sympathetic to Jacobs, he discouraged her from being too candid with others about the circumstances surrounding the birth of her two children: "Your straight-forward answers do you credit; but don't answer every body so openly. It might give some heartless people a pretext for treating you with contempt." The word *contempt*, Jacobs recalled, "burned me like coals of fire." She replied, "God alone knows how I have suffered; and He, I trust, will forgive me."[38]

As Jacobs's comments suggest, those women who wrote of their experiences in slavery spoke eloquently of the power relations that circumscribed their lives and were more actively critical of the rigid religious code that seemed to condemn them for events over which they had no control.[39] In her narrative, *Behind the Scenes; or, Thirty Years a Slave and Four Years in the White House*, Elizabeth Keckley described her situation in one curt paragraph: "I was regarded as fair-looking for one of my race, and for four years a white man—I spare the world his name—had base designs upon me. I do not care to dwell upon this subject, for it is one that is fraught with pain. Suffice it to say, that he persecuted me for four years, and I—I—became a mother."⁴⁰ Jacobs similarly explained, "I wanted to keep myself pure; and, under the most adverse circumstances, I tried hard to preserve my self-respect; but I was struggling alone in the powerful grasp of the demon Slavery; and the monster proved too strong for me." After describing her decision to thwart her owner's advances by choosing an unmarried white gentleman as a lover and ostensible protector, Jacobs asked her free female audience for forgiveness: "Pity me, and pardon me, O virtuous reader! You never knew what it is to be a slave; to be entirely unprotected by law or custom; to have the laws reduce you to the condition of a chattel, entirely subject to the will of another." She confessed, "I know I did wrong. No one can feel it more sensibly than I do. The painful and humiliating memory will haunt me to my dying day." However, Jacobs concluded, "In looking back, calmly, on the events of my life, I feel that the slave woman ought not to be judged by the same standard as others."⁴¹ Like Jacobs, Keckley placed the blame for her "suffering" and "mortification" squarely on the shoulders of the peculiar institution: "If my poor boy ever suffered any humiliating pangs on account of birth, he could not blame his mother, for God knows that she did not wish to give him life; he must blame the edicts of that society which deemed it no crime to undermine the virtue of girls in my then position."⁴²

For elite and aspiring northern free black readers, stories about slavery's assault on the morality, virtue, and marital bonds of young African American women and men raised troubling questions not just about the state of their souls but also about the current and future health of the race. Because women have often served as allegorical figures of the nation in modern and ancient nationalist discourses, descriptions of the systematic abuse of enslaved African American women at the hands of slaveholders functioned as a powerful symbol for the persecution of the race.⁴³ For some, this was not simply a metaphor but a matter of scientific concern. After describing the physical and emotional difficulties endured by enslaved women, particularly while pregnant, Hosea Easton worried about what effects might linger and pass from mother to child. "Can it be believed to be possible," he asked in his 1837 treatise, "for such a one to bring perfect children into the world?" He continued, "If we are permitted to decide that natural causes produce natural effects, then it must be equally true that unnatural causes produce unnatural effects. The slave system is an unnatural cause, and has produced its unnatural effects, as displayed in the deformity of two and a half millions of beings, who have been under its soul-and-body-destroying influence, lineally, for near three hundred years; together with all those who have died their progenitors since that period." He continued, "Slavery, in its effects, is like that of a complicated disease, typifying evil in all its variety—in its operations, omnipotent to destroy—in effect, fatal as death and hell." Moreover, "When I think of nature's laws, that with scrupulous exactness they are to be obeyed by all things over which they are intended to bear rule ... I wonder that I am a man; for though of the third generation from slave parents, yet in body and mind nature has never been permitted to half finish her work."[44] Slavery, in other words, not only marred the past and blighted the present; if allowed to continue in this vein, it threatened to destroy the future.

"AM I NOT A MAN AND A BROTHER?"

In addition to portraying slavery's negative impact on African American children and families and dramatizing slaveholders' power to force young sisters and daughters into a life of immorality and sin, representations of slavery also underscored black conduct writers' anxieties regarding the state of young African American men. While slave narratives featured the successful journey to freedom and autonomy of a single individual, they also included "numerous examples of white men's power over slave men's bodies" that represented, as Kristin Hoganson has argued, "an impotence caused by the inability to resist masters."[45] The most popular piece of antislavery iconography in the Anglo-American abolitionist community was an image of the manacled slave with the caption, "Am I Not a Man and a Brother?" As literary scholar Paul Gilmore notes, the depiction shows a supplicant, an object of pity, rather than a subject with the ability to act on his own. Moreover, descriptions of violent restraint and sadistic punishment carried unambiguously sexual connotations for early-nineteenth-century readers accustomed to reading displays of power as pornography.[46] Consequently, these descriptions also serve as a backdrop against which black personal conduct discourse must be read. While black conduct writers and activists stressed the importance of independence and held up male authors of slave narratives as black self-made men worthy of emulation, slave narratives also depicted successive scenes of dependent black sons, husbands, and fathers unable to marry the women of their choice; prevented from reaping the benefits of their labor; trained to rely on theft, sophistry, and spirits; and powerless to protect themselves from violent, predatory, and despotic masters.

Enslaved men were unable not only to defend themselves but also to do what free men were expected to do according to law and custom: protect the dependents in their families—particularly their female dependents—from violence and abuse. The law placed free white wives and daughters "under the protection" of their husbands and fathers, and the state assumed the wife's lack of free will and duty to depend on her husband and obey his wishes.[47] Husbands legally controlled both the body and the labor of their wives and remained responsible for most crimes they committed.[48] As the head of the household, then, fathers and husbands were entitled to gain satisfaction for assaults on their property, which included—in legal terms—dependent wives and daughters. Enslaved husbands and fathers, however, had none of these legal rights, which belonged instead to the slaveholder. For example, as Catherine Clinton writes, "If a rapist was suspected of sexual assault of a slave woman, he was charged with 'assault and battery' and, in the case of conviction, damages were paid to her owner, as would be the case in any other 'property damage.'"[49] But enslaved husbands and fathers had no recourse.

Therefore, descriptions of the abuse experienced by enslaved women not only crystallized the immorality of slavery for northern readers but also, as Hazel V. Carby writes, underscored the "denial" of "the manhood of the male slave."[50] The *Colored American* demonstrated the connection between these concepts when it printed "A Few Plain Questions for Plain Folks":

> Can a slave marry without his owner's consent? If so, quote the law; give chapter and verse.
> Can a slave prevent the sale of his wife if the owner pleases? If so, quote the law.
> Can a slave, with impunity, refuse to flog his wife with her person all exposed, if his owner pleases to command him? If so, quote the law.
> Can a slave obtain redress, if *his master* deprives him of his goods? If so, quote the law.
> Can a slave attend either public or private worship, without the risk of punishment, if his master forbids him? If so, quote the law.
> These are plain questions, which every slave owner knows can only be answered in one way.
> When, then, any individual gets up to tell you how well the slaves are treated, or how happy under such circumstances slaves may be, tell him that he insults your understanding, that he outrages your republican feeling, and that he dishonors God.

Claiming his right to these gender privileges, the author signed his letter, "A Husband and a Father."[51] And in 1844, James McCune Smith summed up the antislavery argument's impact on black patriarchal authority in a letter to the *New York Tribune*: "The slave has no right to his own person," and "the slave has no right to his own wife."[52] In Pennington's assessment, "Whatever may be the ill or favoured condition of the slave in the matter of mere personal treatment, it is the chattel relation that robs him of his manhood, and transfers his ownership in himself to another. It is this that transfers the proprietorship of his wife and children to another. It is this that throws his family history into utter confusion, and leaves him without a single record to which he may appeal in vindication of his character, or honour."[53] Given the solubility of the marriage bond and the inability of fathers to protect their daughters, incidents described in slave narratives suggested that enslaved African American men could never completely fulfill their duties and obligations as heads of households, protecting and caring for their dependents. As Hoganson notes, "The slave narratives used by Garrisonians to promote their cause depicted the slave man's inability to protect his family as a reflection of his own submissiveness."[54] Slave narratives, like white-authored abolitionist literature, highlighted a troubling form of enslaved male subjugation even as they celebrated those who threw off the chains of slavery.[55]

Male narrators eloquently recounted the anguish they experienced under these circumstances. After quoting several state laws detailing the legal authority of master over slave, William Craft explained that "should the bondman, of his own accord, fight to defend his wife, or should his terrified daughter instinctively raise her hand and strike the wretch who attempts to violate her chastity, he or she shall, saith the model republican law, suffer death." When describing these "worst features" of slavery, he wrote, "it is common practice in the slave States for ladies, when angry with their maids, to send them to the calybuce sugar-house, or to some other place established for the purpose of punishing slaves, and have them severely flogged." Furthermore, "it is a fact, that the villains to whom those defenceless creatures are sent, not only flog them as they are ordered, but frequently compel them to submit to the greatest indignity. Oh! if there is any one thing under the wide canopy of heaven, horrible enough to stir a man's soul, and to make his very blood boil, it is the thought of his dear wife, his unprotected sister, or his young and virtuous daughters, struggling to save themselves from falling a prey to such demons!"[56] Narrators further suggested that this powerlessness created a sense of profound anxiety and distress in enslaved men, damaging the natural bonds of affection between husbands and wives. Even after being sold to the same plantation as his wife, for example, Bibb recalled that he was far from happy. "It was not that I was opposed to living with Malinda, who was then the centre and object of my affections. But to live where I must be eye witness to her insults, scourgings and abuses, such as are common to be inflicted upon slaves, was more than I could bear. If my wife must be exposed to the insults and licentious passions of wicked slavedrivers and overseers; if she must bear the stripes of the lash laid on by an unmerciful tyrant; if this is to be done with impunity, which is frequently done by slaveholders and their abettors, Heaven forbid that I should be compelled to witness the sight."[57] For this reason, literary historian William L. Andrews notes, "To be the husband of a slave was to bind oneself emotionally to an exquisite form of misery."[58]

On occasion, descriptions of male repression and subjugation moved into the realm of the overtly pornographic. While living in New York City soon after the passage of the 1850 Fugitive Slave Law, Jacobs encountered a fugitive named Luke on his way to Canada. The two had lived near each other in North Carolina, and Jacobs "rejoiced" to see that he, too, had "escaped from the black pit" of slavery. In fact, Jacobs was "peculiarly glad" to see Luke on the road to freedom, since he had experienced "extreme hardships" at the hands of his young, weak, and bedridden but despotic master, who had lost the use of his legs after years of "excessive dissipation." According to Jacobs, Luke's master "kept a cowhide beside him, and, for the most trivial occurrence, he would order his attendant to bare his back, and kneel beside the couch, while he whipped him till his strength was exhausted. Some days [Luke] was not allowed to wear any thing but his shirt, in order to be in readiness to be flogged." And when the young master grew too weak and ill to discipline Luke, he would call the town constable into his bedroom and watch while the constable administered the corporal punishment. According to Jacobs, "A day seldom passed without his receiving more or less blows." Jacobs then abandoned the restraint that characterizes much of her narration to describe a scene of blatant sexual violence: "As he lay there on his bed, a mere degraded wreck of manhood, he took into his head the strangest freaks of despotism; and if Luke hesitated to submit to his orders, the constable was immediately sent for. Some of these freaks were of a nature too filthy to be repeated. When I fled from the house of bondage, I left poor Luke still chained to the bedside of this cruel and disgusting wretch."[59] Jacobs's report of Luke's experiences shows him to be "symbolically castrated, by virtue of his subjugation as a slave, his feminized/maternal duties to his master, and his master's sexual abuse."[60] This depiction contrasts mightily with Douglass's heroic account of his two-hour physical altercation with the "slave breaker" Covey, a fight that Douglass later characterized as "the turning point" in his life as a slave, the victory that "recalled to life" his "crushed self-respect" and "self-confidence" and renewed his "determination to be A FREEMAN."[61]

By contrast, recurring representations of naked, chained, and submissive young men; disordered and threatened families; and fathers who lacked the most basic paternal authority would have been extraordinarily troubling for black middle-class readers. Indeed, northern black writers worried that generations of these experiences had doomed African Americans to a kind of weakness and timidity. Delany, for example, insisted that "the degradation of the slave parent has been entailed upon the child, induced by the subtle policy of the oppressor, in regular succession handed down from father to son—a system of regular submission and servitude, menialism and dependence, until it has become almost a physiological function of our system, an actual condition of our nature."[62] And when he criticized northern blacks for being too passive about fighting for their rights, too inclined to say, "*First* seek ye the Kingdom of heaven and its righteousness, and ALL other things shall be added," Delany argued that this tendency was "but the result of oppression and degradation, a legitimate offspring, an unerring compliance with the hell-originated mandates" of the institution of slavery. "The slaveholder and pro-slavery man-debasing hypocrites of the country, have so taught our fathers, and they, unfortunately, in turn, have taught them to us."[63]

Male narrators in particular worried about the "slavish" traits they retained in freedom. In his personal narrative, Ward wrote, "It is almost impossible to spend youth, manhood, and the greater part of life, in such a condition as that of the American slave, and entirely escape, or to any great extent ever become free from, the legitimate influences of it upon the whole character." He went on, "Indeed, though I recollect nothing of slavery, I am every day showing something of my slave origin. It is among my thoughts, my superstitions, my narrow views, my awkwardness of manners. Ah, the infernal impress is upon me, and I fear I shall transmit it to my children, and they to theirs! How deeply seated, how far reaching, a curse it is!"[64] In May 1843, Douglass similarly remarked that slavery had instilled in him "a disposition I never can quite shake off, to cower before white men."[65]

Making the political personal, Jacobs's tale and similar stories underscored why it was imperative for all African Americans, including the aspiring and elite, to embody a challenge to slavery and place their lives in the service of the freedom struggle. And northern black editors hoped that slave narratives would heighten readers' commitment to the antislavery cause. In March 1861, the *Weekly Anglo-African* published an excerpt from Jacobs's *Incidents in the Life of a Slave Girl*; after favorably reviewing the book, editor Thomas Hamilton declared, "No one can read these pages without a feeling of horror, and a stronger determination arising in them to tear down the cursed system which makes such records possible. Wrath, the fiery messenger which goes flaming from the roused soul and overthrows in its divine fury the accursed tyrannies of earth, will find in these pages new fuel for the fire, and new force for the storm which shall overthrow and sweep from existence American slavery."[66]

MAKING THE POLITICAL PERSONAL

The slave narratives that black newspaper editors recommended to their readers consistently argued that slavery perverted proper domestic and family relations, chipped away at women's virtue, and reduced African American fathers to an unmanly and dependent condition. The various examples of sexual exploitation and family disruption were terribly distressing for northern black audiences, for whom slavery was neither a theoretical state nor an abstract condition but rather recent family history, a constant possibility, and a continuing presence in their lives. The process of reading and writing slave narratives forced northern African Americans to relive and reimagine those experiences with the full knowledge that others continued to live under these circumstances. In this context, African American public figures such as Garnet expressed concerns not only about those who remained enslaved in the South but also about slavery's ability to continue to tear apart families in the North and to transmit its pernicious effects to future generations. These circumstances ensured that northern free black readers would interpret slave narratives in profoundly personal terms.

In light of the belief that the future of the race rested on the actions of aspiring African American men and women, they had a duty to do whatever possible to bring an end to the peculiar institution. This perspective heightened the need to live antislavery principles day in and day out as well as suggested that other, more satisfying ways might exist to act on antislavery credentials.

Indeed, after describing slavery's impact on African American wives, husbands, and children in his "Address to the Slaves," Garnet "referred to the fate of Denmark Vesey and his accomplices—of Nat Turner; to the burning of McIntosh, to the case of Madison Washington, as well as to many other cases—to what had been done to move the slaveholders to let go their grasp, and asked what more could be done—if we have not waited long enough—if it were not time to speak louder and longer—to take higher ground and other steps."[67]

CHAPTER FOUR

Domestic Literature and the Antislavery Household

> At a time, alas! when every thing displeased me; when every object was disgusting; when my sufferings had destroyed all the energy and vigour of my soul; when grief had shut from my streaming eyes the beauties of nature; when frequent disappointments had bowed my soul, and rendered the whole universe a dreary tomb; when prejudice had barred the door of every honourable employment against me, and slander too held up her hideous finger; when I wished that I had not been born, or that I could retire from a world of wrongs, and end my days far from the white man's scorn; the kind attentions of a woman, were capable of conveying a secret charm, a silent consolation to my mind. Oh! nothing can render the bowers of retirement so serene and comfortable, or can so sweetly soften all our woes, as a conviction that woman is not indifferent to our fate.
>
> —"Female Tenderness," *Freedom's Journal* (1827)

Long married to a successful caterer and blessed with three children, Solomon Northup could not wait to leave behind Bayou Boeuf, Louisiana, the scene of his twelve-year captivity in slavery, and return to the "happy and prosperous life" he had once led as a farmer, carpenter, fiddler, and family man in Upstate New York. In the closing paragraphs of his 1853 narrative, *Twelve Years a Slave*, Northup described the moment he, his wife, and two of his children were reunited. As he entered their "comfortable cottage" in Saratoga Springs, his younger daughter, Margaret, only seven years old at the time of his kidnapping, failed to recognize him. For his part, Northup was stunned by the change in Margaret's appearance, for the "little prattling girl" he remembered was now "grown to womanhood—was married, with a bright-eyed boy standing by her side." Then Northup learned that "not forgetful of his enslaved, unfortunate grand-father, she had named the child Solomon Northup Staunton." Next, Northup's eldest daughter, Elizabeth, entered the room, and his wife, Anne, came running from the hotel in which she worked. They embraced him, "and with tears flowing down their cheeks, hung upon [Northup's] neck." Solomon and Anne's youngest son, Alonzo, was not present for the reunion, for he had traveled to the boomtowns of western New York in hopes of earning enough money to redeem his father from slavery. Still, the scene ends with domestic tranquility restored, with family members reunited and "the household gathered round the fire, that sent out its warm, and crackling comfort through the room."[1]

Northup's decision to end his slave narrative with this family tableau was not inconsequential, for descriptions of domestic space and tropes of familial relationships had long held extraordinary political significance in the United States. During the revolutionary era, for example, American spokesmen used the metaphor of family relationships—specifically those centering on parental obligations to children—to dramatize the North American colonies' disintegrating relationship with imperial Britain. Immediately after the establishment of the republic, political commentators used the example of companionate marriage to evoke the bonds that united the states for mutual happiness and the common good. These familial tropes would continue to be invoked to explain an array of political developments and debates in the nineteenth century, even providing one of the most enduring interpretations of the Civil War: brother against brother. With respect to antislavery politics, however, the connection between domestic discourse and political ideology became even more pronounced. And as Chris Dixon has argued, "Radical abolitionism was premised on the interdependence between domestic life and the outside world."[2] In fact, as historian Mary Ryan demonstrates in her analysis of antebellum domestic literature, "the abolitionist polemicists of the 1830s . . . first invested the question of slavery with domestic sentiments." And by the 1850s, the abolitionist critique of slavery had become so thoroughly intertwined with domestic discourse that the premier abolitionist novel, *Uncle Tom's Cabin*, was itself a work of domestic fiction.[3]

For African Americans such as Northup, home and family held even more personal political significance. Free blacks needed only to contrast their situation with that of their brothers and sisters in the South to recall that the right to have one's marriage protected by law was a privilege millions of African Americans did not share. And this knowledge shaped northern blacks' perceptions of their privileges as free men and women as well as their critique of slavery. In

Figure 3. "Arrival Home, and First Meeting with His Wife and Children." From Solomon Northup, *Twelve Years a Slave: Narrative of Solomon Northup, a Citizen of New York, Kidnapped in Washington City in 1841, and Rescued in 1853, from a Cotton Plantation near the Red River, in Louisiana* (Auburn, N.Y.: Derby and Miller, 1853). Image courtesy of Documenting the American South, the University of North Carolina at Chapel Hill Libraries.

a letter published in the *Colored American*, for example, one free black reader placed black families at the heart of his interpretation of the meaning of freedom. First, he noted, "the dwelling of the black man is protected by the same laws which protect the dwelling of the white man. The colored mother, as well as the white mother, feels that her children are her own." The northern African American "is a free man in his own quiet dwelling, and the children, who play at his door, or gather round his evening fire, are under the protection of the same laws which give peace and security to his white neighbor's dwelling." In addition, northern men and women could make their own marriage choices and have their marriages sanctioned by the state. "No one can deprive the colored husband of his rights, or the colored wife of her protection." The enslaved man, however, "holds his wife but by permission from his master, and when his master says the word, he must give his wife to another, and take another to himself." These personal and familial rights meant a great deal to members of the northern black activist community. As the writer put it, "The free colored man of the north considers it an inestimable privilege that he can be the protector of his daughters, and unite them with their associates in lawful and honorable marriage."[4] In this view, freedom was not only an individual's natural right but also restored proper relations and paternal authority to African American families.

Charged as this idea was with intense political significance, northern black ministers, writers, and activists had much to say about African American domestic concerns long before Northup's sentimental family tableau appeared in print. Didactic pronouncements on child rearing could be found in political pamphlets penned by black ministers, and counsel on courtship, marriage, and family governance was woven into political and religious commentary from editorials in the African American press to speeches at black state and national conventions.[5] As a vignette on "Female Tenderness" that appeared in *Freedom's Journal* in 1827 suggests, African American domestic writers consistently linked middle-class ideals about gender, home, family, and domestic space to the project of living an antislavery life, placing both the free black home and African American women's influence and domesticity in the service of the private day-to-day war free African Americans waged against the nation's proslavery culture.[6] Familial relationships (particularly those between mothers, sisters, and daughters and their male kin), these authors argued, helped individuals live up to their antislavery principles, while the ideal black family served as the engine of the antislavery struggle, an essential part of the race's ascendance from slavery to freedom. Such claims took advantage of the common understanding that families were simultaneously private entities shaped by conjugal love, mutual affection, and ties of kinship and political institutions regulated by the laws of the state.[7] To ensure that aspiring African Americans created ideal families and domestic spaces, black domestic writers urged free African Americans to create the ideal antislavery household by attending to their domestic duties and obligations as husbands and wives, actively employing female influence, and thoroughly inculcating antislavery values in their children. In the process, the free black home and its attendant familial relationships were positioned as a privileged antislavery space and the barometer of the future health of the race.

CREATING AN ANTISLAVERY HOUSEHOLD

By 1857, when Frances Ellen Watkins, a popular young black abolitionist lecturer, published "Report," a poem offering advice to young courting men on ideal female character, and "Advice to the Girls," a humorous poem urging young women to choose "good and kind" husbands with "common sense," she was contributing her insight and wit to a wide-ranging and growing body of African American marriage advice. In fact, by the 1830s, many of the columns and editorials in *Freedom's Journal*, the *Weekly Advocate*, and the *Colored American* were presenting marriage and the establishment of a household as essential for the happiness of young aspiring African American men and women. To underscore this point, *Freedom's Journal* and other newspapers reprinted humorous cautionary tales from contemporary British novels and journals such as the *Gentleman's Magazine*. "The Old Maid's Thermometer," "The Bachelor's Thermometer," the story of "Miss Becky Duguid," and similar tales outlined the tragic consequences that awaited those who put off marriage. "The Bachelor's Thermometer," for example, explained how a handsome but prideful twenty-four-year-old man too pleased with his own virtues to marry the woman he truly loved soon found himself an irritable fifty-something battling gout and an unpleasant gastrointestinal disorder, lonely and pathetic enough to marry his unrefined maid.[8] Likewise, "The Old Maid's Diary" (the less sexually suggestive title the editors of *Freedom's Journal* apparently chose for "The Old Maid's Thermometer") detailed how an amiable and attractive young lady who was so fond of charming all those around her that she refused to settle on one suitor grew up to become an unmarried, "ill-humoured," lonely woman in her forties who turned "all her sensibility to cats and dogs."[9] After reading a reprinted excerpt from Susan Edmoundstone Ferrier's novel, *Marriage*, the readers of *Freedom's Journal* may well have giggled at the lessons learned by "Miss Becky Duguid," who had intended to remain single, bucking tradition and "escap[ing] the snares and anxieties of the married state," the "indifference or the ill-humour of husbands," and "the troubles and vexations of children." "But poor Miss Becky soon found her mistake." She discovered that as an aging unmarried aunt, she was constantly expected to sit with a "dull and sickly wife" or an "ill-natured husband" or to "nurse the children" of her siblings, never invited to "any party of pleasure."[10]

While the leisured circumstances suggested in these stories bore little resemblance to the lives led by the overwhelming majority of northern free blacks, that antebellum black newspapers printed such tales suggests that free black readers (or at least editors) found them both amusing and instructive. In many respects, these tales, which relied heavily on the cultural tropes favored by mainstream middle-class society, used humor to construct and reaffirm the boundaries of an emerging black middle-class community. But they were also intended to warn the young men and women of the race that those who delayed marriage too long or made themselves unappealing to the opposite sex might miss their chances and end up like Tabitha Wilson, "a most venomous backbiting old maid of forty-five."[11]

These decidedly flip descriptions of the consequences of avoiding matrimony were supplemented with letters, stories, and sermons on the results of ill-advised matches. After tiring of paying for slander suits brought against his wife, "Job" used the black press to publicly declare that his wife, "a leading member of this society," is "one of the greatest shrews of whom you ever heard" and that her tongue "goes as steadily as the clack of a mill." He advised other young men to choose their wives more wisely.[12] Speeches reprinted in *Freedom's Journal* also taught young women to be prudent when selecting husbands. In 1827, for example, *Freedom's Journal* reprinted "The Intemperate Husband" from an address delivered before the Massachusetts Society for Suppressing Intemperance. According to the speaker, "when a husband and father forgets the duties he once delighted to fulfil, and by slow degrees becomes the creature of intemperance, there enters into his house the sorrow that rends the spirit—that cannot be alleviated, that will not be comforted." The speaker asked his audience to visualize and "to behold him," in his sad state, "fallen away from the station he once adorned, degraded from eminence to ignominy—at home, turning his dwelling to darkness, and its holy endearments to mockery—abroad, thrust from the companionship of the worthy, a self-branded outlaw—this is the wo that the wife feels is more dreadful than death,—that she mourns over, as worse than widowhood!"[13] Such lectures did far more than remind young men to avoid the grog shop and the bottle. They also made clear that young women who placed themselves under the protection of such husbands would eventually pay a steep price. Similarly, in "The Slovenly Wife," a cautionary tale reminding young women to put the needs of their households above the inanities of fashion, young male readers were taught to be wary of the hidden costs involved in the maintenance of fashionable young wives. Published in the *Colored American* in 1838, the parable described "Hester S.," the "youngest daughter of a respectable mechanic," as a young woman whose "beauty was proverbial.... Too ardent a love for showy dress, in preference to neatness, seemed her only fault." But her husband soon learned that this seemingly minor character flaw had extraordinary consequences. Rather than attending to her household duties, she spent her husband's money on extravagant dresses, driving him into debt. Over time, "his flourishing business and his handsome wife became more and more neglected.... Creditors now visited in lieu of customers. The goods were sold; the shop was soon closed. The husband had become a drunkard, and the once beloved and yet beautiful wife, sinking under the combined effects of poverty, and shame, and remorse, found out too late that she was the unhappy cause of their mutual wretchedness and ruin. Thus ends a true but humble tale, told by A WIFE."[14]

When we connect this discourse with the political function of marriage itself, we see that these decisions to delay marriage or choose inappropriate spouses were not inconsequential to elite and aspiring African Americans. An alcoholic husband would inevitably abandon his responsibilities, leaving his family and home in ruins. A gossiping wife could squander her husband's wealth on slander suits. A wife who cared more about her personal appearance than managing her household might soon lead all the members of the family to poverty, shame, and ruin. Conversely, an "ideal" marriage (and thus a healthy household) promised to improve a man's economic prospects and enlarge his political status. These ideas were hardly new. As historian Nancy Cott reminds us, American political figures had long "assumed that marriage and property-holding and heading a family were closely related as attributes of citizen-voters." And in the republican political theory that continued to influence political and domestic ideologies, a man's ability to function as an independent head of a family with a dependent wife and children served as one of the primary examples of his independence and political capacity—that is, his ability to act as a disinterested citizen who could wield suffrage appropriately and contribute to a virtuous body politic.[15] Legal marriage conferred head-of-household status on husbands, thus cementing their standing as guardians of dependents. Through the marriage vows, the wife gained protection of her husband, and by becoming one with him, she enlarged his political capacity, reaffirming his position as head of the household. In other words, if "participatory citizenship in the American political tradition required" independence, it was defined not solely by land, wealth, and self-mastery but also through the polity of the family.[16] With this idea in mind, black domestic discourse implied that one's marriage choice bore a direct relationship to one's ability to live an antislavery life.

Indeed, slave narratives sometimes highlighted the moments when their narrators changed their marital status, marking this moment as the final stage of their ascent to freedom. For example, both Frederick Douglass and Henry Bibb concluded their self-transformations with the exchange of formal wedding vows with a free black woman. Near the conclusion of his narrative, Bibb noted that he ultimately married the eligible Mary Miles of Boston, his "bosom friend, a help-meet, a loving companion in all the social, moral, and religious relations of life." Bibb also pointed out that other fugitives acted similarly with regard to these personal family matters: "I am happy to state that many fugitive slaves, who ... escape to the free North with those whom they claim as their wives, notwithstanding all their ignorance and superstition, are not at all disposed to live together like brutes, as they have been compelled to do in slaveholding Churches. But as soon as they get free from slavery they go before some anti-slavery clergyman, and have the solemn ceremony of marriage performed according to the laws of the country."[17] Similarly, Douglass recalled that a few days after making his way to New York and finding shelter in the home of David Ruggles, the leader of the city's Vigilance Society, Ruggles sent for Douglass's fiancée, Anna, and soon after her arrival in New York City, "Mr. Ruggles called in the Rev. J. W. C. Pennington, who, in the presence of Mr. Ruggles, Mrs. Michaels, and two or three others, performed the marriage ceremony." After receiving their certificate of marriage, "I shouldered one part of our baggage, and Anna took up the other, and we set out forthwith."[18] These descriptions of marriage functioned as more than just a conventional happy ending for the narrator. They symbolized the final step in the ascendance from slavery to freedom, from the dependence of enslavement to independence. By marrying, former slaves placed themselves fully in the position of independent men, ready to wield the legal privileges of any free man.

To help husbands shore up their status as independent heads of households, black domestic literature focused heavily on the roles and responsibilities of African American wives, urging them to act like proper dependents in two key ways. First, black conduct writers offered a primer on how to avoid the kind of behavior that might subvert a husband's authority. Editors regularly pointed out that a man preferred not to marry a woman with "a babbling tongue" by printing letters from men who swore they would "rather dwell in the dens of the Caucasus, and abide two years at Liberia, than remain one month in the town that is blest with her residence." This was strong condemnation, indeed, given the free black population's overwhelming opposition to the American Colonization Society's plan to remove free African Americans to Liberia.[19] Editors also instructed female readers to nurture happiness in their marriages by remaining pious and good-natured and by deferring to their husbands' authority. The *Colored American* advised wives to "resolve every morning to be cheerful and good-natured," to "dispute not" with their husbands, and to remember that while "submission in a man to his wife is even disgraceful to both . . . implicit submission in a wife to the will of her husband is what she promised at the altar."[20]

These admonitions, as scholars have noted, conformed to the same middle-class domestic ideals and practices celebrated by white conduct writers and failed to challenge prevailing discourses of female inferiority.[21] But these views were not necessarily incompatible with a radical antislavery agenda. William Lloyd Garrison, a founder of the American Antislavery Society and an exemplar of white radical abolitionism, for example, reprinted a series of maxims on spousal duties and obligations in the pages of the *Liberator*, a newspaper with many African American subscribers. Maxim 3 stated, "She never attempts to rule or appear to rule her husband. Such conduct degrades husbands—and wives always partake largely in the degradation of their husbands." Similarly, Maxim 6 proclaimed, "She never attempts to interfere in his business, unless he ask her advice or counsel, and never attempts to control him in the management of it." Husbands, for their part, were counseled to listen to their wives' sound judgment and to enlist them in the battle against economic disaster. For "if she have prudence and good sense he consults her on all great operations, involving the risk of ruin, or serious injury in case of failure." Since "many a man has been rescued from ruin by the wise counsels of his wife," readers were urged to remember that "a husband can never procure a counsellor more deeply interested in his welfare than his wife."[22]

As Maxim 6 suggests, in addition to reminding wives to be appropriately (rather than overly) submissive, abolitionist domestic writers instructed women to help their husbands in the family's economic pursuits, framing these behaviors as essential for the enhancement of the husbands' political capacity. Not only did a husband and father demonstrate his political capacity by virtue of the contrast between his legal status and the dependents in his household, but he also needed to maintain the household's economic independence.[23] Wives were urged to help by economizing and by offering wise advice and counsel when appropriate. Toward these ends, black domestic writers consistently echoed the advice of white domestic writer and abolitionist Lydia Maria Child, who characterized wifely frugality as essential in a "land of precarious fortunes" racked by stock market crashes and boom-and-bust economic cycles and encouraged free black women to attend to the tasks of housework and manage their homes with an eye toward improving their family's financial condition.[24] In "Religion and the Pure Principles of Morality" (1831), Maria Stewart directed free black women to pay close attention to their household expenditures: "Let each one strive to excel in good housewifery, knowing that prudence and economy are the road to wealth. Let us not say we know this, or we know that, and practise nothing; but let us practise what we do know."[25] And "are there not many wives ... who can thus lighten their husband's hearts, and keep their purses heavy?" inquired a piece on frugal housewives reprinted in an 1860 issue of the *Weekly Anglo-African* newspaper. "Look twice before you throw it aside. Don't put those old pantaloons into the carpet rags or the mop until you have patched them once more. Let the tuck down in the little girl's dress; make the old ribbon trim the little bonnet again; get the boots mended; buy a little trimming for that old sack, and it will look as well as new. Contrive and economize, and you will be happier; discipline yourself better, do more good, and set a better example than if you had plenty of money and lived carelessly."[26] Framed in this way, a wife's attention to domestic economy provided a crucial means for women to help their husbands prosper, retain economic independence, and thus demonstrate political capacity.

Wives of this type, black domestic writers suggested, would serve as perfect complements and partners for the mechanics, farmers, doctors, and divines championed as exemplars of antislavery living by the Reverend Samuel Ringgold Ward and others. Consequently, black conduct writers also urged young women to get the proper training to be of service to their husband's pursuit of economic independence. "Each sex," wrote the Reverend Lewis Woodson, "should receive that education which is best calculated to qualify them for a discharge of their appropriate duties."[27] For many people, this idea meant that young African American women should "acquire an education which will fit them to become the wives of an enlightened mechanic, a store keeper, or a clerk."[28] Charles B. Ray emphasized this point almost immediately after the death of his young wife, Henrietta, submitting a series of editorials to the *Colored American* arguing that "our daughters" should receive "a solid education" consisting first and foremost "of the use of the needle, house work, and domestic economy generally." Ray complained that many young African American women lacked the proper knowledge of housewifery, a deficiency he believed to be "the cause of the greatest amount of domestic broils, and contentions, the cause of so many abandoned females [and an impetus for] intemperance, suicide, and to all the prevailing evils of the day." To avoid disaster, Ray suggested that girls first remain at home with their mothers to learn "all the art of domestic cookery" and to "be taught to know how to manage a house, and govern and instruct children." Only after mastering these skills should they be sent away for further education.[29] In the 1850s, Martin Delany made a case for a more expanded list of duties, explicitly insisting that young women be trained to be partners in their husband's economic ventures: "Let our young women have an education; let their minds be well informed; well stored with useful information and practical proficiency, rather than the light superficial acquirements, popularly and fashionably called accomplishments. We desire accomplishments, but they must be *useful*." Rather than simply "transcribing in their blank books recipes for *Cooking*; we desire to see them making the transfer of *Invoices of Merchandise*." These efforts would not only enhance their husbands' independence but also strengthen the larger effort to build up a mighty race. Consequently, he called for young African American women to "come to our aid then; the *morning* of our *Redemption* from degradation, adorns the horizon."[30]

This type of idealized economic partnership is also visible in the *Colored American*'s story of Harry and Mary Hemphill, which illustrated both an ideal version of wifely frugality and its positive impact on the industry and morality of a young man. When the newly wed Hemphills set up housekeeping in the country (away from the temptations Harry would have faced in the city), Mary turned "her whole attention" to things domestic, so that "all went like clock work at home; the family expenditures were carefully made; not a farthing was wasted, not a scrap lost; the furniture was all neat and useful, rather than ornamental; the table plain, frugal, but wholesome and well spread; little went either to the seamstress or the tailor; no extravagance in dress, no costly company-keeping, [and] no useless waste of time in ceaseless visiting." In short, Mary created an ideal home where Harry could seek "repose after the toil and weariness of the day" and forget "the heartlessness of the world, and all the wrongs of men." Harry "devoted himself to business with steady purpose and untiring zeal; he obtained credit by his plain and honest dealing; custom by his faithful punctuality and constant cares; friends by his obliging deportment and accommodating disposition." He ultimately "gained the reputation of being the best workman in the village," the family thrived, "and he and Mary mutually [gave] each other the credit" for their success. The author then charged his younger readers, both male and female, with following the characters' examples: "I pen their simple history in the hope, that as it is entirely imitable, some who read it will try to imitate it."[31]

Once established, these stable and independent households could play important roles for the northern black abolitionist community, serving as key forums for antislavery men and women to gather for abolitionist, literary, and vigilance committee meetings as well as serving as stops on the Underground Railroad.[32] For example, Ruggles attended to "a number of other fugitive slaves," including Douglass, from home, "devising ways and means for their successful escape."[33] Other northern free blacks similarly made their homes havens for fugitives on the flight to freedom. When Ward's parents arrived in New York City on August 3, 1826, with young Samuel in tow, they "lodged the first night" with the parents of Henry Highland Garnet.[34] And when she arrived in Philadelphia after escaping from North Carolina, young Harriet Jacobs received shelter, advice, and instruction on how to proceed to New York from the Reverend Jeremiah Durham and his wife. Jacobs was deeply grateful for the Durhams' kindness and hospitality. "I was tired," Jacobs recalled, and Mrs. Durham's "friendly manner was a sweet refreshment. God bless her! I was sure that she had comforted other weary hearts, before I received her sympathy."[35]

More than simply safe havens, these domestic spaces functioned as political spaces for those African Americans who aspired to place every aspect of their lives in the service of the freedom struggle. While traveling as a correspondent for Douglass's *North Star* in 1848 and 1849, Delany took time out from his description of the many organizations and institutions African Americans had built in western Pennsylvania to praise two of the families who had welcomed him into their homes. These husbands and their "intelligent wives" were more than just kind hosts and hostesses for weary travelers: they were men and women who fashioned their homes into antislavery spaces. In Harrisburg, Delany was hosted by "John Williams, and his intelligent lady," who "most kindly received me the night that stupid ignorance and wicked prejudice debarred me from shelter, and at whose door the antislavery latch-string always hangs out." Delany also thanked "John Wolf, and his amiable, intelligent lady, whose house also keeps the welcome knocker to the Anti-Slavery pilgrim on the door." Delany interpreted the hospitality of these couples as examples of private ways that families who "take high anti-slavery ground, feeling closely identified with their people, and stand ready at any time," could "enter into measures for the support of the cause, and those who are faithfully laboring for our elevation."[36]

DEMOCRATIZING FEMALE INFLUENCE

Black domestic writers not only linked the duties and obligations of spouses to efforts to claim independence for the race but also imbued emerging middle-class ideas about true womanhood and female influence with antislavery meaning. Female influence was a relatively new concept in the early republic, one heavily praised and promoted by mainstream American domestic writers. By midcentury, the concept defined hegemonic gender ideals, serving as a key component of the construction of early-nineteenth-century middle-class domesticity. While white conduct writers instructed newly middle-class white American men to live up to celebrations of "self-made men" (independent agents striving for success in the emerging capitalist marketplace), they expected a class of "true women" (that is, innately pious, moral, virtuous, and submissive women) to preside over a separate domestic sphere that served as a pure and safe space set apart from the forces of the corrupt outside world. Antebellum writers routinely characterized this domestic sphere as women's ideal arena, the space where they would exercise their purifying moral influence on the men in their lives. If women properly fulfilled these duties, their influence would ultimately result in a more moral, pious, and perfect world.[37]

Of course, few African American women had the luxury of remaining cloistered within a domestic sphere. Even if they had wanted to do so, the circumstances in which most free African Americans lived made it difficult for free black women to conform to the strictest interpretations of separate spheres and ideal domesticity. The majority of the married and unmarried free black women residing in the northern states worked for wages—usually in "demanding, undesirable, and poorly paid" positions as domestics or laundresses—or supplemented their families' income by taking in boarders.[38] Free black women across the economic spectrum participated in a variety of associations, among them church-related societies and abolitionist organizations. Consequently, historians agree, black conduct writers' descriptions of women's proper place as the private domestic sphere rather than the public world of wage labor ignored free black women's needs as wage workers and perhaps even helped to limit black women's opportunities to claim more visible leadership roles in the many organizations in which they participated.[39]

While scholars are right to point out the distance between the idealized rhetoric and the reality of free black women's lives, African American domestic writers also redefined the rhetoric of female influence, turning it toward the political needs of the African American population. Rather than insisting on a limited domestic sphere for a small class of elite African American women, black domestic writers instead praised a democratized version of female influence so that all respectable African American women—irrespective of their participation in the public world of wage labor—were deemed purveyors of qualities generally presumed to be reserved for middle-class whites alone. According to *Freedom's Journal*, all women were "formed to adorn and humanize mankind, to sooth his cares, and strew his path with flowers."[40] In this way, African American domestic writers consistently emphasized the most democratic vision of female influence, claiming an ideal to which all African American women could aspire, irrespective of their economic status, prior condition, participation in the wage labor economy, or role in abolitionist and community organizations.

This is especially apparent in a letter on "Female Influence" from "Ellen," published in the September 30, 1837, issue of the *Colored American*. First acknowledging the "delicacy" that its author, "a young and unknown female," had to "overcome" before "writing for the public press," she explained that her "anxiety" for the "elevation of [her] people, and the improvement of [her] sex" compelled her to address the public. The author insisted that women had important roles at every stage of their lives. As mothers, she argued, women should watch carefully over their young sons, "train their minds to virtue," and "instill into them true Moral and Religious principles." As sisters, young women and girls could keep their "brothers in the path in which a mother's care had led them," providing a counterweight to the "rich" and "imaginative fancies" and "buoyant feelings of youth" that might lure even the most virtuous of young men away from the family fold. Finally, as a wives, young women should be willing to "assist" in their husbands' "literary labors," ever ready to offer "judicious counsel and advice" and to "incite" their husbands "to deeds of valor and patriotism." Ultimately, "whether as a mother, sister, or wife," women "can throw a halo around the domestic hearth, and make HOME the delight of man, and the place he will seek with ardour after the toils of the day, or the anxiety and care attendant on business or study." For this reason, the "appropriate sphere for the female to use her influence over man is the domestic fireside. There she can show her power over the lords of creation—there she can shine her true glory." "Whether the female move in the highest walks of society, or toils with laborious assiduity in the peasant's cot," according to this author, "still the influence she exerts is the same. Whether she treads majestically the monarchial palace, or groans beneath the lash of the Southern task-master; whether she roams the Western prairies, the untutored child of nature, or sings the song of love in the luxurious gardens of Persia's golden empire, she has the same heavenly influence over man, which she can exercise for his good or evil—for his misery or his happiness."[41] In this way, "Ellen" and other black domestic writers characterized female influence as an innate attribute of all women, irrespective of race, class, or condition of servitude.

Placing a democratized interpretation of female influence within the framework of specific familial roles and celebrating female influence as innate to all virtuous black mothers, daughters, wives, and sisters performed a specific ideological function for aspiring northern African Americans. By celebrating female influence, black domestic writers created an image of black femininity that challenged the key gender constructions at the heart of the institution of slavery. As historian Jennifer Morgan has demonstrated, enslaved women's reproductive capacity gave British New World slavery its distinctive characteristic of perpetuity. Irrespective of the familial bonds that united and sustained the slave community, the law defined enslaved women simply as the personal property of their white owners, and under this system, enslaved women's bodies produced and reproduced the agricultural and human commodities of slave societies, expanding owners' estates. Categorized as merchandise, enslaved women of African descent could be separated from their families, stripped naked and examined publicly by prospective buyers, and sold as chattel to the highest bidder. Gender offered no protection.[42]

By the nineteenth century, antebellum proslavery writers, intellectuals, scientists, and theologians had constructed the cultural apparatus that framed this harsh economic reality, describing enslaved women in a set of terms far removed from the sentimental phrases used to characterize the nature of the "true women" of the republic. In religious literature, popular novels, historical romances, and natural and social science publications, "proslavery intellectuals created three specific images—the 'mammy,' the 'Jezebel,' and the 'mule'—as preeminent features of the dominant ideology that justified their exploitation of female slaves."[43] And as historian Deborah Gray White has demonstrated, "One of the most prevalent images of black women in antebellum America was of a person governed almost entirely by her libido, a Jezebel character." This cultural trope of a highly sensual and remarkably fertile woman of African descent affirmed and reaffirmed a system where enslaved women were regularly viewed in various states of undress in the fields, at the whipping post, and on the auction block, where their fertility could be discussed in polite conversation, their marital status sundered at will, and their daughters sold off as courtesans to take part in what was politely known as the "fancy trade."[44] As a whole, this discourse insisted that the phrase *slave woman* signified "burden bearing, domestic servitude, and libidinous self-absorption."[45]

These "controlling images" undoubtedly shaped white perceptions of northern free black women as well.[46] Edward Clay's caricatures of elite and aspiring free black women in Philadelphia emphasized features that would have been perceived as the antithesis of the ideal of white womanhood. Instead of wearing chaste and modest dress, Clay's female figures sport ridiculously large hats and wear ostentatious dresses with ridiculously oversized sleeves and absurdly wide skirts. And with but a few exceptions, the characters are short, squat, and drawn with impossibly dark skin, large hands, and giant feet. By contrast, when Clay lampoons Philadelphia's white elites for their ardent love of the latest fashions, his white female caricatures retain their pale skin, delicate features, and, most important, tiny hands and feet—symbols of feminine beauty in the period. Clay asks his reader to laugh at the absurdity of the middle-class black woman. And at a time when female arms and legs were considered so delicate and private that they were politely referred to as "limbs," Clay highlights the singular oddity of the black female body by having his figure receive coal black stockings in response to her request for "flesh coloured" ones.

Even abolitionists, who sought to challenge proslavery arguments by showing that enslaved women suffered horribly, unwittingly helped to shore up these

Figure 4. "Have you any flesh coloured silk stockings, young man?" "Oui, Madame! here is von pair of de first qualité!" From Edward W. Clay, *Life in Philadelphia* (Philadelphia: Simpson, 1829). Courtesy of the Library Company of Philadelphia.

perceptions.[47] As scholars have argued, consistent depictions of violence against partially clothed or nude black women registered as pornographic in the antebellum northern middle-class mind. As historian Catherine Clinton notes, "Whipping itself can be a symbol of male will and lashing a form of sexual sublimation."[48] And constant denunciations of the South as "one great Sodom," a "place in which men could indulge their erotic impulses with impunity," and a culture where enslaved women regularly "lured young slaveholders into illicit attachments," inadvertently helped to confirm the prevailing controlling image of black women as overly sexual seductresses—Jezebels.[49] Consequently, these depictions could not but reinforce the dominant ideological beliefs that rooted deviant sexuality in the body of the black woman.

Such representations of African American women, free or enslaved, thus "existed in an antithetical relationship with the values embodied in the cult of true womanhood."[50] By the late eighteenth century, the terms *slave* and *black* had become synonymous and were often used interchangeably in the United States; similarly, the phrases *enslaved women* and *black women* must have been indistinguishable. In this context, no woman of African descent could ever be the pure, pious, submissive paragon of domesticity celebrated as a true woman by mainstream conduct writers. In other words, even if conventional wisdom dictated that "a true woman was a true woman, wherever she was found," most white Americans believed that this "true woman" upheld the republic with her "frail white hand."[51]

Embodying and personifying a challenge to this racialized interpretation of true womanhood had the potential to take on a subversive meaning for free African American women. It provided a way for aspiring African American women at all stages of their lives to contest proslavery ideologies within their private dwellings. On a day-to-day basis, a wife could place her domesticity in the service of her family rather than a master or employer. Scholar Gayle T. Tate has argued that this domestic labor—"household management, task-orientation, decision making processes, and goal-setting behavior"—functioned as a critical form of black women's activism.[52] Caring for their families in this way might have empowered free black women, particularly those who had grown up with the expectation that their official duty would be serving the families of their owners. But female influence also enabled them to wield a specific form of gendered power within the family circle and to demand a level of respect and deference that they would rarely receive outside the walls of their homes. For aspiring women who worked for wages, this insistence that female influence was innate, that they too were ideal women, would have provided a powerful reminder of their slender and tenuous privileges as free women.

African American domestic writers also regularly placed female influence directly in the service of the larger antislavery enterprise. Indeed, a mother's influence was characterized as so powerful that it could pull a wayward young man off the road to ruin and back onto the path of antislavery living. Thus, by attending to their role within the domestic sphere, mothers served as the first line of defense against the moral corruption of vulnerable young African American men. For example, an essay on "Maternity" in the *Colored American* noted that while "women's charms are certainly many and powerful," motherhood has a power "beyond this world." After discussing men's love for their mothers—"'Tis our first love!"—as well as the glory and sanctity of the state of motherhood itself, the author charged that "he who can enter an apartment, and behold the tender babe feeding upon its mother's beauty, nourished by the tide of life which flows through her generous veins, without a panting bosom and grateful eye, is no man, but a monster . . . and is fit only for the shadow of darkness and the solitude of the desert." The editors of the *Colored American* stated their hopes that "fathers and children" would read the piece, circulate it, and enable it to "be the instrumentality in reclaiming some besotted husband, or long lost profligate son."[53]

Black domestic writers also connected black women's influence within the home to their institution-building efforts in the free black community. For example, on January 7, 1837, in the first issue of the *Weekly Advocate*, an editorialist addressed a piece "To the Females of Colour," urging them to use their "powerful" female "influence" to support the fledgling journal by making it a fixture in their homes: "Let not our hopes of its success be indulged in vain, for want of effort on your part to sustain it."[54] And in 1857, when Mary Still published a pamphlet, *An Appeal to the Females of the African Methodist Episcopal Church*, she placed the "female part of the Church" at the center of a half century of African American community building and antislavery activism, inviting female readers to lend their support to the denomination's new newspaper, *The Christian Recorder*, which had been forced to suspend publication in 1856 as a consequence of lack of funds. Women, she proclaimed, had been central "to the advancement of great moral enterprizes" throughout the history of the world. In fact, "the moral or degraded condition of society depends solely upon the influence of woman, if she be virtuous, pious and industrious, her feet abiding in her own house, ruleing her family well." For Still, "Such a woman is like a tree planted by the river side, whose leaves are evergreen; she extends in her neighborhood a healthy influence, and all men calleth her blessed."[55] While Still doubtless would have disagreed with the previous generation's more limited vision of the scope of female influence, she would have agreed with earlier authors that female influence, rooted as it was in the domestic relationships between wives, mothers, sisters, and daughters and their male kin, made the well-ordered free black home and family a crucial institution for antislavery living.

Circumstantial evidence suggests that this idealization of race-specific female influence may have shaped the courtship and marriage choices of young elite and aspiring African American men and women. In 1837, Henry Highland Garnet described his future wife, Julia Williams, in glowing terms: "Oh what a lively being she is! Modest, susceptible, and chaste, a good Christian and a scholar."[56] John Mercer Langston also portrayed his wife as the embodiment of this ideal. Caroline M. Wall, whom Langston married on October 25, 1854, was a "talented, refined and pleasant person in appearance and conduct.... [W]ith her brothers and younger sister respecting and honoring her authority, while she bore herself with dignity, self-possession and propriety, he discovered in her those elements of genuine womanly character which make the constitution of the true, loving and useful wife. He discovered too, in her conversation and behavior, that she was fully informed as to the condition of the colored people, with whom she was identified in blood in her maternal relationships, and deeply and intelligently interested in their education and elevation."[57] Such a wife would certainly be an ideal partner and helpmeet and an asset in the antislavery struggle.

CHILD REARING

Scholars have noted that social protest, whether "civil rights, anti-slavery, or general social reform," tended to be a family endeavor for antebellum free blacks. Historian Wilma King has argued that "childhood experiences in homes" often shaped "an individual's social consciousness."[58] And James Oliver Horton has found that "if one member of a family was involved" in antislavery activism, then "other family members were likely to take part."[59] Indeed, the evidence supports these claims. For example, William Watkins, who published several letters under the pseudonym "Colored Baltimorean," founded the William Watkins Academy for Negro Youth, an institution that offered a classical curriculum to its students. His niece, Frances Ellen Watkins, whom he adopted after the death of her mother, continued the activist tradition, becoming a famous member of the abolitionist lecture circuit as well as a poet and novelist.[60] Susan Paul and Mary Ann Shadd followed in the footsteps of their activist fathers, Thomas Paul and Abraham Shadd, respectively. William G. Nell, founder of the Massachusetts General Colored Association, helped to mold the political sensibilities of his son, William Cooper Nell, a fixture of the abolitionist community. The Douglass and Easton families spawned multiple generations of activists.[61] And the children and grandchildren of James and Charlotte Forten would grow to become leaders in African American and interracial antislavery gatherings.[62]

So it should come as no surprise that antebellum black writers and ministers paid great attention to child rearing, offering advice and instruction on the proper political, moral, and intellectual education of children and instructing parents to provide the tools that would enable children to become ideal antislavery men and women. At the 1839 annual meeting of the State Temperance Society of Colored Americans, participants resolved "that it is the duty of every female in this society constantly in season, and out of season, to instill into the minds of all the children and youth the principles of temperance."[63] Saying that "work never hurts the child," John Berry Meachum urged "every father or mother, or any head of a family," to "endeavor to raise our children with as much industry as we possibly can." Reminding aspiring mothers and fathers of the importance of social graces, he suggested that parents "see particularly" that their children "are raised up nicely in their manners and their deportment. It takes a long time to get the training of a child out of him, and if it is good we do not want to get it out of him." He also reminded parents to be mindful of the moral needs of their children and to ensure that they did not begin to travel down the wrong path. "We must endeavor," he wrote, "to have our children look up a little, for they are too many to lie in idleness and dishonor. Just as sure as you see a lazy child, and his parent cannot break that child from his laziness, he is very apt to become a disgrace to his parents and to himself, and not fit for any society. So let us endeavor to keep laziness out of our children; let them be raised up honorable men and women." In Rev. Meachum's view, if free black parents did their job properly, they would "instill such principles" in their children "as could never be eradicated by time, place, or circumstance."[64]

To help instill these principles, black domestic writers by the 1840s advised readers to employ the sentimental child-rearing practices that defined middle-class domestic culture. Parents were counseled to eschew corporal punishment, instead appealing to their children's consciences and using persuasion to nurture the development of a moral compass and teach the difference between right and wrong. Meachum thought that the best way to correct a wayward child was to discuss the matter calmly rather than "get in a passion, and in that passion correct the child too severely." And Meachum found it absolutely inappropriate for black parents—particularly mothers—to "strike" their children "over the head" or "knock them to the ground."[65] Such child-rearing techniques not only signified a move away from the patriarchal methods that had formerly held sway but also would have been a particularly pronounced departure from the type of discipline that Meachum and others might have received in their youth at the hands of slaveholders.

In addition to advocating the more gentle forms of discipline in favor in middle-class circles, black domestic writers tended to frame the free black family in deeply sentimental terms. This is especially apparent in Susan Paul's *Memoir of James Jackson, the Attentive and Obedient Scholar, Who Died in Boston, October 31, 1833, Aged Six Years and Eleven Months*, a celebration of the brief life of one of Paul's most promising young students. Paul intended her book to function simultaneously as a primer on conduct for young African American children and a kind of child-rearing treatise for their parents, and her descriptions of young James and his mother to serve as examples for members of the free black community. After James's father, "a respectable" man, passed away, the boy's mother was left alone to provide for several children. Deeply committed to their well-being, James's mother made sure to keep him enrolled in school, even helping him with his studies—both secular and religious—at the end of her long workday. In this way, she served as a model for those who intended to inculcate the value of antislavery living in their children and provided an example of domesticity despite the absence of the comforts that would have characterized a more economically secure middle-class home. According to Paul, young James Jackson was a near-perfect child because he listened to his mother's wisdom: "I wish," Paul wrote, "some of you who read this could see how his eyes would sparkle with pleasure, when he thought he had pleased his dear mother. I am sure you would be sorry that you had given your parents any unnecessary trouble, or spoken unkind words to them, when they desired you to do any thing for them. Your parents always know better than you do what is best for you. Although James was so very young, *he* knew this, and always cheerfully obeyed his mother's commands." She advised her young readers to remember that "the great God can see you and hear you always."

And she highlighted "four words" that she urged them to "treasure up in your memory, and frequently repeat to yourselves, when wicked children would lead you into temptation; the words are *Thou God seest me*." Paul hoped the book would "prompt parents and teachers to store the minds of the children committed to them with religious truth." If they could succeed in this endeavor, she was certain that "God will give you a large reward; yea, a hundred fold. In this life, you shall see your children coming up to be respected in society, and in the world to come, they shall be acknowledged by our Lord as heirs to life eternal."[66]

As Paul's book suggests, black conduct writers argued that the process of creating ideal black children depended on the sound education and morality of African American parents, many of whom would be the primary role models for children required to work rather than attend school.[67] Like white conduct writers, black conduct writers repeatedly reminded parents that children were largely imitative creatures.[68] "Children do little," proclaimed a passage from *Dwight's Theology* reprinted in an 1827 issue of *Freedom's Journal*, "besides imitating others." Consequently, parents needed to provide the best examples within the home. African American readers of *Freedom's Journal* would have learned that "the moral branches of Education can never be successfully taught without the aid of example," and "example has, in a great measure, the same influence upon every part of education." Therefore, failure to provide the best examples would undoubtedly lead to poorly behaved children. "Parents who read, will have reading children. Industrious parents will have industrious children. Lying parents will have lying children."[69] Rev. Meachum advised free black parents to keep in mind that they should "never allow the child to tell you a lie" and remember the power of their example: "If you promise [your children] any thing," you must "keep your word."[70] Maria Stewart agreed: "You must be careful that you set an example worthy of following, for you they will imitate." And she declared that "there are many instances, even among us now, where parents have discharged their duty faithfully, and their children now reflect honor upon their gray hairs."[71]

With the next generation in mind, African American writers, activists, and public speakers urged their audience to attend to personal morality and education precisely for the sake of their children. Still cautioned wives and mothers to safeguard their piety, morality, and virtue, for "if unhappily she should be . . . loud, clamorous, her feet wandering from the path of virtue, neglecting to rule her family, then indeed is the demoralizing effort of a bad influence felt in all avenues of her life."[72] In a letter advocating increased access to education for free black women, one woman informed readers of the *Liberator* "that the offspring of ignorant parents are generally vicious," for when proper "advice or instruction" is not provided in the family circle, and when "inattention and unpardonable carelessness" rule the day, a child "is suffered to run the whole course of vice, until he becomes an outcast from society."[73] And some writers perceived a slippery slope from societal outcast to an early grave. During the National Black Convention of 1833, the Committee on Temperance called for all free blacks to practice "intire abstinence" or face severe consequences. "Those children in tatters, who are cruelly permitted to waste those precious hours, which should be employed in the acquisition of knowledge, who are shivering with cold, or crying for a morsel of bread, are the children of *intemperate parents. These impoverished families, these premature graves*, are the production of strong drink."[74] These charges to safeguard parental morality were not unusual in the period. As historian Mary Ryan points out, concerns about perceived parental moral lapses, particularly alcohol consumption, reflected larger middle-class anxieties about the liminality of their position.[75] But black conduct writers' insistence that personal behavior had antislavery implications suggests that these authors also interpreted success or failure in child rearing in larger, race-specific, and deeply political terms.

These larger concerns remained central to the child-rearing advice in Meachum's 1846 *Address to All the Colored Citizens of the United States*. First, Meachum characterized child rearing as one of the key privileges and duties of freedom. "In times past," he wrote, "your fathers were deprived of [freedom], and of course they could not be charged with not raising their children in the right manner; that is, if they did all they could according to their situation. But as you are free, (thanks be to God for it,) the guilt comes on your head." He urged free black parents to "train up your children in the way they should go" for the good of not simply the family but also the entire "young race." Foremost among these obligations was attending to children's education, a task that Meachum saw as essential for the development of racial unity. Concerned about the low rates of schooling for African American children in the North, Meachum asked, "Look at the young and rising generation. See the great mass of them growing up without education. What is the reason of this?" Although Meachum was clearly aware of the structural barriers to education African American children faced—he would later circumvent Missouri's ban on educating black children by holding classes on a steamboat in the middle of the Mississippi River—he also blamed what he perceived as a low interest in education on a lack of racial pride and unity. Answering, "because the fathers are not united, and the children growing up without union to the great body of their fellow beings of the same color," Meachum despaired, "The mother hath not taught it to the child, and he has nothing to rouse his mind to action." With that in mind, the reverend directed his readers to take Proverbs 22:6 ("Train up a child in the way he should go") "in consideration now and wake up the minds of our children." Meachum then personalized the proverb for the race, reminding his readers, "We are bound by the law of God and man, and our good sense, to train up *our children* in the way they shall go when young, that when they grow old they should not depart from it." As far as Meachum was concerned, racial unity was of primary importance to this agenda: "Union is the strong cord that binds nations together. Then let the mother teach it to the child, and let the father not forget that he is accountable before God for the raising of his children."[76]

By slipping so easily between race and nation, antebellum free blacks such as Meachum created the archetype of what would later be known as a "race home": a politically oriented African American family whose health, prosperity, production, and reproduction functioned both as a metaphor for and a building block of the race. Just as John Adams had argued that the nation's moral foundation rested on its families, Delany proclaimed, "Nations are but great families," and as "it is with families, so it is with nations." He continued, "Each citizen of a nation should bear the same resemblance to the great leading traits which mark the enterprise of that people, as the individual members do to the family to which they belong."[77] As a piece on child rearing published in *Freedom's Journal* concluded, "Patriotism, as well as charity, begins at home."[78] Thus, parents were charged with creating models of virtuous and independent black families, and raising ideal children. Insisting that free black parents needed to provide their children with a key set of skills while impressing on them a sense of "responsibility of race," black conduct writers informed their readers that African American parents bore responsibility for raising children who would be a credit not just to their parents but to the entire race.[79] Like their parents, exemplary children would serve as living refutations of proslavery doctrine. While touring African American communities as a correspondent for the *North Star* in 1848, Delany did not shy away from framing his praise of the children of his Carlisle, Pennsylvania, host, the Reverend W. Webb, in terms of a competition with white Americans: "The children of the family are intelligent and interesting in a high degree, and will challenge comparison with, and might well put to blush, those of their Anglo-Saxon neighbors for good behavior."[80] Given the high stakes of this competition, parents were called on to teach their children to embrace the forms of respectability and spirit of racial unity characterized as essential for living an antislavery life. In the process, these authors implied that the health and future progress of the race rested on successful parental adherence to middle-class child-rearing practices.

TOWARD A BLACK MIDDLE-CLASS DOMESTIC IDEAL

African American writers offered a wealth of domestic advice for aspiring free blacks in the decades preceding the Civil War. They instructed young men and women to choose appropriate partners, to create ideal homes and families, and to fulfill the gender-specific duties expected of members of well-ordered, virtuous, and independent households. The model homes and families celebrated in black domestic discourse certainly differed dramatically from the domestic conditions experienced by the vast majority of free African Americans as well as the millions of enslaved African Americans. But the domestic discourse circulating in African American print culture was not meant to accurately reflect current domestic conditions. Like personal conduct discourse, domestic advice was intended to offer guidance about how to remake one's family into an institution that was the antithesis of slavery and thus a vehicle for engaging in the most personal of antislavery politics.

The link between antislavery living and the emergence of an African American domestic ideal is illustrated in an 1832 vignette on "Family Worship" published in the *Liberator*. The piece was written by Sarah Mapps Douglass, an unmarried twenty-six-year-old African American schoolteacher living in Philadelphia. Douglass used the essay to paint a sentimental family tableau that bears a close resemblance to the final scenes of Northup's *Twelve Years a Slave*. The piece invited readers to imagine themselves gazing unobserved on a family gathered together for morning prayers. Looking past the honeysuckle vine, "through the open window into the cottage," readers/viewers would see the mother reading "from the book of books," the father offering a "humble prayer," and the "meek and loving" children seated near their parents. Although the family was not entirely at peace—"their eldest son is absent," having "strayed from the fold"—the quiet family moment was characterized as nothing less than a domestic ideal for the free black population. Douglass praised the members of her fictional family for their "humble, unostentatious piety" and urged "all the families of our people" to follow this lead. And she concluded by inviting respectable readers to "lift the latch" and "enter the abode," joining this domestic scene.[81]

As Douglass's piece suggests, the personal politics involved in living an antislavery life required more than individual acts; rather, they demanded a family commitment. In this brief scene, Douglass captured the many tropes embedded in the conduct discourse that taught aspiring free blacks how and why to place their domestic and family lives in the service of the antislavery struggle. Douglass took great pains to locate the family in a setting that symbolized virtue and independence, placing her characters in a "cottage," rural architecture that distances them from the urban environment. The cottage also signifies a middling economic status for the family, for like their piety, the Lindsey home is "unostentatious" and "humble" rather than decadent and opulent. Douglass even drapes the home in a honeysuckle vine, drawing on the biblical trope of the vine and fig tree, a phrase that enjoyed some popularity in the late eighteenth century and was regularly invoked during discussions of independence by men including George Washington and Richard Allen, founder of Philadelphia's Mother Bethel African Methodist Episcopal Church. Moreover, by having the parents lead their children in the ritual of family prayer, Douglass clearly suggests that families who regularly assembled together to pray were engaging in a practice with ramifications that extended far beyond their cottage and their individual spiritual well-being. Indeed, Douglass argued that despite the private domestic setting, these personal family moments were crucial spaces for the project of living an antislavery life. "O lady, would that we might see all the families of our people so engaged!" she wrote, "how would the sunshine of such an example disperse the mists of prejudice which surround us! Yes, religion and education would raise us to an equality with the fairest in our land." Finally, as far as Douglass was concerned, these parents would be instilling the principles that would keep their children on the path of respectability so crucial to free black middle-class forms of personal politics. In fact, Douglass assured her readers that the "wayward son" would soon remember the hours spent in prayer with his family and return home, "kneeling again at his parent's knees," receiving "their blessing as he was wont to do when a happy and sinless child."[82]

Such vignettes suggested that men and women could embody their resistance to the peculiar institution by claiming their roles as ideal mothers and fathers, brothers and sisters, sons and daughters. From this perspective, the economic partnerships involved in companionate marriage could help young men become independent self-made men. Female influence could be turned toward protecting the morality of vulnerable young men and creating a domestic space that served as a bulwark against the racism of the outside world. And attention to proper child-rearing techniques would serve as a means to build a new generation committed to working for the good of the race. Such behavior may have done little directly to challenge the expansion of southern slavery and the growth of national racism, but its value lay in the psychological power it gave to free men and women, reminding them daily that they were not enslaved and were therefore duty-bound to place their lives in the service of the antislavery struggle. By creating a body of domestic discourse, writers and editors advocated another way for elite and aspiring African Americans to engage privately in personal politics, away from the gaze of white observers. Moreover, by placing that personal politics at the center of a black middle-class domestic ideal, African American domestic discourse suggested that antislavery living could be a family and thus collective enterprise as well as an individual one.

CHAPTER FIVE

Transnationalism, Revolution, and the *Anglo-African Magazine* on the Eve of the Civil War

> We are among those who believe that freedom is destined, ultimately, to triumph . . . yet we are fully satisfied that this great object will not be attained, without great labor, toil, and sacrifice. Tyranny never releases its victim without a struggle.
> — *Anglo-African Magazine* (September 1859)

When Thomas Hamilton of Brooklyn, New York, launched the *Anglo-African Magazine* in 1859, he offered "the first literary magazine produced by and for the black community," opening a new phase in African American literary history. The magazine, which appeared monthly during 1859 and irregularly from 1860 to 1865, ultimately provided a public forum for some of the most prominent figures in antebellum northern black life, including Edward Wilmot Blyden, Mary Ann Shadd Cary, Martin Delany, James McCune Smith, Daniel Alexander Payne, Frances Ellen Watkins, and Sarah Mapps Douglass. These and other well-known authors contributed fiction and poetry, philosophical and scientific essays, political and social commentary, and analysis of African American historical subjects. Like the African American newspapers that came before it, the *Anglo-African Magazine* offered an array of essays designed to mold the tastes, culture, and manners of its readers. With these goals in mind, Hamilton provided a "mixture of articles grave and gay, things serious, and . . . things juicy" for his audience of elite and aspiring African Americans. In the process, the *Anglo-African Magazine* helped to define the literary character of the northern black middle classes.[1]

In keeping with the fact that black conduct and domestic discourse consis-

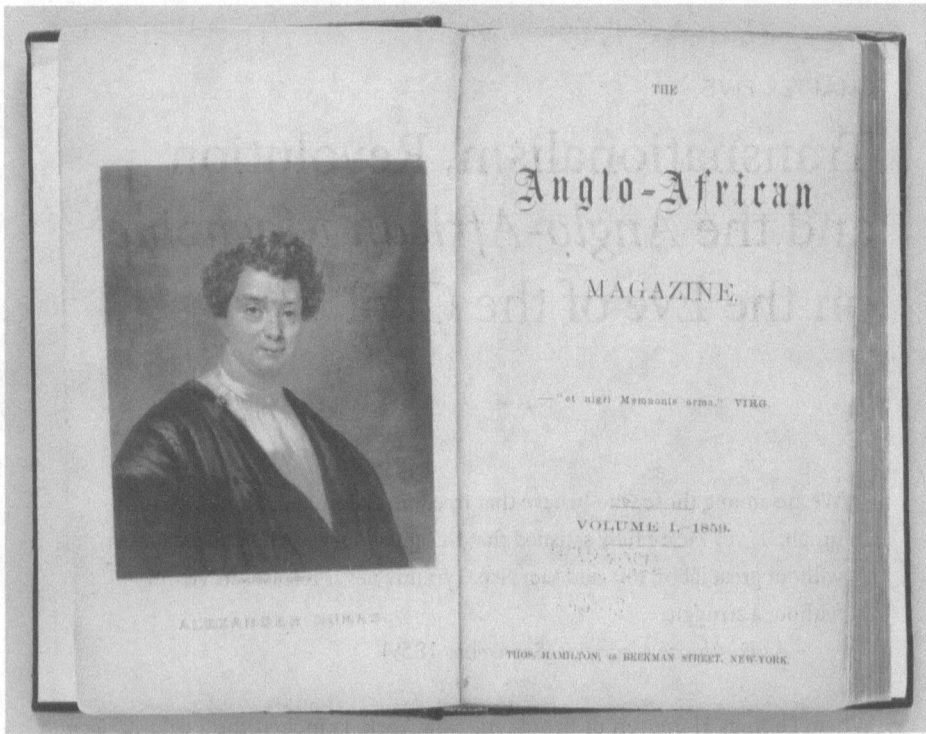

Figure 5. The frontispiece of volume 1 of the *Anglo-African Magazine*, which Thomas Hamilton issued as a bound collection in 1859. It contained an image of Alexandre Dumas, the author *The Three Musketeers* (1844) and *The Count of Monte Cristo* (1844), who was of French and African ancestry. The Latin *et nigri Memnonis arma* inscription comes from Virgil's *Aeneid* and refers to "the arms of black Memnon," an Ethiopian warrior-king who distinguished himself in battle during the Trojan War. Courtesy of Manuscripts, Archives, and Rare Books Division, Schomburg Center for Research in Black Culture, the New York Public Library, Astor, Lenox, and Tilden Foundations.

tently linked the personal with the political, Hamilton's magazine had a sharp political edge. Just as the editors of *Freedom's Journal* had hoped to do some three decades earlier, Hamilton sought to provide an independent voice for members of the northern free black community. Hamilton also intended his publication to boost the spirits of his readers, northern black men and women who had deep antislavery sentiments and who were now grappling with the implications of the 1850 Fugitive Slave Act, which sent waves of fugitives and their families fleeing the United States, and the 1857 *Dred Scott* decision, in which the U.S. Supreme Court essentially rendered free African Americans stateless, unable to sue in federal court, obtain passports, or claim any rights that "whites were bound to respect." As Hamilton wrote in his introduction to the magazine's inaugural issue, "In addition to an exposé of the condition of blacks, this Magazine will have the aim to uphold and encourage the now depressed hopes of thinking black men, in the United States—the men who, for twenty years and more have been active in conventions, in public meetings, in societies, in the pulpit, and through the press, cheering on and laboring on to promote emancipation, affranchisement and education." Hamilton realized that after decades of activism, his readers were disheartened to see "as the apparent result of their work and their sacrifices, only Fugitive Slave laws and Compromise bills, and the denial of citizenship on the part of the Federal and State Governments." Therefore, many were increasingly inclined to consider emigrating from the land of their birth. Hamilton believed that despite the difficulties they faced, northern black activists were "wrong to despond, wrong to change the scene of the contest" and "set up a breast-work in distant regions." The "sterner and fiercer the conflict," he proclaimed, "the sterner and steadier should be the soldiers engaged in it."[2] And in an effort to prepare his soldiers for the conflict, the *Anglo-African Magazine* championed a radical political sensibility for elite and aspiring African American readers.

    This chapter explores the origins of this militant identity and assesses its place in the *Anglo-African Magazine*. The magazine's articles expanded on a number of revolutionary themes that had appeared both alongside and within slave narratives and black conduct and domestic discourse from the 1820s through the 1850s. Throughout this period, black writers and activists drew on the history of the African diaspora to forge a usable revolution that blended the highest ideals of virtue and sacrifice with black liberation theology. At the same time, African American leaders took inspiration from classical Roman tales as well as the republican uprisings and independence movements taking place in Europe at the time.³ The *Anglo-African Magazine* pulled together all these strands, weaving a distinctive political narrative for aspiring African Americans. By reading the fiction and history published in the *Anglo-African*, black readers could imagine themselves as the heirs to an ancient revolutionary tradition and as soldiers on the front lines of a transnational freedom struggle, ready to ride into battle on the eve of the Civil War.

BLACK FOUNDING FATHERS

Historians have long noted that antebellum African American activists continually claimed the American Revolution as their own, skillfully deploying revolutionary-era symbolism in their public discourse and placing its ideals in the service of emancipation and abolition. From this perspective, both the Declaration of Independence, which justified the right to throw off oppressive forms of government, and the subsequent war against England underscored the legitimacy of the African American freedom struggle.⁴ In addition, writers and intellectuals such as William C. Nell would publicize the history of African American participation in the founding of the republic by celebrating Crispus Attucks Day and publishing a formal history of African American military service as evidence of black participation in the creation of the young republic.⁵ These representations of African American service and sacrifice were intended to counter white Americans' tendency to "ignore many of the prominent and significant facts in the early history of their country," insist "that this government rested solely upon a white basis," and shape "their legislation to practically enforce the atrocious doctrine" that "colored men have no rights that white men are bound to respect."⁶

But despite its utility as a rhetorical device that justified their inalienable right to liberty, the American Revolution was incomplete. Indeed, that characterization perhaps was the most generous way of assessing the gap between the articulated ideals of the Declaration of Independence and the reality of antebellum African Americans' lives under the Constitution in a slaveholding republic. Therefore, as they celebrated the nation's African American founders, venerating black Revolutionary War martyrs such as Attucks and Peter Salem and veterans such as James Forten, black writers remained mindful that the heroism of these figures contrasted mightily with the hypocrisy of the country they helped to create. And from the late eighteenth century onward, northern African Americans vociferously pointed out the irony and injustice of this fact when addressing white audiences.⁷ Forten articulated these sentiments in his 1813 pamphlet, *Letters from a Man of Colour*, proclaiming that the idea "that GOD created all men equal" is "one of the most prominent features" in the Declaration of Independence, and the Constitution," and arguing on behalf of the most expansive interpretation of that phrase: this "idea embraces the Indian and the European, the Savage and the Saint, the Peruvian and the Laplander, the white Man and the African, and whatever measures are adopted subversive of this inestimable privilege" are "in direct violation of the letter and spirit of our Constitution."⁸ Delegates to the 1845 New York State Convention pointed out that these African American men had served honorably during the American Revolution and the War of 1812 before asking, "Are we to be thus looked to, for assistance in the 'hour of danger,' but trampled under foot in the time of peace? Did our fathers fight for American liberty that their children might be disfranchised and loaded with insults?"⁹ Similar rhetorical questions formed the centerpiece of Frederick Douglass's powerful 1852 speech, "What to the Slave Is the Fourth of July?" Given the nation's continuing support for slavery and racism, Douglass could only declare in response, "This Fourth of July is yours, not mine." And as David Walker asked after quoting the text of the Declaration of Independence near the end of his *Appeal to the Coloured Citizens of the World*, "See your Declaration Americans!!! Do you understand your own language?"¹⁰ The gap between the nation's founding rhetoric and the reality of African Americans' lives made the revolution at best an ideal now corrupted by the forces of slavery and at worst nothing more than a "fraud," a "sham," and evidence of the utmost "hypocrisy."¹¹

With this idea in mind, African American writers and public speakers forged a distinctly radical African American revolutionary tradition—what historian Manisha Sinha calls an "alternative tradition of radicalism" that contained both a powerful call for freedom and a pointed critique of the nation in which they lived.¹² Finding the American Revolution too flawed to stand alone as a usable revolution and taking inspiration from their interpretation of Christianity, northern black writers looked beyond George Washington, Thomas Jefferson, and Patrick Henry for models of true revolutionaries past. When describing ideals of heroism and patriotism for northern black audiences, northern black writers praised instead Joseph Cinque, the African leader of an 1839 revolt by slaves aboard the *Amistad* en route from the west coast of Africa to Cuba; and Madison Washington, a slave from Virginia who led an 1841 revolt aboard a domestic slave-trading vessel, the *Creole*, bound for the markets of New Orleans.

These writers also often highlighted the actions of leaders of southern insurrections—Gabriel Prosser, Denmark Vesey, and Nat Turner—by characterizing these rebels as romantic heroes and contrasting them with Thomas Jefferson and George Washington, the slaveholding leaders of the American Revolution. The editors of the *Colored American* praised Cinque as a "noble hero" who "has placed himself side by side with Patrick Henry, John Hancock, Thomas Jefferson, and Samuel and John Adams." "Were he not an African," they continued, "a black man, his fame would be emblazoned forth on the tide of time, and written in high eulogium by the historian's pen."[13] Similarly, in his 1843 "Address to the Slaves" at the National Black Convention in Buffalo, New York, Henry Highland Garnet paid tribute to the lives and exploits of Vesey; "the patriotic Nathaniel Turner"; Cinque, "the hero of the Amistad"; and Madison Washington, "that bright star of freedom."[14] In 1852, Frederick Douglass took a similar approach in "The Heroic Slave," his fictionalized account of the 1841 revolt aboard the *Creole*. Douglass characterized Madison Washington as "a man who loved liberty as well as did Patrick Henry,—who deserved it as much as Thomas Jefferson,—and who fought for it with a valor as high, an arm as strong, and against odds as great, as he who led all the armies of the American colonies through the great war for freedom and independence."[15]

In addition to lionizing those Africans and African Americans who fought to throw off their chains in the United States, northern free blacks identified with Caribbean revolutionaries. Free black writers quickly embraced the Haitian Revolution, holding it up as a true revolution, in contrast with the war for independence that had established the slaveholding republic in which they lived. Walker, Delany, and others celebrated the leaders of the Haitian Revolution, particularly Toussaint-Louverture and Jean-Jacques Dessalines, and interpreted their success in overturning a slave society and establishing a free black nation as an example of the positive possibilities of slave insurrection and a model for their enslaved southern brethren.[16] Northern writers also offered great praise for Cuban poet Gabriel de la Concepción Valdés, known as Plácido, who was executed for his purported role in an 1844 Cuban slave conspiracy. Douglass called Plácido "the black Revolutionist from Cuba" and insisted that "his genius, and his heroic death will doubtless be regarded by his race as precious legacies," examples of a diasporic commitment to freedom.[17]

Northern free blacks also skillfully employed Afro-Christianity to sharpen their critique of America's unfinished revolution and infuse their freedom struggle with a divine authority. African Americans, free and enslaved, north and south, had long received particular strength from the book of Exodus and made its tale of Moses delivering the Hebrews from slavery in Egypt the centerpiece of U.S. Afro-Christianity.[18] In this view, biblical prophecy revealed that God would not simply liberate his people but also ultimately punish white Americans for their sins against their darker brothers and sisters, just as God had punished the Egyptians who enslaved the Hebrews. Consequently, African American writers warned white Americans that God would rebuke them for mistreating his chosen people, failing to live up to their revolutionary ideals, and thus violating the nation's covenant with God.[19] As the Reverend Nathaniel Paul warned in his 1827 Albany address commemorating the abolition of slavery in New York, "our liberties, says Mr. Jefferson, are the gift of God, and they are not to be violated but with his wrath."[20] In her 1831 essay, "Religion and the Pure Principles of Morality, the Sure Foundation on Which We Must Build," Maria Stewart exhorted African Americans to "sheath your swords, and calm your angry passions. Stand still and know that the Lord he is God." She reminded African Americans that "vengeance is [God's,] and he will repay." Therefore, "fret not yourselves because of the men who bring wicked devices to pass," for "they shall be cut down as the grass, and wither as the green herb."[21] Similarly, David Walker assured readers of his *Appeal* "that God will accomplish it—if nothing else will answer, he will hurl tyrants and devils into *atoms*, and make way for his people."[22] Such statements continually reminded northern free blacks that the day of liberation and divine retribution for the sins of slavery and racism was at hand and provided religious justification for any steps African Americans might take to hasten that day.

By blending revolutionary-era ideals with Afro-Christianity and the history of the African diaspora, African American writers and public speakers reminded their audiences of the unfinished American Revolution while casting leaders of slave rebellions as activists, true patriots, and messianic agents of God. For elite and aspiring African Americans, these founding fathers of the African diaspora, men who had taken up arms on behalf of freedom, served as consummate examples of how to live an antislavery life. While proslavery sympathizers found these leaders to be brutal and savage, northern black writers characterized them as thoughtful, educated, and even kind and virtuous citizen-soldiers defending the honor of their race on the field of battle. And authors urged the men and women of their generation to celebrate this history, commit it to memory, and transmit it to their children. When the editors of the *Colored American* thanked Robert Purvis for his gift of a mezzotint of

Cinque, they said, "We shall be proud to have our apartments graced with the portrait of the noble *Cinque*, and shall regard it as a favor to our descendants, to transmit to them his likeness."[23] African Americans gathering in Buffalo in March 1841 to celebrate the release of the *Amistad* captives agreed that they "highly approve[d] of the intrepid act of Joseph *Cinque*, who preferred death rather than slavery," and resolved "that Joseph *Cinque's* name shall live to tell to succeeding generations."[24] As Nell wrote in an 1859 essay on "Colored American Patriots," these figures offered "proof that the colored American has ever proved loyal, and ready to die, if need be, at Freedom's shrine."[25] And when J. N. Still, a member of Brooklyn's black community, wrote to the *Provincial Freeman* in 1856 to request funds for a traveling exhibition of scenes from *Uncle Tom's Cabin*, he promised that his next endeavor would not focus on "that deplorable and humiliating aspect of the colored man's case, represented in that work." Rather, he vowed that the next exhibit he sponsored would contain "very different scenes, representing . . . a far more hopeful aspect of the black man, than has ever been presented to the American public. . . . There have been places where, and times when the black man of modern times has proven himself the *patriot*, the *statesman*, and the *warrior*. As such, then, let him be known to the world that may acknowledge it, and to our youth, that they may imitate their example and copy their virtues."[26] To Still and others, these patriots, statesmen, and warriors were not simply admirable but also models for emulation.

Throughout the 1840s and 1850s, northern black activists consistently voiced their admiration for these particular examples of black freedom fighters and sought to enact alternative revolutionary principles in a variety of ways. Catherine and John Mercer Langston, for example, named their son after black revolutionaries.[27] And when elite and aspiring African Americans discussed their reasons for protecting and rescuing fugitive slaves, they invariably spoke in terms of revolution.[28] After his trial and conviction for his role in the celebrated 1858 Oberlin-Wellington fugitive slave rescue, John's older brother Charles Henry Langston explained to the court, "Being identified with that man by color, by race, by manhood, by sympathies, such as God had implanted in us all, I felt it my duty to go and do what I could toward liberating him. I had been taught by my Revolutionary father—and I say this with all due respect to him—and by his honored associates, that the fundamental doctrine of this government was that *all* men have a right, to life and liberty, and coming from the Old Dominion I brought into Ohio these sentiments, deeply impressed upon my heart."[29]

Other northern African Americans began taking more formal and collective steps to prepare for their role in the coming uprising. By 1851, black convention delegates were endorsing black military companies as essential for "racial defense." In New York City, a successful African American barber, Henry W. Johnson, suggested that African American men begin learning military tactics, and "the convention at which he was speaking recommended the formation of military companies for defensive purposes."[30] Throughout the region, black men began joining together, arming themselves, and drilling in city streets.[31] In Boston, sixty-five men petitioned the state legislature for permission to form an independent African American military company not only to defend the state of Massachusetts but also to "place us in a position that we may command respect."[32] Some African Americans christened their military companies with the names of African American heroes, such as the "Attuck Blues, the first Colored Military Company ever organized in Cincinnatti," in 1854,[33] and the Garnet Guards of Harrisburg, Pennsylvania, and Douglass Guards, of Reading, Pennsylvania, a company numbering "some twenty or thirty persons, all warlike men."[34] As residents of a nation that celebrated military service, and acutely aware of the contemporary ideological connections among concepts of citizenship, suffrage, manhood, and participation in the militia, the Boston petitioners based their request on their rights "as men" who were "proud of, and conscious of the inherent dignity of manhood; as men, who, knowing our rights, dare, at all hazards, to maintain them."[35] As far as these men were concerned, their alternative interpretation of revolution was sanctioned by God, and they were charged with the responsibility of living up to a radical militant ideal.

TRANSNATIONAL DISCOURSES OF REVOLUTION

In addition to linking Christianity with historic figures from the African diaspora, antebellum northern blacks aligned themselves with classical Roman and contemporary European republican movements. Indeed, as Mitch Kachun has demonstrated, northern free blacks spent the first half of the nineteenth century embracing a host of international political movements as their own and incorporating references to these uprisings into their abolitionist lexicon.[36]

In the 1820s, for example, African Americans in New York City held fancy dress balls in support of Greek revolutionaries waging a war of independence from the Ottoman Empire. One such ball took place on January 1, 1824, a day that commemorated both the abolition of the Atlantic slave trade in the United

States and the founding of the independent republic of Haiti and thus held profound symbolism for northern African Americans—particularly black New Yorkers in the midst of the transition from slavery to freedom. The organizers recognized that January 1 "cannot fail most powerfully to recall to the descendants of Africans, the blessings of freedom." Three years later, during the final months of slavery in New York state, black New Yorkers held another benefit ball on behalf of the Greek revolution. This time, they linked the Greek struggle with the abolition of slavery even more firmly by decorating the hall with banners from the New York Manumission Society.[37]

This pattern continued through the 1840s and 1850s, as republican and nationalist movements swept through Europe. When Johnson addressed Rochester's 1848 First of August Celebration (commemorating the end of slavery in the British Caribbean), he placed "the march of liberty" in the context of that year's February Revolution in France. "Fellow-citizens," he said, "we are not only here today to commemorate the dawn of liberty in the British West India Islands; but also to rejoice over the progress of liberty in other lands—if you please, over the birth of a new [French] republic."[38] The printers, carpenters, blacksmiths, shoemakers, editors, merchants, painters, farmers, laborers, barbers, physicians, masons, students, clergymen, and grocers who composed the delegates to the 1848 National Convention in Cleveland, Ohio, also claimed the French Revolution as their own, modifying the French motto, "Liberté, egalité, fraternité," in accordance with their needs and closing their convention with "three cheers" for "Elevation—Liberty—Equality, and Fraternity."[39] A number of African Americans also saw the Irish reform movement as a cause in keeping with their own, traveling to the Emerald Isle to raise support for the abolitionist cause.[40] The belief that African Americans and Irish republicans were freedom fighters of the same stripe inspired the men and women who gathered on the evening of October 14, 1850, at Philadelphia's Brick Wesley African Methodist Episcopal Church to protest the Fugitive Slave Act. They closed by "adopting fully the noble sentiment of the Irish Patriot" and borrowing an Irish poem:

> Whether on the scaffold high,
> Or on the battle's van,
> The fittest place where man can die,
> Is where he dies for man.[41]

This final stanza punctuated their resolve to fight to the death to protect themselves and their brethren and resist any attempt to reduce them to slavery.

Northern free blacks were also swept up in the national excitement over Louis Kossuth, a Hungarian who led a failed Magyar uprising against the Ottoman Empire in 1848 and was jailed and subsequently exiled. Between 1848 and 1852, Americans followed Kossuth's story with great interest, and when he traveled to the United States on an 1851 fund-raising tour, people flocked to hear his speeches. The excitement over Kossuth influenced the major writers of the day: Whitman, Emerson, and Hawthorne referenced and even celebrated Kossuth and other European republican figures.[42] For these writers and other white Americans, events in Europe represented signs of American liberty radiating outward, the next steps in the inexorable march of free republican principles that began with the creation of the United States. And white admirers saw in Kossuth and other European revolutionaries and nationalists romantic heroes in the mold of their beloved George Washington.[43]

Northern black activists and writers were equally impressed with Kossuth's revolutionary effort, and black convention speeches and political fiction contain passing positive references to Kossuth, Hungary, and Austria. Unlike white Americans, however, who regularly interpreted European political events in terms of the American Revolution, northern free blacks viewed Kossuth's effort in light of their own freedom struggle. In 1851, when black New Yorkers formed a Committee of Thirteen to defend fugitives in the wake of the Fugitive Slave Act, they drafted an address to Kossuth characterizing his Hungarian liberation movement as a "kindred effort" with their fight.[44] And during his triumphant visit to New York City, a delegation of African Americans led by a prosperous restaurateur, George Downing, who had recently renamed an item on his oyster cellar's menu Kossuth Oysters, insisted on a personal audience with the Hungarian hero, telling him that northern blacks believed that the Hungarian Revolution was a universal battle in keeping with their own fight for freedom—the "common cause of crushed, outraged, humanity."[45] Even though Kossuth deeply disappointed the delegation by refusing to issue a formal statement condemning American slavery, African Americans continued to cast themselves as "colored Hungarians" when expressing their continued commitment to the freedom struggle.[46] Consequently, in 1852, when a group of free blacks met at the Third Christian Church in New Bedford, Massachusetts, to publicly denounce the American Colonization Society, they resolved to "pledge to each other our lives, our fortunes, and our sacred honor, not to support the American Colonization Society. . . . [O]ur duty as colored Hungarians is plain before us; here we were born, here we will live, by the help of the Almighty, and here we will die, and let our bones lie by our fathers."[47]

In addition to characterizing European revolutions as kindred freedom struggles, African American activists also made great rhetorical use of these events, referencing them in an effort to sharpen their critique of the nation's hypocrisy. For despite the best efforts of black and white abolitionists, most white Americans exhibited little sympathy regarding the plight of the 3.5 million enslaved men and women living within the nation's borders, and few seemed troubled by the fact that the laws of the land barred fugitives from obtaining their own liberty. How committed to liberty and justice could Americans be if they praised European rebels but ignored the "American Hungarian" in their midst? "And yet," as Johnson exclaimed in his 1848 First of August Address, "this is called a free republic; and Americans call themselves republicans! Oh, is not this inconsistency the most irreconcilable—guilt the most abandoned—hypocrisy the most unblushing!"[48] As Hezekiah Ford Douglas put it in an exchange with William Howard Day during the 1851 Ohio State Convention, the "American Hungarian" fled from "despotism" that was far worse than that which could be found in Russia or Austria and that was enforced by the Constitution.[49] And after recounting the story of Madison Washington and the revolt he led aboard the *Creole*, Samuel Ringgold Ward asked, "What lacked these men of being Tells, Mazzinis, and Kossuths in their way, except for white or whitish skins?"[50]

The contrast between white Americans' excitement about European revolutions and their (at best) indifference to the horrors of American slavery galled northern free black activists, who resolved "that we will hold up to the scorn of the civilized world that hypocrisy which welcomes to our shores the refugees from Austrian tyranny, and at the same time would send the refugees from American Slavery back to a doom, compared with which, Austrian tyranny is mercy."[51] Johnson and others understood that although "they boast, long and loud, of 'virtuous liberty,' and we are told, 'whenever a human being pines in chains, these Americans drop their tears,'" it is clear that "the American people exhaust the great fountain of national sympathy for the oppressed of other lands, but are careful to keep none in reserve for the downtrodden and oppressed of their own country." Johnson enumerated examples of this hypocrisy in his 1848 address, boldly asserting that "if the oppressed of other lands engage in a noble struggle for liberty, (if they be white,) they receive the warmest sympathies of the American people. When Greece was struggling for liberty, not only did almost every pulpit in our land resound with eloquent pleadings in her behalf, but the whole country was filled with melting tones of sympathy for the oppressed Greeks, and contributions were made to aid them in their noble struggle." Moreover, "When Poland attempted to strike off the fetters of tyranny, and the best blood of her children mingled with her green soil—when her patriotic sons kissed the statues of their heroes and swore upon the green graves of their venerated sires—Poland shall be free! And when at last, through treachery, she again sank beneath the cold iron grasp of her despotic masters—mark again, how the tear of sympathy flowed from every American eye." Finally, "when we received intelligence of the late revolution in France, what great rejoicing there was in this country." But despite their "loud cry of freedom and equal rights," Americans "delight to deal in oppression. Trampling in the dust the great principles contained in their Declaration of Independence, they countenance and sustain one of the most grinding and crushing systems of oppressions that ever stained the dark annals of crime, or shocked the high majesty of heaven."[52]

Although these nineteenth-century European uprisings were particularly useful in sharpening African Americans' critiques of the nation's hypocrisy, such comparisons also offered a particular type of inspiration, demonstrating that revolution—whether the imperfect American Revolution or the model Haitian Revolution—was not merely a late-eighteenth-century phenomenon. Rather, it was a living possibility, currently taking place in other parts of the globe. Thus, while Haiti's history offered northern free blacks proof that New World slavery was doomed to fail and that the man of African descent would continue to rise "and claim his rights," the events of the day made it clear that revolutionary change was, as prophesied, achievable in their lifetimes.[53]

Indeed, African Americans living an antislavery life could also find examples of the courage and character they deemed essential for revolution in their own backyard, where enslaved men and women chose death over enslavement, the truest example of virtue and sacrifice that could be expected from a revolutionary. When the black and abolitionist press highlighted incidents where fugitive slaves chose to murder members of their families rather than see them returned to bondage, black abolitionists were quick to characterize these men and women as heroes rather than victims. When Delany described for the *North Star*'s readers "a most heart-rending occurrence," he cast the young father and mother of a family of three in unmistakably heroic terms. After being sold, "the parents learned that their darling babe, but twenty months old, was to have been left behind." At this point, "the frantic and heroic mother—God bless her!—asked her husband for his pocket-knife, which was very small—cut the throat of her child—held her neck to her husband while he deliberately cut her throat—then—O! yes, then like a man and a hero, deliberately cut his own throat."[54] With that, Delany transformed an account of the horrors of slavery into a celebration of enslaved women's and men's willingness to sacrifice their loved ones and empower themselves by choosing death over enslavement. In this view, enslaved African Americans who made these choices embodied the ultimate antislavery stance; unable to secure their liberty, they chose death.

In addition, when northern black writers wrote about these events, they characterized these men and women as exemplars of a heroic and ancient republican tradition. William Wells Brown asked, "What has the brother not done, upon the Slave-plantation, for the purpose of protecting the chastity of a dearly beloved sister?" and "What has the father not done to protect the chastity of his daughter? What has the husband not done to protect his wife from the hands of the tyrant?" Answers to such rhetorical questions were often placed in classical Roman terms by invoking the mythic story of Virginius, the Roman who murdered his daughter, Virginia, to save her from enslavement. Like Virginius, Brown answered: "The mother has taken the life of her child, to preserve that child from the hands of the Slave-trader. The brother has taken the life of his sister, to protect her chastity. As the noble Virginius seized the dagger, and thrust it to the heart of the gentle Virginia, to save her from the hands of Appius Claudius of Rome, so has the father seized the deadly knife, and taken the life of his daughter, to save her from the hands of the master or of the Negro-driver."[55] Brown's analogy must have resonated deeply with those taught to place their lives in the service of the antislavery cause. Indeed, when recounting the murder-suicide of the enslaved family in Kentucky, Delany wrote, "A noble woman! . . . worthy, thrice worthy to be associated in history with the noble wife of Asdrubal!" And he called the father a "most noble man!—a Virginius!" and proclaimed that "the manly and heroic deed that thou hast perpetrated shall live in the heart of every true friend of humanity and lover of liberty!"[56]

Although hearing about these assertions of will might have offered some catharsis to northern black readers, they also suggested that enslaved men and women were far more revolutionary than their free brothers and sisters. And if elite and aspiring African Americans were truly to embody the spirit of the past and carry it into the present, they might need to be willing to die to live a fully antislavery life. Elite and aspiring free blacks often spoke in terms of their intent to live up to these standards, proclaiming their desire to make the ultimate sacrifice for the cause of freedom. According to Frances Ellen Watkins, such a role meant that "I could consent to part with a portion of the blood from my own veins" if "the liberation of the slave demanded it."[57] Black Philadelphians pledged to fight to the death against the Fugitive Slave Act: it was "our sacred duty, a duty that we owe to ourselves, our wives, our children, and to our common nature, as well as to the panting fugitive from oppression, to resist this law at any cost and at all hazards; and we hereby pledge our lives, our fortunes, and our sacred honor so to do."[58] At the 1856 Ohio State Convention, the members of the Ladies' Anti-Slavery Society of Delaware, Ohio, forwarded an address by their spokeswoman, twenty-year-old Sara Stanley, in appreciation of the efforts being made by the men on the convention floor.[59] "Press on!" she urged. "Manhood's prerogatives are yours by Almighty fiat." After enumerating the importance of republican principles and her disgust with the violation of African Americans' rights in the North and their continued enslavement in the South, she positioned free black women as supporters of manly displays of martial valor to come. "It was a Spartan mother's farewell to her son, 'Bring home your shield or be brought upon it.' To you we would say, be true, be courageous, be steadfast in the discharge of your duty. The citadel of Error must yield to the unshrinking phalanx of truth. In our fireside circles, in the seclusion of our closets, we kneel in tearful supplication in your behalf. As Christian wives, mothers and daughters ... we pledge ourselves to exert our influence unceasingly in the cause of Liberty and Humanity." Finally, she offered her society's encouragement and support by using the rhetoric of battle, charging the delegates to "be courageous; be steadfast; unfurl your banner to the breeze—let its folds float proudly over you, bearing the glorious inscription, broad and brilliant as the material universe: 'God and Liberty!'"[60]

By placing their diasporic struggle within this broader transnational and historic context, northern free blacks forged a genealogy of resistance, an international freedom struggle that extended from the ancient world to the present day. As Osborne P. Anderson wrote in his 1861 memoir, the fight for liberty exhibited at Harpers Ferry could be seen "coming down through the nations," irrespective of "national boundaries or peculiarities." In fact, "it has been proclaimed and enforced by the patriarch and the warrior of the Old World" as well as "the enfranchised freeman and the humble slave of the New." In Anderson's view,

[Liberty's] nationality is universal; its language every where understood by the haters of tyranny; and those that accept its mission, every where understand each other. There is an unbroken chain of sentiment and purpose from Moses of the Jews to John Brown of America; from Kossuth, and the liberators of France and Italy, to the untutored Gabriel, and the Denmark Veseys, Nat Turners and Madison Washingtons of the Southern American States. The shaping and expressing of a thought for freedom takes the same consistence with the colored American—whether he be an independent citizen of the Haytian nation, a proscribed but humble nominally free colored man, a patient, toiling, but hopeful slave—as with the proudest or noblest representative of European or American civilization and Christianity.[61]

As Osborne's proclamation suggests, he and other northern free blacks saw the fight for liberty as rooted in biblical authority. Moreover, this unbroken chain of freedom fighters made Africans throughout the diaspora—slave and free, north and south—heirs to a radical tradition, participants in a transnational freedom struggle that began with the liberation of the Hebrews in Egypt, continued with the acts of heroic Romans such as Virginius, reached its apogee with the Haitian Revolution, and continued to be embodied in the courageous actions of the enslaved and free men and women of the current generation.

CREATING MODERN REVOLUTIONARIES IN THE ANGLO-AFRICAN MAGAZINE

Throughout 1859, contributors to the *Anglo-African* returned to these transnational revolutionary themes, making them a fixture of Hamilton's magazine. The fiction and the history published in the *Anglo-African Magazine* served as particularly useful media for explicitly linking the past with the present and spelling out a distinct radical role for elite and aspiring free black readers. Reading these tales, African Americans could imagine themselves in the role of the protagonists, heirs to an ancient, transnational freedom struggle, ready and willing to sacrifice all on the altar of liberty. Such an identification was essential for aspiring African Americans who had long thought of themselves as the vanguard of the race, best positioned to help those still enslaved.

These lessons formed the centerpiece of the "Afric-American Picture Gallery," a series of seven essays by William J. Wilson that appeared in the *Anglo-African Magazine* in 1859. Wilson, a Brooklyn resident like Hamilton, was a schoolteacher and an active figure in antebellum black public life. Wilson also served as a delegate to several state and national black conventions, including the National Convention of the Colored Men of America in Rochester in 1853 and the National Convention in Washington, D.C., in 1869.[62] Under the pen name Ethiop, he regularly published correspondence in *Frederick Douglass's Paper* and Hamilton's other journal, the *Weekly Anglo-African*.

For the "Afric-American Picture Gallery," Wilson chose to blend past and present, history and politics, fact and fiction in a most creative way. Wilson positions himself as a sketch artist/curator commenting on the portraits and sculptures displayed in a secret gallery. Sitting in an easy chair at the center of the space, pencil and paper in hand, he promises to narrate what he sees "in this almost unknown Gallery." His essays offer not a traditional history but a usable history for free black readers: in the first installment, Ethiop notes that he will not discuss every image on display; rather, "Let us take a survey, and speak only of what strikes us most forcibly in our present mood."[63] As the narrator vividly describes oil paintings, marble busts, pen-and-ink drawings, and charcoal sketches, the reader learns of incidents from the African American past: the first cargo of African slaves known to arrive in British North America in 1619, the first black convention in 1831, the triumphs of actor Ira Aldridge.

Wilson used these essays to highlight black founding fathers and mothers from the revolutionary era—martyr Crispus Attucks, entrepreneur James Forten, poet Phillis Wheatley (who, "lady visitors to the Gallery," he writes "would do well" to study), and Bishop Richard Allen, founder of the African Methodist Episcopal Church—and gives a special place of honor to a portrait of Toussaint-Louverture, who provided a "useful and touching lesson" for the race.[64] Like other northern black writers in the period, Wilson reflects on the higher patriotism of these African American heroes, contrasting them with the hypocrisy of America's greatest eighteenth-century national heroes, Thomas Jefferson and George Washington. "A picture of Thomas Jefferson brings before the mind in all its scope and strength that inimitable document, the Declaration of Independence," he wrote, "and in addition, carries us forward to the times, when its broad and eternal principles, will be fully recognised by, and applied to the entire American people. I had these conclusions forced upon me by looking not upon either the picture of Washington or Jefferson in the gallery. Far from it; but by a most beautiful portrait of one of the greatest men the world ever saw—Toussant L'Overture."[65] He also speaks eloquently of the dignity and beauty of Cinque and provides a stirring characterization of Turner.

In so doing, Wilson joins the ranks of other northern blacks who placed rebellious slaves within a revolutionary tradition that included nineteenth-century icons as well as heroes of the American war for independence and the Haitian Revolution.

The essays also surveyed the political debates of the period by cleverly blending descriptions of the past with the concerns of the present. The narrator finds himself regularly interrupted by passers-by—men and women, philosophers, doctors, professors and fugitives, critics and admirers of the gallery both black and white—who engage him in conversation. The narrator and his interlocutors take on debates such as the value of a separate black press, condition versus color, the best choice of a name for people of African descent living in America, and passive versus redemptive Christianity. Here the essays move from description to dialogue, with conversations that carefully stage or dramatize discussions taking place throughout the black public sphere, and the narrator finds himself enraged, bemused, amused, insulted, and affirmed by those who enter his gallery.

Although the narrative form is unusual, it is not surprising that Wilson would take such an inventive approach. He was deeply interested in the arts and had long insisted that he and his compatriots "tell our own story, write our own lecture, paint our own picture, chisel our own bust." As he saw it, "The encouragement and self-reliance [the arts] will inspire will do more to push us forward than all the speculations about our 'manifest destiny,' &c., that has emanated from the brains of all the fools white or black in Christendom."[66] And he called for "a room for readings, or drawings, paintings, or sculpturings, or music" created by his people "to be opened in the heart of Gotham" for their enjoyment.[67] Wilson thought that African American visual culture could offer useful lessons: "Pictures are teachings by example. From them we often derive our best lessons."[68] Therefore, Ethiop filled his gallery with exemplary figures from African American history.

The heroic figures Ethiop placed in his gallery were not simply meant to serve as casual reading for elite and aspiring black readers. They also served as powerful calls to political action and militancy. Wilson underscores this point in a conversation between the narrator and Bill in the final "Afric-American Picture Gallery" essay. While meditating on the meaning of the images displayed in his gallery, the narrator is interrupted by Bill, a fugitive who bursts into the gallery, emotionally overwrought after spying his old master on a New

York City street. Bill then explains that some years earlier, he strangled slave catchers hired by this master, affirming that "God had implanted the principles of liberty in my bosom, [and] both in seeking and maintaining that liberty, I had determined to remove every obstacle that obtruded itself between me and it." In a language that would have made David Walker proud, Bill proclaimed, "I did, therefore, nothing more than my duty, to my manhood, and to my God." And with that, Ethiop concluded both the installment and the series, placing a portrait of Bill in a place of honor at the northern end of the gallery.[69]

Ethiop thus reminds readers that the heroes he described were not just figures passively to be admired but examples for northern free blacks to follow. As Wilson's narrator says early in the series, "These pictures . . . serve as simple reminders of what the people of color were, now are, and will yet be."[70] Thus, Ethiop links the efforts of revolutionaries past with contemporary black abolitionists' efforts: "It is of this class comes our Nat Turners. . . . It is of this class come the Margaret Garners, who rather than their babes even shall clank a chain, prefer to send them up to their God who gave them. It is of this class comes our Douglasses and our Browns, and a host of other spirits now cast upon the regions of the North."[71] And he encourages his elite and aspiring black readers to embody the attributes of these revolutionaries in preparation for the coming struggle, noting that the gallery is not yet full: "The walls are spacious, and contain ample room for more, and, in many instances, better paintings; and many niches yet vacant for busts and statues."[72] Wilson's comments suggest that northern blacks increasingly believed that if their heroes past and present exhibited the highest forms of virtue, sacrifice, and love of liberty, perhaps men and women in their own communities should cultivate the same principles and actions and prepare themselves to take positions of honor in the pantheon of heroes.

Martin Delany also used these mutually reinforcing themes as the basis for *Blake; or, The Huts of America*, which the *Anglo-African Magazine* published in serial form between 1859 and 1862. The novel, set in 1853, told the story of Henry Blake, a fugitive who left his owner after the sale of his wife and traveled across the South, planning a slave insurrection, invoking the spirit of generations of black revolutionaries, and framing them as messianic agents of God. "From plantation to plantation" he went, "sowing the seeds of future devastation and ruin to the master and redemption to the slave, an antecedent more terrible in its anticipation than the warning voices of the destroying Angel in commanding the slaughter of the firstborn of Egypt." When Blake arrived in the Great Dismal Swamp region of North Carolina, he was met by "some of Virginia and North Carolina's boldest black rebels," and "a number of the old confederates of the noted Nat Turner," who "hailed the daring young runaway as the harbinger of better days." There, "the names of Nat Turner, Denmark Veezie, and General Gabriel [Prosser]" all "were held . . . in sacred reverence." Even though some of the rebels "claim[ed] to have been patriots in the American Revolution," they considered Prosser, Vesey, and Turner "to be the greatest men who ever lived." In keeping with the ideals of liberation theology, the revolutionaries combined their belief in divine retribution with the ideal of manly self-assertion in their rallying cry, "Arm of the Lord, awake!"[73]

Delany's decision to have Blake consult with black revolutionaries and set his plan in motion after the disruption of his family was not inconsequential. Depictions of male revenge executed on behalf of loved ones appeared quite frequently in the fiction produced by northern blacks in the period. For example, in "Patrick Brown's First Love," a short story published anonymously in the *Anglo-African Magazine*, the actions of the eponymous hero suggest that the most personal ties of love and affection might provide the greatest spark for the coming revolution. The now elderly Brown tells the narrator that "in his early youth," he had loved an enslaved woman, Keziah, "with a mild, passionate, and boundless love." But when a slave trader attempted first to seduce and subsequently to bind, gag, and rape Keziah during their journey into the Lower South, Brown stabbed and "disemboweled" the trader using the man's own knife. Keziah saved herself by choosing death before dishonor and was found the next morning lying next to the body of the slave trader, "unstained by his guilty touch, with death—beautiful; oh! How beautiful!—on her virgin brow." And after murdering the slave trader, Brown spent the rest of his life executing his successive owners. Like Keziah, Blake's wife, Maggie, refused to comply with the sexual demands of her owners. But rather than death, Maggie endured a succession of sales and violent beatings. When Blake ultimately located his wife on a Cuban plantation, the once beautiful Maggie was aged, graying, and badly scarred by the beatings of her new owner, whose advances she repeatedly and consistently refused. Like her husband, Maggie retained her honor at all costs.[74]

Delany and the author of "Patrick Brown's First Love" clearly believed that women's ability to retain their chastity and sacrifice everything made them virtuous heroines and worthy wives for would-be revolutionaries. Echoing the views of the author of "Female Influence," an 1837 essay in the *Colored American*, such displays of feminine virtue and sacrifice spurred fathers, sons, and brothers to further action, to "deeds of valor and patriotism."[75] Thus, after reuniting with Maggie, Blake tells her, "As God lives, I will avenge your wrongs" and hastens his plans for insurrection and revolution.[76] The narrator of "Patrick Brown's First Love" concludes with an appeal to Roman lore, saying that in the near future, "some black-bosomed Virginius, crazed at the sight of his deflowered daughter, or some flame-colored hero, maddened at the sight of the wife of his bosom outraged in his very presence, will raise his bloody arm, and kindle the wild revenge of the ten thousands, in like manner maddened; and there will be a short and bloody end to slavery."[77] For readers accustomed to accounts of ideal chaste wives and independent husbands, virtuous republican gender ideals acquired a militant, revolutionary spirit in moments of crisis. These works of fiction provided a striking counterpoint to the reports of abuse detailed in slave narratives, for the virtue and sacrifices of these fictional characters could be understood as acts that saved the race from corruption. As virtue triumphs in these allegories, so, by extension, does the race.

The history and fiction published in the *Anglo-African Magazine* must have given aspiring African Americans who sought to live an antislavery life a great deal to consider on the eve of the Civil War. By linking black heroic figures of the diaspora with European nationalists of the period, militarizing gender ideals, and casting contemporary heroic slaves as classic heroes from antiquity, contributors to the *Anglo-African Magazine* continued the process of recasting the idea of revolution itself, moving it beyond American exceptionalism and redefining it as an international freedom struggle that aspiring free blacks could exemplify as long as they exhibited virtue and maintained a willingness to sacrifice. And celebrating this type of revolution ultimately provided a new set of opportunities and imperatives for northern free blacks whose interpretations of theology called them to service, who sought to live Ward's vision of an antislavery life, and who intended to embody the antithesis of proslavery ideology.

FREE BLACK PERSONAL POLITICS ON THE EVE OF THE CIVIL WAR

In the decade preceding the Civil War, as the nation moved inexorably toward dissolution, northern black writers insisted that a long-prophesied day of revolution was at hand. Even African American émigrés to Canada agreed that "revolution is the boldest and probably the most glorious alternative," and though waging war against slaveholders was less practical than emigration, "it is the right of the colored Americans."[78] William J. Wilson expressed a similar sentiment in an 1859 essay on "The Anglo-African and the African Slave Trade": "We even now live in a day of calculation, and the day of exact reckoning is approaching: a day when, whether men will or no, the just measure shall be meted out to all, not only in heaven, but here on earth; and this our portion of it will not surely be forgotten." According to Wilson, "The exact *when*, and the precise *how*, are alone in the bosom of God," and "we are content to let them rest there." In the interim, however, "it behooves every one to be on the alert; to be on the watch-tower or in the drill, or measuring strength; and with book in hand, comparing and noting the result."[79] If rebellious slaves were engaging in God's work—striking a physical blow to liberate the race from slavery—northern blacks could not remain passive. In 1858, John Rock, a physician and dentist famous for being denied a passport by Secretary of State Lewis Cass, succinctly framed this sentiment at Boston's Faneuil Hall: "Sooner or later the clashing of arms will be heard in this country." At that point, "150,000 freemen capable of bearing arms, and not all cowards and fools," will join "three quarters of a million slaves," and "wild with the enthusiasm caused by the dawn of the glorious opportunity of being able to strike a genuine blow for freedom," they "will be a power that white men will be 'bound to respect.'"[80] Circumstances demanded that free black northerners embody the spirit of revolution and prepare to join their enslaved brothers and sisters in a battle for freedom.

For aspiring black readers who sought to place their lives in the service of the antislavery struggle and to embody resistance to the proslavery ideology dominating the national consciousness, the revolutionary identity put forward in the *Anglo-African Magazine* offered inspiration at a moment of crisis. For decades, northern black writers and public figures had found that the history of the African diaspora offered up outstanding examples of antislavery living. They consequently highlighted the stories of black citizen-soldiers, praising these men and women as true revolutionaries, exemplary figures, and models for aspiring African Americans to emulate to place their lives in the full service of the freedom struggle. Northern black writers also situated members of their generation at the end of the arc of a transnational revolutionary trajectory and characterized their generation's actions as modern-day manifestations of the kind of iconic patriotic acts necessary for the fulfillment of the Scriptures prophesying their people's deliverance from oppression. In the process, black writers, ministers, and public figures expanded the concept of antislavery living to include the most radical of identities for aspiring free blacks: antislavery revolutionaries and race patriots, modern manifestations of an ancient, international freedom struggle, men and women ready to lay down their lives in service of the cause. Contributors to the *Anglo-African Magazine* produced historical fiction that amplified these arguments in ways that recast the meaning of service, suggesting that additional, radical forms of northern free black agency were essential for the fulfillment of divine prophecy.

Indeed, Delany crystallized these hopes and directives in *Blake*. Near the end of the novel, Blake finally reunites with Maggie in Cuba and reveals his true identity. He was not a slave but Carolus Henrico Blacus, a free black sailor and cousin of Plácido who had been kidnapped and sent to toil on a southern plantation. His ultimate goal: to unite the free and enslaved Africans of Cuba and lead a redemptive diasporic rebellion that would spread from Cuba to the southern United States.[81] This sense of purpose, this belief that free African Americans could embody the spirit of revolutionaries past, would further radicalize elite and aspiring free blacks during the 1850s and prepare them for their new roles as freedom's soldiers during the Civil War and in the coming decades.

Epilogue

Beginning in the early nineteenth century, as a small population of free African Americans carved out a space for their communities in the North, they also created a print culture that spoke to the cultural and political concerns of an emerging black middle class. African American writers, ministers, newspaper editors, and public figures repeatedly placed middle-class forms of self-fashioning, domestic family practices, and transnational political discourse in the service of the fight to end slavery and expand African American civil and political rights. In essays, speeches, memoirs, and fiction, these authors advised aspiring African Americans to live up to their antislavery principles by following advice on matters of personal and domestic conduct, fashioning themselves into ideal men and women, and transforming themselves into living, breathing refutations of the arguments used to justify the institution of slavery and its concomitant racism. These writers further urged readers to enact their antislavery principles as independent men in the public sphere; to cultivate these principles within the bosom of the family circle; to claim their roles as virtuous mothers, fathers, brothers, and sisters; and to imagine themselves as heirs to an international revolutionary tradition that stretched back to antiquity, ready to sacrifice in the name of freedom.

These ideas ultimately also shaped the way leading black activists interpreted the Civil War and characterized the role they believed northern blacks should play in the conflict. Like many white antislavery advocates, prominent African Americans agreed that the national crisis bore the stamp of divine retribution for the sin of slavery. Indeed, one man wrote to the *Christian Recorder*, the journal of the African Methodist Episcopal Church, to point out the "correspondence existing between the war in the United States and the Egyptian plagues," and he prophesied that "the inexpressible tortures inflicted upon ancient Egypt" and "the bloody streets of France in 1792, will all hardly bear a comparison to what will befall this nation."[1] But when the Civil War began in

1861, black public figures urged African Americans to join their brethren in the South as members of an international community of freedom fighters. In August of that year, Thomas Hamilton captured the sense of expectancy in the air when he wrote, "Colored men whose fingers tingle to pull the trigger, or clutch the knife aimed at the slaveholders in arms, will not have to wait much longer."[2] Frederick Douglass expressed the sentiments of many black abolitionists when he declared, "LET THE SLAVES AND FREE COLORED PEOPLE BE CALLED INTO SERVICE, AND FORMED INTO A LIBERATING ARMY, to march into the South and raise the banner of emancipation among the slaves."[3] In January 1862, when Martin Delany suggested to a crowd of black New Yorkers, "Let our war cry be 'insurrection,'" his "declaration was received with tremendous applause."[4] And after 1863, when the Emancipation Proclamation transformed Union policy and the federal government officially sanctioned black enlistment, the editor of the *Christian Recorder* proclaimed, "Now is the time for us to fly to arms! to arms!" The *Recorder* continued, "It is better to die warriors than to die slaves."[5]

During the Civil War, free northern blacks placed their antislavery efforts in the service of the nation, recruiting African American troops for the Union and enlisting in the colored regiments. Northern free blacks—some volunteers, some conscripts—accounted for 18 percent of the 180,000 African American Union soldiers, serving in higher proportions than whites in many districts.[6] When explaining their support for black service or personal decisions to enlist, elite and aspiring free blacks expressed joy at the prospect of embodying their antislavery principles by becoming freedom's soldiers, aiding their brothers and sisters in bondage, taking up arms against the society that hoped to enslave them, and following in the footsteps of their hero, Toussaint-Louverture.[7] When James Forten's son, Robert, returned unannounced from his self-imposed exile in England to the United States, he explained his decision to enlist and become a recruiting officer for the Union by asking, "When now on the eve of the triumph of freedom how could I, or any other colored man in whose bosom a love of country, race, and liberty dwells, remain in a foreign land? I am come to break the bonds of the slave and aid in the triumph of liberty."[8] In January 1863, Hezekiah Ford Douglas wrote to *Frederick Douglass's Monthly*, explaining, "I enlisted six months ago in order to be better prepared to play my part in the great drama of the Negro's redemption."[9]

Always aware that their few educational and material advantages moved them into the higher classes of free African Americans, elite and aspiring northern blacks immediately positioned themselves as the patrons of freedmen and freedwomen as the South became liberated. Some worried about the former slaves' ability to secure the political rights and material foundation believed necessary for manly independence. One black Minnesota resident wrote to the *Weekly Anglo-African* to suggest "that we of the North should look after our forsaken and unlettered brethren. They are unable to contend for their own rights, and I think that we should organize for that very purpose." He recommended that specific prominent African Americans, including Frederick Douglass, Charles L. Remond, William Wells Brown, and J. W. Loguen, press the federal government to give freedmen possession of abandoned land.[10] Other black leaders, particularly those connected with the African Methodist Episcopal and African Methodist Episcopal Zion Churches, exhibited a deep concern about the moral and spiritual state of southern blacks and began sending northern blacks as missionaries to contraband camps and liberated territories.[11] Many elite African Americans expressed interest in the education of freedmen and freedwomen, urging "persons of our own color" to fill "the positions of teachers" in the South and recommending "to the educated portion of our people the importance of seeking such positions as soon as possible."[12] Consequently, as early as 1862, middle-class and prominent northern blacks began traveling to the South to work with emancipated slaves as teachers, missionaries, and political allies.[13] Frederick Douglass, Henry Highland Garnet, Alexander Crummell, and John Mercer Langston relocated to Washington, D.C. While Martin Delany worked as an officer of the Freedmen's Bureau in South Carolina, Douglass would edit the *New National Era* newspaper and return to the lecture circuit, where his speech on "Self-Made Men" continued to receive great acclaim. Frances Ellen Watkins Harper extended her lecture circuit into the southern states after combat between Union and Confederate troops ceased.[14] And Charlotte Forten and other African American women arrived as teachers and missionaries under the auspices of organizations such as the Freedmen's Aid Society, the African Methodist Episcopal and African Methodist Episcopal Zion Churches, and the American Missionary Aid Society.

For these now unambiguously elite African Americans, the Civil War offered a chance to fulfill a long-awaited prophetic role that had become an essential part of their identity. For decades, they had sought to transform themselves into ideal free men and women, to embody resistance to slavery, and to place every aspect of their lives in the service of the freedom struggle. They saw themselves as having a duty to act and execute divine will, to place their lives and homes in the service of the fight for freedom, and to take up positions in their generation's pantheon of heroes. As African Americans trained to believe in the transformative power of self-improvement, these men and women now hoped to spread their faith in the virtues they extolled to the South's newly freed men and women.[15] In the process, aspiring northerners would help to plant the seeds for a brand of uplift ideology that would come to inform the politics and identity of a new generation of African American activists in the South: the race men and women of the post-Reconstruction era.

NOTES

Abbreviations

AAM   *Anglo-African Magazine*
BAP   C. Peter Ripley, Roy E. Finkenbine, Michael F. Hembree, and Donald Yacavone, eds. *The Black Abolitionist Papers*. 5 vols. Chapel Hill: University of North Carolina Press, 1985–92.
BAPC   George E. Carter, C. Peter Ripley, and Jeffrey Rossbach, eds. *The Black Abolitionist Papers, 1830–1865*. Microfilm. Sanford, N.C.: Microfilming Corporation of America, 1981.
BSC   Philip S. Foner and George E. Walker, eds. *Proceedings of the Black State Conventions, 1840–1865*. 2 vols. Philadelphia: Temple University Press, 1979–80.
CA   *Colored American*
FJ   *Freedom's Journal*
NNC   Howard Bell, ed. *Minutes of the Proceedings of the National Negro Conventions, 1830–1864*. New York: Arno, 1969.
NS   *North Star*
WAA   *Weekly Anglo-African*

Introduction

1. In a study of the free black population in antebellum cities, Leonard Curry found that approximately 2 percent of all employed free men of color were engaged in professional, managerial, artistic, clerical, or scientific enterprises that required substantial or specific education (*The Free Black in Urban America, 1800–1850: The Shadow of the Dream* [Chicago: University of Chicago Press, 1981], 18–22).

2. For information about the emergence of antebellum black print culture, see Bella Gross, "*Freedom's Journal* and the *Rights of All*," *Journal of Negro History* 17 (July 1932): 241–86; Martin E. Dann, *The Black Press, 1827–1890: The Quest for a National Identity* (New York: Putnam's, 1971); Jacqueline Bacon, *Freedom's Journal: The First African American Newspaper* (Lanham, Md.: Lexington, 2007). Elizabeth McHenry argues that the reading habits of these African Americans tell us a great deal about both their personal and political sensibilities (*Forgotten Readers: Recovering the Lost History of Afri-

can American Literary Societies [Durham: Duke University Press, 2002], esp. chapters 1 and 2).

3. Patrick Rael, *Black Identity and Black Protest* (Chapel Hill: University of North Carolina Press, 2002), 179. Kevin Gaines examines racial uplift ideology in the early twentieth century in *Uplifting the Race: Black Leadership, Politics, and Culture in the Twentieth Century* (Chapel Hill: University of North Carolina Press, 1996).

4. Evelyn Brooks Higginbotham coined the term *politics of respectability* in her study of black Baptist women in the post-Reconstruction era, *Righteous Discontent: The Women's Movement in the Black Baptist Church, 1880–1920* (Cambridge: Harvard University Press, 1993). The literature on early-nineteenth-century racial uplift in the northern black community includes Rael, *Black Identity and Black Protest*, esp. chapters 4 and 5; Elizabeth Rauh Bethel, *The Roots of African-American Identity: Memory and History in Free Antebellum Communities* (New York: St. Martin's, 1997), chapter 5; Frederick Cooper, "Elevating the Race: The Social Thought of Black Leaders, 1827–50," *American Quarterly* 24 (December 1972): 604–25; Robert S. Levine, *Martin Delany, Frederick Douglass, and the Politics of Representative Identity* (Chapel Hill: University of North Carolina Press, 1997).

5. Scholars now agree that the institutions created to facilitate racial elevation would become the core institutions of African American abolitionist activity. R. J. Young argues that "the word that summed up the path activists wished their race to follow was 'elevation.' This term covered temperance reform, education, values like hard work and religious sensibility but can be thought of as African Americans making themselves 'respectable,' both in their own eyes and in those of whites" (*Antebellum Black Activists: Race, Gender, Self* [New York: Garland, 1996], 110–11). In his study of the Reconstruction era, Eric Foner notes that "the small black political leadership of ministers, professionals, and members of abolitionist societies, had long searched for a means of improving the condition of Northern blacks while at the same time striking a blow against slavery.... Free blacks were advised to forsake menial occupations, educate themselves and their children, and live unimpeachably moral lives, thus 'elevating' the race, disproving the idea of black inferiority, and demonstrating themselves worthy of citizenship" (*Reconstruction: America's Unfinished Revolution, 1863–1877* [New York: Harper and Row, 1988], 26). Rael agrees with these characterizations and goes further, arguing that the ideal of elevation formed the cornerstone of black protest thought before the Civil War. According to Rael, the leadership of the northern black community consistently proclaimed that individual improvement of one's physical state, intellect, and personal morality should remain the goal of each member of the free black population and should be used as a tool in the struggle to combat growing antiblack sentiment in the North (*Black Identity and Black Protest*, 127). Jane H. Pease and William H. Pease argue that this pattern—the belief that the elevation of the race and the fight against slavery were

inseparable battles—ultimately distinguished white abolitionist ideology from black abolitionism. According to Pease and Pease, despite black abolitionists' insistence that the issues were inseparable, white abolitionists tended to view the northern black campaign for civil rights as a secondary concern and focused primarily on the abolition of southern slavery (*They Who Would Be Free: Blacks' Search for Freedom, 1830-1861* [Urbana: University of Illinois Press, 1990]).

6. Recent scholarship has suggested that discourses of respectability helped to shape the processes of African American class formation. Instead of calling for respectability, New York's poor and laboring African Americans preferred to use informal demonstrations, expressive street culture, and parades to raise black consciousness and publicly object to the racial, economic, and political status quo. The division between those New York City blacks who preferred the "respectable" church service over a public procession and others was played out in the pages of the *Freedom's Journal* and is discussed by Shane White in "'It Was a Proud Day': African Americans, Festivals, and Parades in the North, 1741-1834," *Journal of American History* 81 (June 1994): 13-50; Leslie M. Harris, *In the Shadow of Slavery: African Americans in New York City, 1626-1863* (Chicago: University of Chicago Press), 122-28.

7. I use the term *aspiring* to denote middle-class men and women. Historians are increasingly moving away from sociological explanations of class in favor of approaches that analyze "middle class" as a cultural process, a set of behaviors and a shared constellation of values and aspirations that began to coalesce in the early nineteenth century. For examples of this approach, see Jennifer L. Goloboy, "The Early American Middle Class," *Journal of the Early Republic* 25 (Winter 2005): 543-44; Paul E. Johnson, *A Shopkeeper's Millennium: Society and Revivals in Rochester, New York, 1815-1837* (1978; New York: Hill and Wang, 2004); Karen Halttunen, *Confidence Men and Painted Women: A Study of Middle-Class Culture in America, 1830-1870* (New Haven: Yale University Press, 1982).

8. Samuel Ringgold Ward, *Autobiography of a Fugitive Negro: His Anti-Slavery Labours in the United States, Canada, and England* (1855; New York: Arno, 1968), 43.

9. Scholarship on the post-Reconstruction era has demonstrated just how important these ideas were to the political activities of a range of elite and aspiring African Americans. This work includes Deborah Gray White, *Too Heavy a Load: Black Women in Defense of Themselves, 1894-1994* (New York: Norton, 1999), chapters 1-3; Higginbotham, *Righteous Discontent*; Glenda Elizabeth Gilmore, *Gender and Jim Crow: Women and the Politics of White Supremacy in North Carolina, 1896-1920* (Chapel Hill: University of North Carolina Press, 1996); Michele Mitchell, *Righteous Propagation: African Americans and the Politics of Racial Destiny after Reconstruction* (Chapel Hill: University of North Carolina Press, 2004); Gaines, *Uplifting the Race*; Victoria W. Wolcott, *Remaking Respectability: African American Women in Interwar Detroit* (Chapel Hill: University

of North Carolina Press, 2001). As these scholars have demonstrated, members of the African American leadership consistently embraced and espoused an ideology of "racial uplift" in the decades after the end of Reconstruction in an effort to strengthen the black population and transform the status of Africans in America. According to Gaines, racial uplift must be considered a black middle-class ideology, and many advocates of uplift viewed class distinctions as evidence of African American progress on a journey from chattel slavery to prosperity, refinement, and—ultimately—equality and power (*Uplifting the Race*, 14–15). A range of African American activists from Booker T. Washington to Marcus Garvey insisted that African American men and women build their own institutions, promote education, and teach industry, dignity, and virtue to their children. Some, like Washington, believed that these efforts would demonstrate the race's fitness for full American citizenship and thus serve to dismantle Jim Crow. Others, like Garvey, saw these efforts as the first steps toward black independence and the creation of "a mighty race" that would challenge European supremacy around the world. Middle-class African Americans, particularly women, were especially amenable to these arguments and made the "uplift of the race" a driving force behind their intraracial community activism. Moreover, much of the uplift rhetoric of the post-Reconstruction era centered on the sanctity of marriage, the creation of the ideal black home and family, and the policing of African American sexual purity—all key concerns of the "aspiring classes" of African Americans. These scholars have found that this discourse had a disproportionate impact on African American women whose reproductive power was viewed as "the crucial site of race building," essential for the social and political progress of the race. See Gaines, *Uplifting the Race*, 12.

10. Much of the more recent literary analysis examines the relationship between slave narratives and other generic forms such as autobiography, sentimental novels, domestic literature, abolitionist fiction, and twentieth-century neoslave narratives. For the advantages of this approach, see Dickson D. Bruce Jr., *The Origins of African American Literature, 1680–1865* (Charlottesville: University Press of Virginia, 2001). See also Audrey Fisch, ed., *The Cambridge Companion to the African American Slave Narrative* (Cambridge: Cambridge University Press, 2007).

11. Most of the research on representations of gender and family in slave narratives focuses on the narratives by enslaved women. In fact, it is generally understood that this interest in family, women's issues, and sexuality distinguishes the published memoirs of women such as Harriet Jacobs from those of men such as Frederick Douglass. See Frances Foster, "'In Respect to Females': Differences in the Portrayals of Women by Male and Female Narrators," *Black American Literature Forum* 15 (Summer 1981): 66–70; Sandra Gunning, "Harriet Jacobs, Frederick Douglass, and the Slavery Debate: Bondage, Family, and the Discourse of Domesticity," in *Harriet Jacobs and Incidents in the Life of a Slave Girl: New Critical Essays*, ed. Deborah M. Garfield and Rafia Zahar (New York: Cam-

bridge University Press, 1996), 131–55; Jennifer Fleischner, *Mastering Slavery: Memory, Family, and Identity in Women's Slave Narratives* (New York: New York University Press, 1996). But when we compare Jacobs's account with other black-authored antislavery literature, we see that she was not the only African American to write about home and family in the decades before the Civil War. As Charles J. Heglar argues, fugitives such as Henry Bibb and William and Ellen Craft also placed home and family at the center of their slave narratives (*Rethinking the Slave Narrative: Slave Marriage and the Narratives of Henry Bibb and William and Ellen Craft* [Westport, Conn.: Greenwood, 2001]).

12. To date, very little research has examined African American domestic discourse. Frances Smith Foster has recently published an anthology of poems, fiction, and letters by African Americans from Phillis Wheatley to Jessie Fauset on courtship, marriage, and family. But Foster does not connect this discourse to the larger political concerns of the free black community or to African American middle-class formation. See Frances Smith Foster, ed., *Love and Marriage in Early African America* (Lebanon, N.H.: Northeastern University Press, 2008).

13. John Ernest, *Liberation Historiography: African American Writers and the Challenge of History, 1794–1861* (Chapel Hill: University of North Carolina Press, 2004), 305. While much scholarship has examined the relationship between magazines and middle-class identity in the late nineteenth century, a close reading of the *Anglo-African Magazine* suggests that magazines and a politicized black middle-class identity were beginning to be linked much earlier. See Richard Ohmann, *Selling Culture: Magazines, Markets, and Class at the Turn of the Century* (New York: Verso, 1998); Ellen Gruber Garvey, *The Adman in the Parlor: Magazines and the Gendering of Consumer Culture, 1880s–1910s* (New York: Oxford University Press, 1996).

14. In recent years, scholars have highlighted the ways that transatlantic intellectual currents and political movements have shaped African American identity, nationalism, and activism. Much of this work has focused on Anglo-American interactions. See Paul Gilroy, *The Black Atlantic: Modernity and Double Consciousness* (Cambridge: Harvard University Press, 1993); R. J. M. Blackett, *Building an Antislavery Wall: Black Americans in the Atlantic Abolitionist Movement, 1830–1860* (Baton Rouge: Louisiana State University Press, 2002); Mitch Kachun, "'Our Platform Is as Broad as Humanity': Transatlantic Freedom Movements and the Idea of Progress in Nineteenth-Century African American Thought and Activism," *Slavery and Abolition* 24 (December 2003): 1–23; Van Gosse, "'As a Nation, the English Are Our Friends': The Emergence of African American Politics in the British Atlantic World, 1772–1861," *American Historical Review* 113 (October 2008): 1003–28.

15. Scholars have traditionally argued that northern black political culture progressed rather naturally from integrationist campaigns at the beginning of the century to separatist ones by the 1850s. Some observers have seen this story as one of black

political maturation, where the movement away from white influences and institutions constituted a process of growing race consciousness, political maturation, and ultimately nationalism. For example, Harry Reed argues that black political awareness developed in five distinct stages, beginning with the creation of separate black churches, followed by the creation of other self-help organizations, the creation of black newspapers that provided a communications network and shaped cultural tastes, and the organization of conventions that allowed the leadership to put forth a national platform for political change. In Reed's analysis, all of these developments lead inexorably toward black nationalist and emigrationist movements, which he considers to be the most sophisticated expression of black political consciousness (*Platform for Change: The Foundations of the Northern Free Black Community, 1775–1865* [East Lansing: Michigan State University Press, 1994], 4–5). Other scholars have seen this trajectory as a narrative of declension, with black spokespersons giving in to despair in response to the insensitivity of white abolitionists and the hostile climate of the 1850s. Pease and Pease, for example, argue that divisions developed between black and white allies because white abolitionists failed to examine their racial prejudices as well as to support northern black efforts to "elevate the race" by encouraging "economic and social mobility for Northern blacks" and working "to acquire the franchise," "insure civil rights," and "establish a sense of black identity and community." These divisions, coupled with the rapidly declining status of northern blacks, ultimately caused black abolitionists to embrace separatist and black nationalist programs (*They Who Would be Free*, 16).

16. Howard H. Bell, "The American Moral Reform Society, 1836–1841," *Journal of Negro Education* 27 (Winter 1958): 34–40; Julie Winch, *Philadelphia's Black Elite: Activism, Accommodation, and the Struggle for Autonomy, 1787–1848* (Philadelphia: Temple University Press, 1988), 108–29.

17. In *Martin Delany*, Levine makes the case that similar calls for "elevation" appeared in competing black political discourses, transcending the strategies of assimilation and emigration hotly debated in the 1850s. In her discussion of Delany's life, Nell Irvin Painter points out that "elevation" was "one of Delany's favorite concepts throughout his life," meaning "the acquisition of gentlemanly culture and correct speech, of upright morals, independent thought, and "manly religion" ("Martin R. Delany: Elitism and Black Nationalism," in *Black Leaders of the Nineteenth Century*, ed. Leon Litwack and August Meier [Urbana: University of Illinois Press, 1988], 152). James Brewer Stewart argues that by the 1840s, respectability continued to be valued but was placed in the service of a more explicitly political agenda ("The Emergence of Racial Modernity and the Rise of the White North, 1790–1840," *Journal of the Early Republic* 18 [Summer 1998]: 214–15).

18. My definition of personal politics is shaped by scholars who demonstrate that cultural practices such as dress, music, and language can have profound political signifi-

cance in certain social contexts. See, for example, Robin D. G. Kelley, "The Riddle of the Zoot: Malcolm Little and Black Cultural Politics during World War II," in *Race Rebels: Culture, Politics, and the Black Working Class* (New York: Free Press, 1994), 161–81; Martin Summers, *Manliness and Its Discontents: The Black Middle Class and the Transformation of Masculinity, 1900–1930* (Chapel Hill: University of North Carolina Press, 2004).

19. Graham Russell Hodges, *Root and Branch: African Americans in New York and East Jersey, 1613–1863* (Chapel Hill: University of North Carolina Press, 1999), 205–13; Shane White and Graham White, *Stylin': African American Expressive Culture from Its Beginnings to the Zoot Suit* (Ithaca: Cornell University Press, 1998), 91–104.

20. Joanne Pope Melish demonstrates that northern blacks used the same language as white reformers and colonizationists when they insisted that the "degraded condition" of African Americans reinforced whites' racism. She notes that this discourse must also be seen as contributing to the creation of racial ideologies in New England. See Joanne Pope Melish, *Disowning Slavery: Gradual Emancipation and "Race" in New England, 1780–1860* (Ithaca: Cornell University Press, 1998), 241–44.

21. Halttunen, *Confidence Men*, 117; C. Dallet Hemphill, *Bowing to Necessities: A History of Manners in America, 1620–1860* (New York: Oxford University Press, 1999), 129–36.

22. Mitchell, *Righteous Propagation*, 108.

23. Erica Armstrong Dunbar finds that the semiprivate albums containing the art, prose, and poetry composed by intimate friends contain sentimental verses on family and domestic themes, excellent penmanship, genteel turns of phrase, and a general concern with respectability (*A Fragile Freedom: African American Women and Emancipation in the Antebellum City* [New Haven: Yale University Press, 2008], 120–47).

24. Joseph Willson, *The Elite of Our People: Joseph Willson's Sketches of Black Upper-Class Life in Antebellum Philadelphia*, ed. Julie Winch (University Park: Pennsylvania State University Press, 2000), 100.

25. Ibid., 99–100.

26. Ward, *Autobiography of a Fugitive Negro*, 43.

CHAPTER ONE. African American Advice Literature and Black Middle-Class Self-Fashioning

1. Vermont first outlawed the enslavement of persons "born in this country or brought from over the sea" in its 1777 constitution, and the Massachusetts supreme court outlawed the institution in 1783 after ruling that slavery violated the state constitution. In 1780, Pennsylvania passed the first legislation providing for the gradual emancipation of slaves, and Rhode Island and Connecticut followed suit in 1784, with New York and New Jersey adopting similar gradual emancipation plans in 1799 and 1804, respec-

tively. For a discussion of the movement toward emancipation in the postrevolutionary era, see Ira Berlin, *Many Thousands Gone: The First Two Centuries of Slavery in North America* (Cambridge: Harvard University Press, 1998), 228–55. For information on the creation of free black political and community institutions in the antebellum North, see Benjamin Quarles, *Black Abolitionists* (New York: Da Capo, 1979); Harry Reed, *Platform for Change: The Foundations of the Northern Free Black Community, 1775–1865* (East Lansing: Michigan State University Press, 1994); James Oliver Horton and Lois E. Horton, *In Search of Liberty: Culture, Community, and Protest among Northern Free Blacks, 1700–1860* (New York: Oxford University Press, 1997).

2. The literature on antebellum black protest culture is vast. For two key interpretations, see Patrick Rael, *Black Identity and Black Protest in the Antebellum North* (Chapel Hill: University of North Carolina Press, 2002); Horton and Horton, *In Search of Liberty*.

3. John Berry Meachum, *Address to All the Colored Citizens of the United States* (Philadelphia: King and Baird, 1846), 11–12, 48, 45, 9, 6.

4. Karen Halttunen, *Confidence Men and Painted Women: A Study of Middle-Class Culture in America, 1830–1870* (New Haven: Yale University Press, 1982), 29.

5. For scholarship on conduct and the emergence of middle-class culture in the northeastern United States, see Stuart Blumin, *The Emergence of the Middle Class: Social Experience in the American City, 1760–1900* (New York: Cambridge University Press, 1989); Paul E. Johnson, *A Shopkeeper's Millennium: Society and Revivals in Rochester, New York, 1815–1837* (1978; New York: Hill and Wang, 2004); Mary Ryan, *Cradle of the Middle Class: The Family in Oneida County, New York, 1790–1865* (New York: Cambridge University Press, 1981); Halttunen, *Confidence Men and Painted Women*; C. Dallett Hemphill, *Bowing to Necessities: A History of Manners in America, 1620–1860* (New York: Oxford University Press, 1999).

6. Scholars have long understood that conduct discourse—even when addressed to members of the working class—was primarily consumed by middle-class whites. However, scholars of African American history usually see this discourse as directed toward the masses of laboring African Americans. But as Michele Mitchell adroitly argues, this type of discourse was most likely consumed by those African Americans most interested in improving themselves—in other words, those who aspired to rise in class and status (*Righteous Propagation: African Americans and the Politics of Racial Destiny after Reconstruction* [Chapel Hill: University of North Carolina Press, 2004], 108).

7. In his analysis of northern black discourses of self-improvement, Frederick Cooper notes that *Freedom's Journal* covered local community events, weddings, and deaths and published articles on important black national and international figures as well as frequent short stories, jokes, and essays on self-improvement. He finds the array of topics so surprising that he concludes, "*Freedom's Journal* can be better understood as a journal designed to serve a developing black community than as a paper of pro-

test" ("Elevating the Race: The Social Thought of Black Leaders, 1827–50," *American Quarterly* 24 [December 1972]: 606, 607). Jacqueline Bacon offers a fine analysis of the journal's range of political, self-improvement, and domestic articles in *Freedom's Journal: The First African American Newspaper* (Lanham, Md.: Lexington, 2007). Though he sees African American newspapers as primarily political texts, Martin Dann agrees that *Freedom's Journal* and all subsequent antebellum black newspapers provided important educational and social resources for their audience (*The Black Press, 1827–1890: The Quest for a National Identity* [New York: Putnam's, 1971], 13). In her analysis of the reading habits of northern free blacks, Elizabeth McHenry explains that these newspapers, along with other forms of antebellum black print culture, were designed to form the "literary character" of African American members, making them into exemplary citizens (*Forgotten Readers: Recovering the Lost History of African American Literary Societies* [Durham: Duke University Press, 2002], chapters 1 and 2).

8. *FJ*, August 3, 1827.
9. *CA*, March 16, 1839.
10. Mitchell, *Righteous Propagation*, 108.
11. "Hand Books for Home Improvement," *WAA*, May 26, 1860.
12. According to Henry Bibb, those defending "Slavery" won the debate. He noted that "it is a hard matter to maintain one side of this question before an audience, nine-tenths of whom are fugitives from slavery, whose prejudices are strongly against the system of slavery" (*Voice of the Fugitive*, September 29, 1851, in *BAPC*, 7:122).
13. McHenry, *Forgotten Readers*, 138–39.
14. Peter Hinks, *To Awaken My Afflicted Brethren: David Walker and the Problem of Antebellum Slave Resistance* (University Park: Pennsylvania State University Press, 1996), 81.
15. Frederick Douglass, *Narrative of the Life of Frederick Douglass, an American Slave, Written by Himself* (1845; New York: Signet, 1997), 116.
16. Hinks, *To Awaken My Afflicted Brethren*, 81.
17. For analysis of racism in the North, see George M. Fredrickson, *The Black Image in the White Mind: The Debate on Afro-American Character and Destiny, 1817–1914* (Hanover, N.H.: Wesleyan University Press, 1987); Leon Litwack, *North of Slavery: The Negro in the Free States* (Chicago: University of Chicago Press, 1961); John Wood Sweet, *Bodies Politic: Negotiating Race in the American North, 1730–1830* (Baltimore: Johns Hopkins University Press, 2003), 312–96; Joanne Pope Melish, *Disowning Slavery: Gradual Emancipation and "Race" in New England, 1780–1860* (Ithaca: Cornell University Press, 1998).
18. *CA*, October 13, 1838.
19. "Speech of the Reverend Theodore S. Wright, at the Anniversary of the New York State Antislavery Society," *New York Evangelist*, November 4, 1837, in *BAPC*, 2:263.
20. Ibid.

21. Joseph Willson, *The Elite of Our People: Joseph Willson's Sketches of Black Upper-Class Life in Antebellum Philadelphia*, ed. Julie Winch (University Park: Pennsylvania State University Press, 2000), 112.

22. Hosea Easton, *Treatise on the Intellectual Character and Civil and Political Condition of the Colored People of the U. States; and the Prejudice Exercised towards Them; with a Sermon on the Duty of the Church to Them* (Boston: Knapp, 1837), 44, 40.

23. Ibid., 44, 45.

24. For information on the Jennings incident, see Shirley Yee, *Black Women Abolitionists: A Study in Activism, 1828–1860* (Knoxville: University of Tennessee Press, 1992) 134.

25. McHenry, *Forgotten Readers*, 86.

26. *FJ*, March 16, 1827.

27. "The Object of the NORTH STAR," *NS*, December 3, 1847.

28. "The Provincial Freeman," *WAA*, February 25, 1860.

29. Ibid., October 1, 1859.

30. "To Young Men," and "Bringing Slaves to the United States," *CA*, July 7, 1838.

31. "Who Does Not Know Tabitha Wilson," and "Slavery in the West Indies," *FJ*, May 11, 1827.

32. "Letters to Country Girls," *NS*, May 4, 1849. Feminist and abolitionist Jane Grey Swisshelm wrote an advice column for farmers' young wives and daughters that was published in the *Pittsburgh Saturday Visitor* in the 1840s and 1850s. Her column was meant to be an alternative to the popular domestic advice books written by Catharine Beecher and Lydia Maria Child. Both Beecher's *A Treatise on Domestic Economy, for the Use of Young Ladies at Home, at School*, and Child's *The American Frugal Housewife, Dedicated to Those Who Are Not Ashamed of Economy*, dispensed advice for young women living in towns and cities. Swisshelm turned her attention to rural women for whom managing the household included housework and occasional field labor. According to her biographer, Swisshelm's "advice was intended to encourage her middle-class rural female readers to construct their gendered identities within a social context that called for respectability but discouraged the pursuit of gentility" (Sylvia D. Hoffert, *Jane Grey Swisshelm: An Unconventional Life, 1815–1884* [Chapel Hill: University of North Carolina Press, 2004], 164–66).

33. Howard Holman Bell, *A Survey of the Negro Convention Movement, 1830–1861* (New York: Arno, 1969).

34. *The Constitution of the American Society of Free Persons of Colour, for Improving Their Condition in the United States; for Purchasing Lands; and for the Establishment of a Settlement in Upper Canada, Also the Proceedings of the Convention, with Their Address to the Free Persons of Colour in the United States* (Philadelphia: Allen, 1831), 5, in *NNC*.

35. Nathaniel Paul, "An Address, Delivered on the Celebration of the Abolition of

Slavery, in the State of New-York, July 5, 1827," 18–20, in *Negro Protest Pamphlets*, ed. Dorothy Porter (New York: Arno, 1969).

36. Theodore S. Wright, "The Slave Has a Friend in Heaven, Though He May Have None Here," in *Lift Every Voice: African American Oratory, 1787–1900*, ed. Philip S. Foner and Robert James Branham (Tuscaloosa: University of Alabama Press, 1998), 163–65.

37. "Responsibility of Colored People in the Free States," *CA*, March 4, 1837.

38. *WAA*, January 7, 1860.

39. "Elevation," *NS*, May 4, 1849.

40. Charlotte Forten Grimké, *The Journals of Charlotte Forten Grimké*, ed. Brenda Stevenson (New York: Oxford University Press, 1988), May 30, 1854, 63, July 30, 1857, 241.

41. *Liberator*, September 1, 1832, in *BAPC*, 1:220.

42. These images were ubiquitous in the early republic. See Melish, *Disowning Slavery*, 171–83; Sweet, *Bodies Politic*, 380–85; Rael, *Black Identity and Black Protest*, 161–65.

43. See Melish, *Disowning Slavery*, 171–83; Rael, *Black Identity and Black Protest*, 161–65; Shane White and Graham White, *Stylin': African American Expressive Culture from Its Beginnings to the Zoot Suit* (Ithaca: Cornell University Press, 1998), 114–16; Gary B. Nash, *Forging Freedom: The Formation of Philadelphia's Black Community, 1720–1840* (Cambridge: Harvard University Press, 1988), 254–59; Erica Armstrong Dunbar, *A Fragile Freedom: African American Women and Emancipation in the Antebellum City* (New Haven: Yale University Press, 2008), 132–33.

44. Willson, *Elite of Our People*, 130.

45. Emma Jones Lapsansky, "Since They Got Those Separate Churches: Afro-Americans and Racism in Jacksonian Philadelphia," *American Quarterly* 32 (Spring 1980): 56.

46. Hilary J. Moss, "Education's Inequity: Opposition to Black Higher Education in Antebellum Connecticut," *History of Education Quarterly* 46 (Spring 2006): 16–35.

47. Wilson Jeremiah Moses, *The Golden Age of Black Nationalism, 1850–1925* (New York: Oxford University Press, 1978), 63–64.

48. James Brewer Stewart, "The New Haven Negro College and the Meanings of Race in New England, 1776–1870," *New England Quarterly* 76 (September 2003): 345–46.

49. *First Annual Report of the American Anti-Slavery Society*, May 6, 1834, in *BAPC*, 6:814.

50. Douglass continued, "We have been often dragged or driven from the tables of hotels where colored men were officiating acceptably as waiters; and from steamboat cabins where twenty or thirty colored men in light jackets and white aprons were frisking about as servants among the whites in every direction. On the very day we were brutally assaulted in New York for riding down Broadway in company with ladies, we saw several white ladies riding with *black servants*. These servants were well-dressed, proud looking men, evidently living on the fat of the land—yet they were servants. They rode

not for their own, but for the pleasure and convenience of white persons. They were not in those carriages as friends or equals" (*NS*, June 13, 1850).

51. Ibid.

52. *Impartial Citizen*, April 11, 1849, in *BAPC*, 5:1057.

53. Quoted in Dorothy Sterling, ed., *We Are Your Sisters: Black Women in the Nineteenth Century* (New York: Norton, 1984), 131.

54. James Forten to Nathaniel P. Rogers, March 29, 1839, in *BAPC*, 3:46–47; Willson, *Elite of Our People*, 99.

55. "Irwin's Letter," *NS*, February 2, 1849.

56. Rael, *Black Identity and Black Protest*, 130–35.

57. Willson, *Elite of Our People*, 112.

58. Martin Delany, "Domestic Economy," *NS*, March 23, 1849.

59. The literature addressing antebellum reform movements in the North and their relationship to the market revolution and evangelical Protestantism is vast. For particularly useful studies, see Ryan, *Cradle of the Middle Class*; Charles Sellers, *The Market Revolution: Jacksonian America, 1815–1846* (New York: Oxford University Press, 1991); Ronald G. Walters, *American Reformers, 1815–1860* (New York: Hill and Wang, 1997); Johnson, *Shopkeeper's Millennium*.

60. For the role of religion in northern black communities, see Horton and Horton, *In Search of Liberty*, chapter 6; Eddie S. Glaude Jr., *Exodus!: Religion, Race, and Nation in Early Nineteenth-Century Black America* (Chicago: University of Chicago Press, 2000).

61. Austin Steward, *Twenty-Two Years a Slave and Forty Years a Freeman: Embracing a Correspondence of Several Years, while President of Wilberforce Colony* (1857; Syracuse: Syracuse University Press, 2002), 72.

62. John Mercer Langston, *From the Virginia Plantation to the National Capitol; or, The First and Only Negro Representative in Congress from the Old Dominion* (1894; New York: Kraus, 1969), 115.

63. After powerful conversion experiences in 1827 and in 1843, Truth was at times an itinerant preacher and a member of a variety of Christian utopian communities, including the Kingdom of Matthias, the Millerites, and the Northampton Association of Education and Industry (Nell Irvin Painter, *Sojourner Truth: A Life, a Symbol* [New York: Norton, 1996], 26–95).

64. David Blight, *Frederick Douglass' Civil War: Keeping Faith in Jubilee* (Baton Rouge: Louisiana State University Press, 1989), 87.

65. For discussion of this particular religious theme and its role in the northern free black community before the Civil War, see Albert J. Raboteau, *A Fire in the Bones: Reflections on African-American Religious History* (Boston: Beacon, 1995), 41–43. See also Glaude, *Exodus!*; Moses, *Golden Age of Black Nationalism*, 22–23; Mia Bay, *The White Image in the Black Mind: African-American Ideas about White People* (New York: Oxford University Press, 2000), 47–49.

66. *NS*, January 19, 1849.
67. *CA*, March 6, 1841.
68. Maria W. Stewart, *Maria W. Stewart, America's First Black Woman Political Writer: Essays and Speeches*, ed. and intro. Marilyn Richardson (Bloomington: Indiana University Press, 1987), 6–20.
69. Hinks, *To Awaken My Afflicted Brethren*, 236, 105–8, 174–75; David Walker, *David Walker's Appeal* (1830; Baltimore: Black Classic, 1993), 50.
70. Meachum, *Address*, 4–5; *Proceedings of the Convention, of the Colored Freemen of Ohio, Held in Cincinnati, January 14, 15, 16, 17, and 19, 1852*, in *BSC*, 276.
71. "Self-Elevation," *Impartial Citizen*, March 14, 1849, in *BAPC*, 5:1003.
72. "Elevation," *NS*, May 4, 1849.

CHAPTER TWO. **Slave Narratives and the Black Self-Made Man**

1. Dickson Bruce Jr., *The Origins of African American Literature, 1680–1865* (Charlottesville: University Press of Virginia, 2001), 220–27; Ann Fabian, *The Unvarnished Truth: Personal Narratives in Nineteenth-Century America* (Berkeley: University of California Press, 2000), 80; Richard S. Newman, *The Transformation of American Abolition: Fighting Slavery in the Early Republic* (Chapel Hill: University of North Carolina Press, 2002), 26.
2. See Elizabeth McHenry, *Forgotten Readers: Recovering the Lost History of African American Literary Societies* (Durham: Duke University Press, 2002), chapters 1 and 2.
3. *Liberator*, July 21, 1832, in *BAPC*, 1:204–5.
4. Charlotte Forten Grimké, *The Journals of Charlotte Forten Grimké*, ed. Brenda Stevenson (New York: Oxford University Press, 1988), July 26, 1857, 240.
5. Samuel Ringgold Ward, *Autobiography of a Fugitive Negro: His Anti-Slavery Labours in the United States, Canada, and England* (1855; New York: Arno, 1968), 42–43.
6. Robert S. Levine argues that slave narratives share much of Benjamin Franklin's autobiography's emphasis on self-improvement, reliance on the Protestant work ethic, and elevation from one's humble beginnings. Levine also finds that "in Douglass's and many other slave narratives of the antebellum period, the Franklinian model is ultimately put to the service of linking the individual uplift of the black persona to the revolutionary cause of freedom" ("The Slave Narrative and the Revolutionary Tradition of American Autobiography," in *The Cambridge Companion to the African American Slave Narrative*, ed. Audrey Fisch [New York: Cambridge University Press, 2007], 106).
7. Ward, *Autobiography of a Fugitive Negro*, 43.
8. Waldo E. Martin Jr. has placed the ideal of the self-made man at the center of Douglass's discourse, particularly with respect to his speeches during and after Reconstruction (*The Mind of Frederick Douglass* [Chapel Hill: University of North Carolina Press, 1984] 253–64).

9. E. Anthony Rotundo, *American Manhood: Transformations in Masculinity from the Revolution to the Modern Era* (New York: Basic Books, 1993), 18–25; Michael Kimmel, *Manhood in America: A Cultural History*, 2nd ed. (New York: Oxford University Press, 2006), 18–21; Gail Bederman, *Manliness and Civilization: A Cultural History of Gender and Race in the United States, 1880–1917* (Chicago: University of Chicago Press, 1995), 10–13.

10. The literature on the ways republicanism continued to inform discourses in the early nineteenth century is vast. See, for example, Jan Lewis, "The Republican Wife: Virtue and Seduction in the Early Republic," *William and Mary Quarterly*, 3rd ser., 44 (October 1987): 689–721; Daniel J. McInerney, *The Fortunate Heirs of Freedom: Abolition and Republican Thought* (Lincoln: University of Nebraska Press, 1994); Sean Wilentz, *Chants Democratic: New York City and the Rise of the American Working Class, 1788–1850* (New York: Oxford University Press, 1984); Steven J. Ross, "The Transformation of Republican Ideology," *Journal of the Early Republic* 10 (Autumn 1990): 323–30; Eric Foner, *Free Soil, Free Labor, Free Men: The Ideology of the Republican Party before the Civil War*, 2nd ed. (New York: Oxford University Press, 1995), 14–15, 27. For a critique of these arguments, see Daniel T. Rodgers, "Republicanism: The Career of a Concept," *Journal of American History* 79 (June 1992): 11–38.

11. David R. Roediger, *The Wages of Whiteness: Race and the Making of the American Working Class*, rev. ed. (New York: Verso, 1999), 47–54; Joyce Appleby, *Inheriting the Revolution: The First Generation of Americans* (Cambridge: Harvard University Press, 2000), 142.

12. See George M. Fredrickson, *The Black Image in the White Mind: The Debate on Afro-American Character and Destiny, 1817–1914* (Hanover, N.H.: Wesleyan University Press, 1987), esp. chapters 1–3; Mia Bay, *The White Image in the Black Mind: African American Ideas about White People, 1830–1925* (New York: Oxford University Press, 2000), 38–50; Bruce Dorsey, *Reforming Men and Women: Gender in the Antebellum City* (Ithaca: Cornell University Press, 2002), 8–9; Paul Gilmore, *The Genuine Article: Race, Mass Culture, and American Literary Manhood* (Durham: Duke University Press, 2001), 56–59; Kristin Hoganson, "Garrisonian Abolitionists and the Rhetoric of Gender, 1850–1860," *American Quarterly* 45 (December 1993): 579; Leslie M. Harris, *In the Shadow of Slavery: African Americans in New York City, 1626–1863* (Chicago: University of Chicago Press, 2003), 98–99; Joanne Pope Melish, *Disowning Slavery: Gradual Emancipation and "Race" in New England, 1780–1860* (Ithaca: Cornell University Press, 1998), 95–118.

13. Shane White, *Stories of Freedom in Black New York* (Cambridge: Harvard University Press, 2002), 51–126.

14. *Report of the Proceedings of the Colored National Convention*, Cleveland, 1848, 19, in *NNC*.

15. Austin Steward, *Twenty-Two Years a Slave and Forty Years a Freeman: Embracing*

a Correspondence of Several Years, while President of Wilberforce Colony (1857; Syracuse: Syracuse University Press, 2002), 80.

16. Martin Delany, *The Condition, Elevation, Emigration, and Destiny of the Colored People of the United States* (1852; Baltimore: Black Classic Press, 1993), 43.

17. *Report of the Proceedings of the Colored National Convention*, Cleveland, 1848, 5, 13, 19, in *NNC*. See also Harris, *In the Shadow of Slavery*, 232.

18. *Minutes and Proceedings of the First Annual Convention*, Philadelphia, 1831, 10, in *NNC*.

19. See Rotundo, *American Manhood*, 3–4; Patrick Rael, *Black Identity and Black Protest in the Antebellum North* (Chapel Hill: University of North Carolina Press, 2002), 131–32.

20. *CA*, April 15, 1837.

21. Leon Litwack, *North of Slavery: The Negro in the Free States* (Chicago: University of Chicago Press, 1961), 175.

22. John Berry Meachum, *Address to All the Colored Citizens of the United States* (Philadelphia: King and Baird, 1846), in *BAPC*, 5:45.

23. *CA*, June 16, 1838.

24. Ibid., February 9, 1839.

25. Steward, *Twenty-Two Years a Slave*, 80.

26. Harris, *In the Shadow of Slavery*, 178.

27. Although African Americans remained intrigued by other emigration efforts, most believed that rather than guaranteeing free black independence, emigration under the auspices of the white-controlled American Colonization Society would reduce all African Americans to a completely dependent status and ensure that slaveholders maintained complete control of the government. Those who did leave, however, continued to explain their decision in terms of their quest for ideal black manhood. See Bruce Dorsey, "A Gendered History of African Colonization in the Antebellum United States," *Journal of Social History* 34 (Fall 2000): 77–103.

28. For discussions of black ambivalence about emigration and hostility to the American Colonization Society, see Gary B. Nash, *Forging Freedom: The Formation of Philadelphia's Black Community, 1720–1840* (Cambridge: Harvard University Press, 1988), 237–41; Julie Winch, *Philadelphia's Black Elite: Activism, Accommodation, and the Struggle for Autonomy, 1787–1848* (Philadelphia: Temple University Press), 37–41; James Oliver Horton and Lois E. Horton, *In Search of Liberty: Culture, Community, and Protest among Northern Free Blacks, 1700–1860* (New York: Oxford University Press, 1997), 187–202.

29. Dorsey, "Gendered History of African Colonization," 91.

30. *Liberator*, January 28, 1832.

31. Delany, *Condition*, 187.

32. *Report of the Proceedings of the Colored National Convention*, Cleveland, 1848, 19, in *NNC*.

33. Harris notes a similar discrepancy during the Black National Convention of 1833, where the delegates (all of whom were male) made no reference to the education of women when discussing education for the race (*In the Shadow of Slavery*, 178).

34. *CA*, November 23, 1839.

35. Dorsey, *Reforming Men and Women*, 102.

36. Barbara Welter, "The Cult of True Womanhood, 1820–1860," *American Quarterly* 18 (Summer 1966): 151–74.

37. *FJ*, November 9, 1827.

38. "To Young Men," *CA*, July 7, 1838.

39. "Means of Elevation," *CA*, June 22, 1839.

40. Maria Stewart, "An Address Delivered at the Boston Masonic Hall," February 27, 1833, in *Maria Stewart, America's First Black Woman Political Writer: Essays and Speeches*, ed. Marilyn Richardson (Bloomington: Indiana University Press, 1987), 60.

41. *CA*, February 16, 1839.

42. Dorsey, *Reforming Men and Women*, 19. Wilentz explores the masculine culture of early-nineteenth-century working-class life in *Chants Democratic*.

43. *CA*, June 16, 1838.

44. "Colored Young Women of New York," *WAA*, November 26, 1859.

45. Lawrence Levine, "William Shakespeare and the American People: A Study in Cultural Transformation," in *The Unpredictable Past: Explorations in American Cultural History* (New York: Oxford University Press, 1993), 147–52.

46. Patricia Cline Cohen, *The Murder of Helen Jewett: The Life and Death of a Prostitute in Nineteenth-Century New York* (New York: Knopf, 1998), 68–69.

47. White, *Stories of Freedom*, 80–82.

48. *CA*, April 25, 1840.

49. "To Young Men," *Weekly Advocate*, February 11, 1837.

50. *CA*, June 22, 1839.

51. *Mirror of Liberty*, July 1838, in *BAPC*, 2:514; Rev. Charles Gardner ("man of color, and pastor of a Presbyterian church in Philadelphia"), reprinted in the *Fourth Annual Report of the American Anti-Slavery Society*, 14–15, in *BAPC*, 2:49–51.

52. Stewart, "Address," 60.

53. *CA*, June 22, 1839.

54. Dorsey, *Reforming Men and Women*, 8–9; Rotundo, *American Manhood*, 179.

55. Rotundo, *American Manhood*, 179.

56. Howard H. Bell, "The American Moral Reform Society, 1836–1841," *Journal of Negro Education*, 27 (Winter 1958): 34–40.

57. "Moral Work for Colored Men I," *CA*, December 2, 1837.

58. *Weekly Advocate*, February 18, 1837.

59. For more examples of the differences as well as similarities between African American men's and women's literary societies, see McHenry, *Forgotten Readers*, 50–79. For examples in later decades, see Emma Jones Lapsansky, "'Discipline to the Mind': Philadelphia's Banneker Institute, 1854–1872," in *A Question of Manhood: A Reader in U.S. Black Men's History and Masculinity*, ed. Darlene Clark Hine and Earnestine Jenkins (Bloomington: Indiana University Press, 1999), 1:399–414.

60. In *Sketches of the Higher Classes of Colored Society*, published in 1841, Joseph Willson notes that in Philadelphia, men's societies including the Philadelphia Library Company of Colored Persons, the Rush Library Company and Debating Society, and the Demosthenian Institute sponsored debates and other public activities. The women's literary societies he highlights did not (*The Elite of Our People: Joseph Willson's Sketches of Black Upper-Class Life in Antebellum Philadelphia*, ed. Julie Winch [University Park: Pennsylvania State University Press, 2000], 111–17).

61. Rotundo, *American Manhood*, 68.

62. *Liberator*, February 7, 1835.

63. Willson, *Elite of Our People*, 111–17.

64. *CA*, February 2, 1839.

65. Joel Schor, *Henry Highland Garnet: A Voice of Black Radicalism in the Nineteenth Century* (Westport, Conn.: Greenwood, 1977), 11; *Liberator*, April 19, 1834.

66. Frederick Cooper also noted, "The success of self-improvement may have itself contributed to the increased emphasis on political agitation" because these small organizations "provided opportunities for potential leaders to develop skills of oratory and organization" ("Elevating the Race: The Social Thought of Black Leaders, 1827–50," *American Quarterly* 24 [December 1972]: 619).

67. "It was not until the 1830's that an articulate, self-confident generation of leaders emerged. A professional and business group of some relative affluence came into existence in this decade. There were now Negro teachers, doctors, editors, ministers, and entrepreneurs who, by participation in newly-organized anti-slavery societies, developed sophistication as a group and experience and ability in a protest movement" (Rhoda Golden Freeman, *The Free Negro in New York City in the Era before the Civil War* [New York: Garland, 1994], 94).

68. *Convention of the Colored Inhabitants of the State of New York*, Albany, August 18–20, 1840, in *BSC*, 15. Rael has found that delegates to the antebellum state and national black conventions reflected the elite of the northern black community, included a higher percentage of property owners, and had greater literacy rates than the general northern black population (*Black Identity and Black Protest*, 38–44).

69. Here I draw on Fabian's analysis of the instructive role of the personal narrative (*Unvarnished Truth*). William L. Andrews has argued that certain male-authored slave

narratives emphasized the importance of acquisition of middle-class values (*To Tell a Free Story: The First Century of Afro-American Autobiography, 1760–1865* [Urbana: University of Illinois Press, 1988], 111–14).

70. "Books," *WAA*, February 25, 1860.

71. "Jermain W. Loguen's Book," *WAA*, December 3, 1859.

72. Frederick Douglass, *My Bondage and My Freedom* (1855; New York: Penguin, 2003), 24.

73. David Leverenz, *Manhood and the American Renaissance* (Ithaca: Cornell University Press, 1990), 128–29. See also Martin, *Mind of Frederick Douglass*, 253–78.

74. Samuel Ringgold Ward was born in Maryland in 1817, the son of enslaved parents. He and his family escaped to New Jersey in 1820 but were forced to flee farther north as a consequence of the frequent kidnappings in the region. They arrived in New York City on August 3, 1826, "and lodged the first night with relations, the parents of the Rev. H. H. Garnett, now of Westmoreland, Jamaica" (Ward, *Autobiography of a Fugitive Negro*, 26). In May 1839, "I was licensed to preach the gospel by the New York Congregational Association, assembled at Poughkeepsie. In November of that same year, I became the travelling agent of first the American and afterwards the New York Anti-slavery Society; in April, 1841, I accepted the unanimous invitation of the Congregational church of South Butler, Wayne, co., N.Y., to be their pastor; and in September of that year I was publicly ordained and inducted as minister of that Church" (31). Ward ultimately studied classics and theology and became a Congregational minister serving white congregations in Upstate New York.

75. James W. C. Pennington (1807–70) was born James Pembroke, enslaved in Maryland. He escaped to the North in 1827 and changed his name, settling in Brooklyn in 1829. In 1835, he moved to Connecticut. He was rejected by Yale Divinity School on the grounds of race but was allowed to attend lectures informally and was ordained in 1838. In 1840, he became the minister of the Talcott Street Congregational Church in Hartford. He moved to New York City in 1848 and became pastor of the First Colored Presbyterian Church, which would later become Shiloh. He traveled extensively through Europe as a delegate to the 1843 Peace Conference in London and the 1849 Peace Congress in Paris. His friends purchased his freedom in 1851 (Willson, *Elite of Our People*, 143–45). Pennington published *The Fugitive Blacksmith* in 1849. When he published his *Textbook* (1841), he "formalized an African-American intellectual tradition" (Elizabeth Rauh Bethel, *The Roots of African-American Identity: Memory and History in Antebellum Free Communities* [New York: St. Martin's, 1997], 167–68).

76. William Wells Brown was born on a plantation near Lexington, Kentucky, in 1814. He held a series of jobs in Kentucky and Missouri before he turned twenty, working as a servant, a field hand, and an assistant to several professionals and as a handyman for a slave trader. That work allowed him to see many aspects of slavery from St. Louis to New Orleans. He escaped on New Year's Day 1834. He worked on a steamboat

on Lake Erie and acted as a conductor for the Underground Railroad in Buffalo. In 1843, he became a lecturer for the Western New York Anti-Slavery Society. In 1847, he moved to Boston, where he wrote the first version of his autobiography. He would revise and expand it several times before 1850 (William Wells Brown, *From Fugitive Slave to Free Man: The Autobiographies of William Wells Brown*, ed. William Andrews [Columbia: University of Missouri Press, 1993], 3). See also the introduction to William Wells Brown, *The Black Man: His Antecedents, His Genius, and His Achievements* (1863; New York: Arno, 1969).

77. Andrews, *To Tell a Free Story*, 107.
78. Delany, *Condition*, 128, 130, 112.
79. *Frederick Douglass' Paper*, October 2, 1851, in *BAPC*, 7:124.
80. Ward, *Autobiography of a Fugitive Negro*, 26, 28, 30.
81. Henry Bibb, *Narrative of the Life and Adventures of Henry Bibb, an American Slave, Written by Himself* (1849; Madison: University of Wisconsin Press, 2001), 174.
82. See Brown, *Black Man*, 276–78.
83. James W. C. Pennington, *The Fugitive Blacksmith; or, Events in the History of James W. C. Pennington, Pastor of a Presbyterian Church, New York, Formerly a Slave in the State of Maryland, United States*, 3rd ed. (1850; Westport, Conn.: Negro Universities Press, 1971), 51, 55.
84. *Emancipator*, July 20, 1833, in *BAPC*, 1:201.
85. Frederick Douglass, *Narrative of the Life of Frederick Douglass, an American Slave, Written by Himself* (1845; New York: Signet, 1997), 50–51, 55–56.
86. Pennington, *Fugitive Blacksmith*, 55.
87. Andrews, *To Tell a Free Story*, 99.
88. Brown continued, "There are few characters more worthy of the student's study than that of Henry Bibb" (*Black Man*, 87).
89. "Books," *WAA*, February 25, 1860.
90. Douglass, *My Bondage and My Freedom*, 24–25.
91. Martin, *Mind of Frederick Douglass*, 256.
92. Fabian, *Unvarnished Truth*, 85.
93. Solomon Northup, *Twelve Years a Slave*, ed. Sue Eakin and Joseph Logsdon (1853; Baton Rouge: Louisiana State University Press, 1968), 19–20.
94. Ibid., 206–15.
95. *Liberator*, August 26, 1853, quoted in ibid., ix.

CHAPTER THREE. **Antislavery Discourse and the African American Family**

1. Quoted in Jean Fagan Yellin, *Harriet Jacobs: A Life* (New York: Basic Books, 2004), 124.
2. Harriet Jacobs, *Incidents in the Life of a Slave Girl, Written by Herself* (1861; Cambridge: Harvard University Press, 1987), 2.

3. See Ronald Walters, *The Antislavery Appeal: American Abolitionism after 1830* (1978; New York: Norton, 1984), 91–110; Charles J. Heglar, *Rethinking the Slave Narrative: Slave Marriage and the Narratives of Henry Bibb and William and Ellen Craft* (Westport, Conn.: Greenwood, 2001).

4. Walters, *Antislavery Appeal*, 95.

5. *NS*, June 8, 1848.

6. Stanley Harrold, *The Rise of Aggressive Abolitionism: Addresses to the Slaves* (Lexington: University Press of Kentucky, 2004), 70.

7. In 1848, Garnet published a new edition of *David Walker's Appeal* and included the "Address to the Slaves of the United States of America." See Henry Highland Garnet, *Walker's Appeal, with a Brief Sketch of His Life* (New York: Tobitt, 1848), 90–96, in *BAPC*, 5:545–48.

8. Garnet, "Address to the Slaves of the United States of America," in *BAPC*, 5:548. Despite its effect when read on the convention floor, the delegates ultimately declined to adopt Garnet's "Address" by a nineteen to eighteen vote, with several abstentions. Led by Frederick Douglass, who at this point in his career continued to oppose the idea of slave insurrection and instead preferred to combat slavery through the Garrisonian tactic of moral suasion, well-known figures such as William Wells Brown and Charles Lenox Remond voted to reject Garnet's "Address" (*Minutes of the National Convention of Colored Citizens, Held at Buffalo, 1843*, 13, 18, 19, in *NNC*).

9. *Minutes of the National Convention of Colored Citizens, Held at Buffalo, 1843*, 13, in *NNC*.

10. Chris Dixon, *Perfecting the Family: Antislavery Marriages in Nineteenth Century America* (Amherst: University of Massachusetts Press, 1997), 32.

11. Frederick Douglass, *Narrative of the Life of Frederick Douglass, an American Slave, Written by Himself* (1845; New York: Signet, 1997), 20.

12. James W. C. Pennington, *The Fugitive Blacksmith; or, Events in the History of James W. C. Pennington, Pastor of a Presbyterian Church, New York, Formerly a Slave in the State of Maryland, United States* (1849; Westport, Conn: Negro Universities Press, 1971), 2.

13. Steven Mintz, *Huck's Raft: A History of American Childhood* (Cambridge: Harvard University Press, 2004), 75–83.

14. Frederick Douglass, *My Bondage and My Freedom* (1855; New York: Penguin, 2003), 34–35.

15. Jacobs, *Incidents*, 143–47.

16. Henry Bibb, *Narrative of the Life and Adventures of Henry Bibb, an American Slave, Written by Himself* (1849; Madison: University of Wisconsin Press, 2001), 43.

17. Ibid., 458–59.

18. Sojourner Truth, *Narrative of Sojourner Truth*, ed. Margaret Washington (New York: Vintage, 1993), 25, 4, 15.

19. Henry Highland Garnet, "Address to the Slaves of the United States of America," in *BAP*, 3:405.

20. William Wells Brown, *Narrative of William W. Brown, a Fugitive Slave* (1847), in *Slave Narratives*, ed. William L. Andrews and Henry Louis Gates Jr. (New York: Penguin, 2001), 415.

21. Bibb, *Narrative*, 44.

22. James W. C. Pennington, "Letter" (1844), in *BAPC*, 4:720–21.

23. Mark S. Weiner, *Black Trials: Citizenship from the Beginnings of Slavery to the End of Caste* (New York: Knopf, 2004), 141–42.

24. "Kidnapping in Pennsylvania," *Douglass's Monthly*, July 1859, http://www.accessible.com/accessible/print?AADocList=1&AADocStyle=STYLED&AAStyleFile=&AABeanName=toc1&AANextPage=/printFullDocFromXML.jsp&AACheck=2.100.1.0.16 (accessed September 5, 2010).

25. Samuel Ringgold Ward, *Autobiography of a Fugitive Negro: His Anti-Slavery Labours in the United States, Canada, and England* (1855; New York: Arno, 1968), 13.

26. Solomon Northup, *Twelve Years a Slave*, ed. Sue Eakin and Joseph Logsdon (1853; Baton Rouge: Louisiana State University Press, 1968), 252.

27. *Liberator*, March 26, 1841; Carter G. Woodson, *The Mind of the Negro as Reflected in Letters Written during the Crisis, 1800–1860* (1926; Eastford, Conn.: Martino Fine Books, 2010), 262.

28. Jacobs, *Incidents*, 170.

29. Charles Ball, *Slavery in the United States: A Narrative of the Life and Adventures of Charles Ball, a Black Man* (1837; New York: Negro Universities Press, 1969), 515–17.

30. As Kristin Hoganson writes, "Because being fully human was so closely tied to a particular gender identity in the Victorian period, Garrisonians responded to their opponents' arguments against the humanity of black people with gender-specific arguments" that "slave men were inherently masculine and slave women were inherently feminine to refute ideas of their inferiority or immaturity." In this view, bondage "corrupted slaves' essential natures" ("Garrisonian Abolitionists and the Rhetoric of Gender, 1850–1860," *American Quarterly* 45 [December 1993]: 575).

31. Brown, *Narrative of William W. Brown*, 412.

32. William Craft and Ellen Craft, *Running a Thousand Miles for Freedom* (1860; Athens: University of Georgia Press, 1999), 19.

33. Pennington, *Fugitive Blacksmith*, v, vi.

34. Brown, *Narrative of William W. Brown*, 413.

35. Bibb, *Narrative*, 38.

36. Garnet, "Address," in *BAPC*, 5:547.

37. George M. Fredrickson notes that white abolitionists "were Christian moralists first and sociologists of slavery second," and "a sin apparently remained a sin whether it was forced on the individual or not" (*The Black Image in the White Mind: The Debate on*

Afro-American Character and Destiny, 1817–1914 [Hanover, N.H.: Wesleyan University Press, 1987], 35).

38. Jacobs, *Incidents*, 160–61.

39. Yellin suggests as much in her introduction to Jacobs, *Incidents*: "Does [Jacobs] suggest, upon mature reflection, that women like herself should be judged (like men) on complex moral grounds—rather than (like women) on the single issue of their conformity to the sexual behavior mandated by the white patriarchy?" (xxxi). Hazel V. Carby also analyzes this tendency in Jacobs's text in *Reconstructing Womanhood: The Emergence of the Afro-American Woman Novelist* (New York: Oxford University Press, 1987), 58–61.

40. Elizabeth Keckley, *Behind the Scenes; or, Thirty Years a Slave, and Four Years in the White House* (1868; New York: Oxford University Press, 1988), 38–39.

41. Jacobs, *Incidents*, 54, 55–56, 86.

42. Keckley, *Behind the Scenes*, 38–39.

43. Catherine Clinton, "'With a Whip in His Hand': Rape, Memory, and African American Women," in *History and Memory in African American Culture*, ed. Geneviève Fabre and Robert O'Meally (New York: Oxford University Press, 1994), 212–13.

44. Hosea Easton, *Treatise on the Intellectual Character and Civil And Political Condition of the Colored People of the U. States; and the Prejudice Exercised towards Them; with a Sermon on the Duty of the Church to Them* (Boston: Knapp, 1837), 24, 26.

45. Hoganson, "Garrisonian Abolitionists," 567.

46. Paul Gilmore, *The Genuine Article: Race, Mass Culture, and American Literary Manhood* (Durham: Duke University Press, 2001), 55, 56; Walters, *Antislavery Appeal*, 76–77.

47. Nancy Isenberg, *Sex and Citizenship in Antebellum America* (Chapel Hill: University of North Carolina Press, 1998), 121.

48. Linda K. Kerber, "A Constitutional Right to Be Treated Like American Ladies: Women and the Obligations of Citizenship," in *U.S. History as Women's History: New Feminist Essays*, ed. Linda K. Kerber, Alice Kessler-Harris, and Kathryn Kish Sklar (Chapel Hill: University of North Carolina Press, 1995), 20–22.

49. Clinton, "With a Whip in His Hand," 206–7.

50. Carby, *Reconstructing Womanhood*, 35.

51. *CA*, April 1, 1837.

52. James McCune Smith to the *New York Tribune*, in *National Anti-Slavery Standard*, February 1, 1844, in *BAPC*, 4:750–51.

53. Pennington, *Fugitive Blacksmith*, xii.

54. Hoganson, "Garrisonian Abolitionists," 564.

55. See Gilmore, *Genuine Article*; Walters, *Antislavery Appeal*, 56.

56. Craft and Craft, *Running a Thousand Miles for Freedom*, 11, 7.

57. Bibb, *Narrative*, 42.

58. William L. Andrews, *To Tell a Free Story: The First Century of Afro-American Autobiography, 1760–1865* (Urbana: University of Illinois Press, 1988), 158.

59. Jacobs, *Incidents*, 192.

60. Aliyyah I. Abdur-Rahman, "'The Strangest Freaks of Despotism': Queer Sexuality in African American Slave Narratives," *African American Review* 40 (Summer 2006): 223–37.

61. Douglass, *My Bondage and My Freedom*, 180.

62. Martin Delany, *The Condition, Elevation, Emigration, and Destiny of the Colored People of the United States* (1852; Baltimore: Black Classic, 1993), 47–48.

63. Martin Delany, "Domestic Economy," *NS*, March 23, 1849.

64. Ward, *Autobiography of a Fugitive Negro*, 169–70.

65. Harrold, *Rise of Aggressive Abolitionism*, 15.

66. Yellin, *Harriet Jacobs*, 147.

67. *Minutes of the National Convention of Colored Citizens Held at Buffalo, 1843*, 13, in *NNC*.

CHAPTER FOUR. **Domestic Literature and the Antislavery Household**

1. Solomon Northup, *Twelve Years a Slave*, ed. Sue Eakin and Joseph Logsdon (1853; Baton Rouge: Louisiana State University Press, 1968), 9, 251.

2. Chris Dixon, *Perfecting the Family: Antislavery Marriages in Nineteenth-Century America* (Amherst: University of Massachusetts Press, 1997), 7.

3. Mary Ryan, *Empire of the Mother: American Writing about Domesticity, 1830–1860* (New York: Routledge, 1985), 130.

4. *CA*, November 13, 1841.

5. For selected examples of this domestic discourse, see Frances Smith Foster, ed., *Love and Marriage in Early African America* (Hanover, N.H.: Northeastern University Press, 2008).

6. "Female Tenderness," *FJ*, July 27, 1827.

7. For recent analysis of the deeply political significance of marriage, see Peggy Pascoe, *What Comes Naturally: Miscegenation Law and the Making of Race in America* (New York: Oxford University Press, 2010).

8. "A Bachelor's Thermometer" begins with the man at ages sixteen and seventeen, with "incipient palpitations towards the young ladies" and "blushing and confusion in conversing with them." By age twenty, he has become "very conscious of his own charms and manliness." By twenty-three, he has become so pleased with himself that he "thinks no woman good enough for him." He is rude and superior toward the woman he really loves, and she marries another. In his early thirties, he is "morose and out of humour in

all conversations on matrimony" but "still retains a high opinion of his attractions as a husband." At thirty-five, he makes a fool of himself when he "falls deeply and violently in love with one of seventeen" who rejects him the following year. In his early forties, he embarks on a long, modest courtship with a young widow, who ultimately rejects him, "being as cautious" as he. By his fifties, he has developed an attraction to his housekeeper, who nurses him through his many bouts with gout. By age fifty-five, he is completely under her influence and very miserable. And in his final years, he marries her on his deathbed, "has his will made in her favour," and "makes his exit" from the world. See "A Bachelor's Thermometer," *FJ*, November 9, 1827.

9. The "Old Maid's Diary," begins with the girl at age fifteen, "anxious for coming out, and the attention of the men." By age nineteen, she has become "a little more difficult, in consequence of being noticed." At twenty-one, she "refuses a good offer, because he is not a man of fashion." She goes on flirting with many men, and by twenty-four, she "wonders she is not married." By twenty-nine, "she almost despairs of entering the married state." Six years later, she has become quite "jealous of the praises of women." And by forty, she has grown "very meddling and officious." She rails against "the manners of the age" and falls terribly in love with a Methodist parson who does not return her affections. By age forty-eight, she has adopted a "dependent relation" to "attend on the dogs" and "vents all her ill-humour on this unfortunate relation." See "The Old Maid's Diary," *FJ*, November 2, 1827.

10. "Disadvantages of Single Blessedness," *FJ*, February 28, 1827.

11. "Who Does Not Know Tabitha Wilson," *FJ*, May 11, 1827.

12. "Job's Letter," *FJ*, September 5, 1828.

13. *FJ*, June 29, 1827.

14. *CA*, June 30, 1838.

15. Nancy F. Cott, "Giving Character to Our Whole Civil Polity: Marriage and the Public Order in the Late Nineteenth Century," in *U.S. History as Women's History: New Feminist Essays*, edited by Linda K. Kerber, Alice Kessler-Harris, and Kathryn Kish Sklar (Chapel Hill: University of North Carolina Press, 1995), 110–11.

16. Nancy F. Cott, "Marriage and Women's Citizenship in the United States, 1830–1934," *American Historical Review* 103 (December 1998): 1451, 1452. See also Shirley Samuels, "The Family, the State, and the Novel in the Early Republic," *American Quarterly* 38 (1986): 387–88; Nancy Isenberg, *Sex and Citizenship in Antebellum America* (Chapel Hill: University of North Carolina Press, 1998), 11.

17. Henry Bibb, *Narrative of the Life and Adventures of Henry Bibb, an American Slave, Written by Himself* (1849; Madison: University of Wisconsin Press, 2001), 191, 39.

18. Frederick Douglass, *Narrative of the Life of Frederick Douglass, an American Slave, Written by Himself* (1845; New York: Signet, 1997), 111.

19. *FJ*, November 2, 1827, October 5, 1827.

20. *CA*, February 16, 1839.

21. As historian James Oliver Horton writes in his seminal article on the domestic pronouncements featured in the antebellum black press, "Clearly there was the hope, even the expectation, among some black men that with freedom would come the possibility that black people could form their lives to approximate gender conventions of American society at large" ("Freedom's Yoke: Gender Conventions among Free Blacks," in *Free People of Color: Inside the African American Community* [Washington, D.C.: Smithsonian Institution Press, 1993], 102). These conventions included endorsing separate spheres, praising men as public beings, and insisting that women adhere to "traditional notions about womanhood"—in other words, being sure to "keep well-ordered homes, care for their families, and be generous and good-tempered" (Jacqueline Bacon, *Freedom's Journal: The First African-American Newspaper* [Lanham, Md.: Lexington, 2007], 131–32). Scholars agree on the pervasiveness of this rhetoric in the northern black public sphere and on its central role in helping to define the ideal if not the reality of gendered free black domestic duties and family roles. As historian Shirley Yee argues in her landmark study of black female abolitionists, "The most powerful institutions within the free black community—the press, the schools, and the churches—provided the greatest support for a gender ideology during the antebellum period" (*Black Women Abolitionists: A Study in Activism, 1828–1860* [Knoxville: University of Tennessee Press, 1992], 58). Black women's work and activism in the public sphere, however, went far beyond the boundaries of the domestic sphere.

22. "Maxims," *Liberator*, February 7, 1835.

23. Cott, "Giving Character," 110–11.

24. Barbara Welter, "The Cult of True Womanhood, 1820–1860," *American Quarterly* 18 (Summer 1966): 168.

25. Maria Stewart, "Religion and the Pure Principles of Morality, the Sure Foundation on Which We Must Build" (1831), in *Maria Stewart, America's First Black Woman Political Writer: Essays and Speeches*, ed. Marilyn Richardson (Bloomington: Indiana University Press, 1987), 37–38.

26. *WAA*, February 11, 1860 (originally published in the *Ohio Farmer*).

27. "The West—no. VI," *CA*, July 13, 1839.

28. *CA*, November 23, 1839.

29. Ibid., March 18, 1837.

30. Martin Delany, *The Condition, Elevation, Emigration, and Destiny of the Colored People of the United States* (1852; Baltimore: Black Classic, 1993), 196.

31. *CA*, June 16, 1838.

32. Female literary societies were most likely to hold their meetings in the homes of

their members. See Elizabeth McHenry, *Forgotten Readers: Recovering the Lost History of African American Literary Societies* (Durham: Duke University Press, 2002), 37.

33. Douglass, *Narrative*, 110.

34. Samuel Ringgold Ward, *Autobiography of a Fugitive Negro: His Anti-Slavery Labours in the United States, Canada, and England* (1855; New York: Arno, 1968), 28.

35. Harriet Jacobs, *Incidents in the Life of a Slave Girl, Written by Herself* (1861; Cambridge: Harvard University Press, 1987), 160.

36. *NS*, December 1, 1848.

37. For a discussion of the relationship between the rise of the middle class and domesticity in the Northeast, see Mary Ryan, *Cradle of the Middle Class: The Family in Oneida County, New York, 1790–1865* (Cambridge: Cambridge University Press, 1981); Nancy Cott, *The Bonds of Womanhood: "Woman's Sphere" in New England, 1780–1835*, 2nd ed. (New Haven: Yale University Press, 1997).

38. James Oliver Horton and Lois E. Horton, *In Search of Liberty: Culture, Community, and Protest among Northern Free Blacks, 1700–1860* [New York: Oxford University Press, 1997], 114. In 1860, more than 75 percent of the black female workers in Boston, Buffalo, and Cincinnati were employed as domestic servants.

39. Yee, *Black Women Abolitionists*, 58.

40. *FJ*, April 13, 1827.

41. "Female Influence," *CA*, September 30, 1837.

42. Jennifer Morgan, *Laboring Women: Reproduction and Gender in New World Slavery* (Philadelphia: University of Pennsylvania Press, 2004). See also Deborah Gray White, *Ar'n't I a Woman: Female Slaves in the Plantation South* (1985; New York: Norton, 1999).

43. Rupe Simms, "Controlling Images and the Gender Construction of Enslaved African Women," *Gender and Society* 15 (December 2001): 880.

44. White, *Ar'n't I a Woman*, 27–46.

45. Simms, "Controlling Images," 885.

46. See Patricia Hill Collins, "Mammies, Matriarchs, and Other Controlling Images," in *Black Feminist Thought: Knowledge, Consciousness, and Politics of Empowerment*, 2nd ed. (New York: Routledge, 2000).

47. Hazel V. Carby, *Reconstructing Womanhood: The Emergence of the Afro-American Woman Novelist* (New York: Oxford University Press, 1987), 34–35.

48. Catherine Clinton, "'With a Whip in His Hand': Rape, Memory, and African American Women," in *History and Memory in African American Culture*, ed. Geneviève Fabre and Robert O'Meally (New York: Oxford University Press, 1994), 208.

49. Ronald Walters, *The Antislavery Appeal: American Abolitionism after 1830* (1978; New York: Norton, 1984), 70–76.

50. Carby, *Reconstructing Womanhood*, 23.

51. Welter, "Cult of True Womanhood," 151–52.

52. Gayle T. Tate, *Unknown Tongues: Black Women's Political Activism in the Antebellum Era, 1830–1860* (East Lansing: Michigan State University Press, 2003), 82.

53. *CA*, May 6, 1837.

54. "To the Females of Colour," *Weekly Advocate*, January 7, 1837; emphasis added.

55. Mary Still, *An Appeal to the Females of the African Methodist Episcopal Church*, in *Pamphlets of Protest: An Anthology of Early African American Protest Literature*, ed. Richard Newman, Patrick Rael, and Phillip Lapsansky (New York: Routledge, 2001), 255–57.

56. Joel Schor, *Henry Highland Garnet: A Voice of Black Radicalism in the Nineteenth Century* (Westport, Conn.: Greenwood, 1977), 15.

57. John Mercer Langston, *From the Virginia Plantation to the National Capitol; or, The First and Only Negro Representative in Congress from the Old Dominion* (1894; New York: Kraus, 1969), 142.

58. Wilma King, *African American Childhoods: Historical Perspectives from Slavery to Civil Rights* (New York: Palgrave Macmillan, 2005), 68.

59. James Oliver Horton, "Generations of Protest: Black Families and Social Reform," in *Free People of Color*, 41–51, 48.

60. Melba Joyce Boyd, *Discarded Legacy: Politics and Poetics in the Life of Frances E. W. Harper, 1825–1911* (Detroit: Wayne State University Press, 1994), 36–38.

61. Horton, "Generations of Protest," 41–51.

62. Julie Winch, *A Gentleman of Color: The Life of James Forten* (New York: Oxford University Press, 2002).

63. *CA*, November 9, 1839.

64. John Berry Meachum, *Address to All the Colored Citizens of the United States* (Philadelphia: King and Baird, 1846), 19, 12, 21.

65. Ibid., *Address*, 21.

66. Susan Paul, *Memoir of James Jackson, the Attentive and Obedient Scholar, Who Died in Boston, October 31, 1833, Aged Six Years and Eleven Months*, ed. Lois Brown (1835; Cambridge: Harvard University Press, 2000), 69, 70–71, 104, 67–68.

67. As Rhoda Golden Freeman points out, in a time with rampant poverty and without compulsory education laws, young children may have been sent "to work rather than to the schoolhouse" to supplement a family's income (*The Free Negro in New York City in the Era before the Civil War* [New York: Garland, 1994], 236).

68. Ryan, *Empire of the Mother*, 51.

69. *FJ*, July 13, 1827.

70. Meachum, *Address*, 12, 21.

71. Stewart, "Religion and the Pure Principles," 36.

72. Still, *Appeal*, 257.

73. *Liberator*, July 7, 1832.

74. *Minutes and Proceedings of the Third Annual Convention*, Philadelphia, 1833, 15–16, 18, in *NNC*.

75. Ryan, *Empire of the Mother*, 63–64.

76. Meachum, *Address*, 44, 13–14.

77. *NS*, March 16, 1849.

78. *FJ*, August 3, 1827.

79. Horton, "Freedom's Yoke," 104.

80. *NS*, December 1, 1848.

81. "Family Worship," *Liberator*, September 8, 1832.

82. Ibid.

CHAPTER FIVE. Transnationalism, Revolution, and the *Anglo-African Magazine* on the Eve of the Civil War

1. "Apology (Introductory)," *AAM*, January 1859, 4; Elizabeth McHenry, *Forgotten Readers: Recovering the Lost History of African American Literary Societies* (Durham: Duke University Press, 2002), 137; John Ernest, *Liberation Historiography: African American Writers and the Challenge of History, 1794–1861* (Chapel Hill: University of North Carolina Press, 2004), 305–6.

2. "Apology (Introductory)," *AAM*, January 1859, 3.

3. As William Caleb McDaniel has recently demonstrated, white Garrisonian abolitionists also interpreted political events in Europe in light of the abolitionist movement ("Our Country Is the World: Radical American Abolitionists Abroad" [Ph.D. diss., Johns Hopkins University, 2006]).

4. For examples of northern free black writers who claimed this revolutionary tradition as their own, see Benjamin Quarles, "Antebellum Free Blacks and the 'Spirit of '76,'" *Journal of Negro History* 61 (July 1976): 229–42; Elizabeth Rauh Bethel, *The Roots of African-American Identity: Memory and History in Antebellum Free Communities* (New York: St. Martin's, 1997); Patrick Rael, *Black Identity and Black Protest in the Antebellum North* (Chapel Hill: University of North Carolina Press, 2002), 257–59.

5. William C. Nell, *The Colored Patriots of the American Revolution, with Sketches of Several Distinguished Colored Persons: To Which Is Added a Brief Survey of the Condition and Prospects of Colored Americans* (1855; New York: Arno, 1968).

6. William C. Nell, "Colored American Patriots," *AAM*, January 1859, 30–31.

7. Manisha Sinha, "An Alternative Tradition of Radicalism: African American Abolitionists and the Metaphor of Revolution," in *Contested Democracy: Freedom, Race, and Power in American History*, ed. Manisha Sinha and Penny von Eschen (New York: Columbia University Press, 2007), 9–30; Rael, *Black Identity and Black Protest*, 255–66.

8. "Letter 1 from a Man of Colour," *FJ*, February 22, 1828.

9. *National Anti-Slavery Standard*, October 30, 1845, in *BSC*, 41.

10. Frederick Douglass, "What to the Slave Is the Fourth of July?," in *Lift Every Voice: African American Oratory, 1787–1900*, edited by Philip S. Foner and Robert James Branham (Tuscaloosa: University of Alabama Press, 1998), 246–68; David Walker, *David Walker's Appeal to the Coloured Citizens of the World*, ed. Peter P. Hinks (University Park: Pennsylvania State University Press, 2000), 78.

11. Douglass, "What to the Slave Is the Fourth of July?," 258.

12. Sinha, "Alternative Tradition of Radicalism."

13. "Cinque," *CA*, March 27, 1841, http://www.accessible.com/accessible/print?AADocList=15&AADocStyle=STYLED&AAStyleFile=&AABeanName=toc1&AANextPage=/printFullDocFromXML.jsp&AACheck=3.38.15.2.1 (accessed September 10, 2010).

14. Henry Highland Garnet, "Address to the Slaves of the United States of America," in *BAPC*, 5:548.

15. Frederick Douglass, "The Heroic Slave" (1852), in Ronald T. Takaki, *Violence in the Black Imagination: Essays and Documents* (New York: Putnam, 1972), 37–38.

16. For a discussion of the northern free black interpretation of the Haitian Revolution, see Alfred N. Hunt, *Haiti's Influence on Antebellum America: Slumbering Volcano in the Caribbean* (Baton Rouge: Louisiana State University Press, 1988), 98–101; Bethel, *Roots of African-American Identity*; Rael, *Black Identity and Black Protest*, 222–26; Sinha, "Alternative Tradition of Radicalism," 21–23; Matthew J. Clavin, *Toussaint Louverture and the American Civil War: The Promise and Peril of a Second Haitian Revolution* (Philadelphia: University of Pennsylvania Press, 2010), chapter 6.

17. "Juan Placido," *NS*, December 7, 1849, http://www.accessible.com/accessible/nt?AADocList=11&AADocStyle=&AAStyleFile=&AABeanName=toc1&AANextPage=/printFullDocFromXML.jsp&AACheck=1.12.11.9.1 (accessed September 13, 2010). For information on Plácido and his importance to black American abolitionists, see Ifeoma Kiddoe Nwankwo, *Black Cosmopolitanism: Racial Consciousness and Transnational Identity in the Nineteenth-Century Americas* (Philadelphia: University of Pennsylvania Press, 2005), 48–80.

18. For northern blacks' interpretations of the Exodus story, see Eddie Glaude Jr., *Exodus!: Religion, Race, and Nation in Early Nineteenth-Century Black America* (Chicago: University of Chicago Press, 2000).

19. Wilson Jeremiah Moses, *Black Messiahs and Uncle Toms: Social and Literary Manipulations of a Religious Myth* (University Park: Pennsylvania State University Press, 1982), 46.

20. Nathaniel Paul, "An Address, Delivered on the Celebration of the Abolition of Slavery, in the State of New-York, July 5, 1827," 19, in *Negro Protest Pamphlets*, ed. Dorothy Porter (New York: Arno, 1969).

21. Maria Stewart, "Religion and the Pure Principles of Morality, the Sure Foundation on Which We Must Build," *Liberator*, October 8, 1831, in *Maria W. Stewart, America's First Black Woman Political Writer*, ed. Marilyn Richardson (Bloomington: Indiana University Press, 1987), 28–41. Richardson cites Luke 16:19 and Psalms 37:35 as Stewart's biblical sources for this passage.

22. David Walker, *David Walker's Appeal* (1830; Baltimore: Black Classic, 1993), 50.

23. *CA*, February 27, 1841.

24. "A Meeting of Congratulation," *CA*, April 17, 1841.

25. Nell, "Colored American Patriots," 30–31.

26. *Provincial Freeman*, January 19, 1856.

27. Arthur Dessalines Langston was named by his parents in honor of "the great Haytian hero" (John Mercer Langston, *From the Virginia Plantation to the National Capitol; or, The First and Only Negro Representative in Congress from the Old Dominion* [1894; New York: Kraus, 1969], 157).

28. For a discussion of the relationship between this rhetoric and slave rescues, see Stanley Harrold, *The Rise of Aggressive Abolitionism: Addresses to the Slaves* (Lexington: University Press of Kentucky, 2004), chapter 5.

29. John Mercer Langston, "The Oberlin Wellington Rescue," *AAM*, July 1859, 212.

30. Howard Holman Bell, *A Survey of the Negro Convention Movement, 1830–1861* (New York: Arno, 1969), 120.

31. Mitch Kachun, *Festivals of Freedom: Memory and Meaning in African American Emancipation Celebrations, 1808–1915* (Amherst: University of Massachusetts Press, 2006), 75–77.

32. William J. Watkins, *Our Rights as Men: An Address Delivered in Boston, before the Legislative Committee on the Militia, February 24, 1853, by William J. Watkins, in Behalf of Sixty-Five Colored Petitioners, Praying for a Charter to Form an Independent Military Company*, 11, in *Negro Protest Pamphlets*, ed. Porter.

33. *Provincial Freeman*, September 8, 1855, in *BAPC*, 9:824.

34. *WAA*, September 24, 1859.

35. Watkins, *Our Rights as Men*, 4.

36. Mitch Kachun, "'Our Platform Is as Broad as Humanity': Transatlantic Freedom Movements and the Idea of Progress in Nineteenth-Century African American Thought and Activism," *Slavery and Abolition* 24 (December 2003): 1–23.

37. Shane White, *Stories of Freedom in Black New York* (Cambridge: Harvard University Press, 2002), 195.

38. *NS*, August 21, 1848.

39. *Report of the Proceedings of the Colored National Convention*, Cleveland, 1848, 12, in *NNC*.

40. Gilbert Osofsky, "Abolitionists, Irish Immigrants, and the Dilemmas of Romantic Nationalism," *American Historical Review* 80 (October 1975): 889–912.

41. *BAP*, 4:68–72. The quotation is from "The Place to Die," by Michael J. Barry (1817–89), an Irish poet and magistrate. The poem was originally published in the September 28, 1844, issue of the *Dublin Nation*.

42. See John W. Oliver, "Louis Kossuth's Appeal to the Middle West—1852," *Mississippi Valley Historical Review* 14 (March 1928): 481–95; Timothy M. Roberts, "'Revolutions Have Become the Bloody Toy of the Multitude': European Revolutions, the South, and the Crisis of 1850," *Journal of the Early Republic* 25 (Summer 2005): 259–83; Donald Spencer, *Louis Kossuth and Young America: A Study of Sectionalism and Foreign Policy, 1848–1852* (Columbia: University of Missouri Press, 1977).

43. David Brion Davis, "The Struggle to Preserve a Revolutionary America," in *Revolutions: Reflections on American Equality and Foreign Liberations* (Cambridge: Harvard University Press, 1990), 57–85.

44. Quarles, "Free Blacks," 241.

45. George T. Downing, "May Hungary Be Free," in *The Voice of Black America: Major Speeches by Negroes in the United States, 1797–1971*, ed. Philip S. Foner (New York: Simon and Schuster, 1972), 103; Spencer, *Louis Kossuth and Young America*, 76–77.

46. William F. Cheek and Aimee Lee Cheek, *John Mercer Langston and the Fight for Black Freedom, 1829–1865* (Urbana: University of Illinois Press, 1989), 187.

47. *BAP*, 4:113–15.

48. *NS*, August 21, 1848.

49. *Minutes of the State Convention of the Colored Citizens of Ohio, Convened at Columbus, Jan. 15th, 16th, 17th, and 18th, 1851*, in *BAP*, 4:74–80.

50. Samuel Ringgold Ward, *Autobiography of a Fugitive Negro: His Anti-Slavery Labours in the United States, Canada, and England* (1855; New York: Arno, 1968), 166–68.

51. *BAP*, 4:69.

52. *NS*, August 21, 1848.

53. John Russwurm, "The Condition and Prospects of Haiti" (1826), in *Lift Every Voice*, ed. Foner and Branham, 101–4.

54. *NS*, June 8, 1848.

55. William Wells Brown, "A Lecture Delivered before the Female Anti-Slavery Society of Salem, at Lyceum Hall, November 14, 1847," in *BAPC*, 5:520–21.

56. *NS*, June 8, 1848.

57. Frances Ellen Watkins letter, October 20, 1854, in *A Brighter Coming Day: A Frances Ellen Watkins Harper Reader*, ed. and intro. Frances Smith Foster (New York: Feminist Press, 1990), 45.

58. *BAP*, 4:69.

59. Ellen NicKenzie Lawson and Marlene D. Merrill, comps., *The Three Sarahs: Documents of Black Antebellum College Women* (Lewiston, N.Y.: Mellen, 1985), 49–50.

60. *Proceedings of the State Convention of Colored Men, Held in the City of Columbus, Ohio, January 16th, 17th, and 18th, 1856*, in BSC, 313–14.

61. Osborne P. Anderson, *A Voice from Harper's Ferry: A Narrative of Events at Harper's Ferry; with Incidents Prior and Subsequent to Its Capture by Captain Brown and His Men* (1861; Freeport, N.Y.: Books for Libraries, 1972), 5–6.

62. Wilson is listed as a delegate in the *Proceedings of the Colored National Convention*, Rochester, 1853, 5, in NNC; *The National Convention of the Colored Men of America*, Washington, D.C., 1869, in *Proceedings of the Black National and State Conventions, 1865–1900*, ed. Philip S. Foner and George E. Walker (Philadelphia: Temple University Press, 1986), 349. Wilson is listed as a New Jersey delegate to the 1869 national convention.

63. Ethiop, "Afric-American Picture Gallery," *AAM*, February 1859, 53.

64. Ibid., July 1859, 218, March 1859, 87.

65. Ibid., March 1859, 87.

66. *Frederick Douglass's Paper*, March 11, 1853, in BAPC, 8:164.

67. Ibid., March 25, 1853, 183.

68. Ethiop, "Afric-American Picture Gallery," *AAM*, March 1859, 87.

69. Ibid., October 1859, 321–24.

70. Ibid., March 1859, 90.

71. Ibid., July 1859, 217.

72. Ibid., February 1859, 53.

73. Martin R. Delany, *Blake; or, The Huts of America*, ed. Floyd Miller (1859; Boston: Beacon, 1970), 83, 112–13, 192–95, 224.

74. "Patrick Brown's First Love," *AAM*, September 1859, 286–88; Delany, *Blake*, 177–82.

75. "Female Influence," *CA*, September 30, 1837.

76. Delany, *Blake*, 192.

77. *AAM*, September 1859, 287.

78. However, because African Americans not only were outnumbered by the white population but also generally lived under constant surveillance and without the free means of communication required "to insure concert of action," the Canadian emigrants could not endorse the "sacred cause of Revolution" (*Minutes and Proceedings of the General Convention, for the Improvement of the Colored Inhabitants of Canada, Held by Adjournments in Amherstburgh, C.W., June 16th and 17th, 1853*, in BAPC, 8:303.

79. Ethiop, "The Anglo-African and the African Slave Trade," *AAM*, September 1859, 286.

80. Quoted in Bethel, *Roots of African-American Identity*, 20.
81. Delany, *Blake*, 193.

Epilogue

1. *Christian Recorder*, July 12, 1862.
2. *WAA*, August 24, 1861, in *BAPC*, 13:709.
3. *Douglass' Monthly*, May 1861; Dudley Taylor Cornish, *The Sable Arm: Black Troops in the Union Army, 1861–1865* (Lawrence: University Press of Kansas, 1987), 4.
4. *WAA*, January 25, 1862, in *BAPC*, 14:87.
5. Joseph E. Williams to Elisha Weaver, *Christian Recorder*, August 15, 1863, in *BAPC*, 14:1012.
6. Between 180,000 and 200,000 African American men joined the Union Army, roughly 10 percent of the total Union soldiers. A total of 68,178 of these African American soldiers died—2,751 killed in action and the rest classified as missing in action or as perishing from wounds or disease (David Blight, *Frederick Douglass' Civil War: Keeping Faith in Jubilee* [Baton Rouge: Louisiana State University Press, 1989], 164; Cornish, *Sable Arm*, 288).
7. Matthew J. Clavin, "American Toussaints: Symbol, Subversion, and the Black Atlantic Tradition in the American Civil War," *Slavery and Abolition* 28 (April 2007): 87–113.
8. Quoted in Daniel Payne, *Recollections of Seventy Years* (1888; New York: Arno, 1968), 52, 53.
9. Edwin Redkey, ed., *A Grand Army of Black Men: Letters from African-American Soldiers in the Union Army, 1861–1865* (Cambridge: Harvard University Press, 1992), 24.
10. *WAA*, February 1, 1862, in *BAPC*, 14:101.
11. Leon Litwack, *Been in the Storm So Long: The Aftermath of Slavery* (New York: Random House, 1980), 456–57.
12. *National Equal Rights League Convention*, Cleveland, 1865, in *Proceedings of the Black National and State Conventions, 1865–1900*, ed. Philip S. Foner and George E. Walker (Philadelphia: Temple University Press, 1986), 56.
13. Clarence Walker, *Rock in a Weary Land: The African Methodist Episcopal Church during the Civil War and Reconstruction* (Baton Rouge: Louisiana State University Press, 1982), 50; Wilson Jeremiah Moses, *Black Messiahs and Uncle Toms: Social and Literary Manipulations of a Religious Myth* (University Park: Pennsylvania State University Press, 1982), 67. The African Methodist Episcopal Church sent seventy-seven missionaries to the South between 1863 and 1870. While many northern blacks came south as church missionaries and teachers, Litwack and Foner also find them to be important supporters

of freedmen's and freedwomen's early political efforts. See Litwack, *Been in the Storm So Long*, 509–10; Eric Foner, *Reconstruction: America's Unfinished Revolution, 1863–1877* (New York: Harper and Row, 1988), 286.

14. In his study of freedmen and freedwomen immediately after the Civil War, Litwack points out the presence of Tunis Campbell (Massachusetts to Georgia), Richard Cain (Virginia to Connecticut to South Carolina), Francis Cardozo (South Carolina to Connecticut to South Carolina), Jonathan Wright (Pennsylvania to South Carolina), and Martin Delany (Pennsylvania to South Carolina), all of whom moved to the South during and after the Civil War (*Been in the Storm So Long*, 509–10). Foner notes that moving to the South provided African Americans with a greater possibility of personal advancement while working for the political rights of the race (*Reconstruction*, 286).

15. Blight, *Frederick Douglass' Civil War*, 195–96. Foner asserts that these ideas "anticipated the fully developed conservative ideology associated with Booker T. Washington that would emerge in the post-Redemption South" (*Reconstruction*, 546).

INDEX

abolition of slavery, in the North, 10, 66
Address to All the Colored Citizens of the United States (Meachum), 11–12, 33, 44, 101–5
advice literature. *See* conduct discourse; domestic discourse
"Afric-American Picture Gallery" (Wilson), 124–27
African diaspora, 4, 114–17, 129–31
alcohol consumption, anxieties about, 49–50
Aldridge, Ira, 57, 125
Allen, Richard, 107, 125
American Colonization Society, 45, 89, 119
American Moral Reform Society, 5–6, 51–52
American Revolution, as incomplete, 112–17
Amistad (ship). *See* Joseph Cinque
Anderson, Osborne P., 123–24
Anglo-African Magazine, 4, 109–12, 124–25, 129–31
aspiring classes, of free blacks, 1, 7–9; antislavery consciousness, 22–24; economic insecurity, 15–16
Attucks, Crispus, 112, 125
Autobiography of a Fugitive Negro (Ward), 37–40

Ball, Charles, 69–70
Bibb, Henry, 3, 56–57, 59; on enslaved fathers, 66; on free black marriages, 88; on remembering slavery, 67–68; on slave marriages, 71, 76–77
black conventions, national, 5–6, 52; convention of 1831, on respectability, 21; convention of 1831, on urban conditions, 44; convention of 1833, on temperance, 104; convention of 1843, on Garnet's "Address to the Slaves," 64, 114; convention of 1848, on the French Revolution, 118; convention of 1848, on male independence, 46; convention of 1848, on occupations, 42–43; convention of 1853, 125; convention of 1869, 125
black conventions, state: New York State Convention of 1840, on respectability, 54; New York State Convention of 1845, on the American Revolution, 113; Ohio State Convention of 1851, on revolutionaries, 120; Ohio State Convention of 1852, on respectability, 34; Ohio State Convention of 1856, on revolutionaries, 123
blackface minstrelsy, 24–25
black nationalism, 6. *See also* emigration
Blake, or the Huts of America (Delany), 127–29, 131
Blyden, Edward Wilmot, 109
"bobalition" broadsides, 24
Brown, William Wells, 38, 59, 127, 134; on remembering slavery, 67; on

Brown, William Wells (*continued*)
self-made men, 56–57; on slave marriages, 70–71; on Virginius, 122

Cary, Mary Ann Shadd, 6, 20, 101, 109
Child, Lydia Maria, 90
Christianity: divine retribution, 114–15; racial responsibility, 21–22; and the Second Great Awakening, 31; and self-help, 32–33; and sinfulness of slavery, 71–72
Christian Recorder, The, 99; on the Civil War, 132–33
Cinque, Joseph, 4, 113–14, 116
Civil War, 131–35
Clay, Edward, 24–26, 29, 96–97
Colored Patriots of the American Revolution (Nell), 54, 112
conduct discourse, 2–3, 7, 12–13, 14–15, 35–36; in newspapers 13–14, 19–21. See also black conventions; slave narratives
Cornish, Samuel E., 27
Craft, William and Ellen: on abuse of enslaved women, 76; on motherhood, 70
Crandall, Prudence, 25–27, 58
Creole (ship). See Madison Washington
Crummell, Alexander, 134

Day, William Howard, 120
Delany, Martin, 2, 30, 109, 133–34; *Blake, or the Huts of America*, 127–29, 131; on effects of slavery, 78; on emigration, 46; on enslaved families, 64; on home as an antislavery space, 92–93; on ideal wives, 91; on occupations, 43; on the political significance of the family, 105; on self-made men, 56; on slave suicides, 121–22

Dessalines, Jean-Jacques, 4. See also revolutionaries
domestic discourse, 3–4; on childrearing, 100–106; on courtship 85–87; for wives, 89–93. See also marriage
Douglas, Hezekiah Ford, 120, 133
Douglass, Frederick, 2–3, 16, 38, 92, 127, 134; on education, 58; on enslaved children, 65; "The Heroic Slave," 114; on independence, 78, 88; on the *North Star*, 20; on prejudice, 27; on self-made men, 55–56, 59–61; "What to the Slave is the Fourth of July?," 113
Douglass, Sarah Mapps, 3, 23, 28, 109; on education, 58; on home and family, 106–8
Downing, George, 119
Dred Scott v. Sanford, 16, 111
Durham, Jeremiah, 72, 92

Easton, Hosea, 27; on effects of slavery, 73–74; on prejudice, 18–19
education, attitudes toward, 57–58, 90–91
"Ellen." See female influence
emigration, 6, 45–46, 111, 129–30
"Ethiop." See William J. Wilson

family, political significance of, 75–76, 81–85, 92–93, 106–8. See also marriage
female influence, 93, 95; and activism, 99–100; democratization of, 94–98
Finney, Charles Grandison, 31
Forten, Charlotte (Mrs. Francis J. Grimké), 10, 23, 38, 134
Forten, James, 23, 101, 125; *Letters from a Man of Colour*, 112–13; on prejudice, 28
Forten, Robert, 133
free blacks, northern: 10–11; working

class, 6, 41. *See also* aspiring classes of free blacks
fugitive slave law of 1850, 35, 77, 111, 118, 123

Garner, Margaret, 127
Garnet, Henry Highland, 25–27, 53, 57, 92, 100, 134; "Address to the Slaves," 64, 67, 72, 80, 114; on self-help, 32
Garrison, William Lloyd, 69. See also *Liberator*

Haitian Revolution. *See* revolutionaries
Hamilton, Thomas, 124, 133; on *Incidents in the Life of a Slave Girl*, 79. See also *Anglo-African Magazine*
Harper, Frances Ellen Watkins, 100–101, 109, 123, 134; on courtship, 85
Henry, Patrick, 113–14
home. *See* family

Incidents in the Life of a Slave Girl (Jacobs), 62–63, 79
independence (male), anxieties about, 50–51, 78

Jacobs, Harriet, 3, 65–66, 92; on family bonds, 69; *Incidents in the Life of a Slave Girl*, 62–63, 79; on sexual abuse of enslaved women, 72–73, 77–78
Jefferson, Thomas, 113–14, 125
Jennings, Elizabeth, 19
Jezebel, 96–98
Jocelyn, Simeon, 25
Johnson, H. N., 118, 120

Keckley, Elizabeth, 72–73
kidnapping, of free blacks, 68–70
Kossuth, Louis, 4, 119–20, 124. *See also* revolutionaries

landownership, attitudes toward, 43–45
Langston, Charles Henry, 116
Langston, John Mercer, 100, 116, 134
Letters from a Man of Colour (Forten), 112–13
Liberator, 13, 38; on enslaved families, 63–64; on wives, 89–90
literary societies, 10, 15, 38, 53–54
Loguen, Jermain W., 55, 59, 134
Louverture, Toussaint, 4, 32, 114, 125, 133. *See also* revolutionaries

market revolution, 12
marriage, political significance of, 87–93. *See also* republicanism
Mazzini, Giuseppe, 4, 120
Meachum, John Berry: *Address to All the Colored Citizens of the United States*, 11–12, 21; on childrearing, 101–5; on landownership, 44; on respectability, 33
middle class: on childrearing, 65; emergence of, 12. *See also* aspiring classes of free blacks
military companies, 117
missionaries, 134
morality, male, anxieties about, 47–51

Nell, William Cooper, 101; *Colored Patriots of the American Revolution*, 54, 112; on respectability, 22–23, 34
newspapers, African American. *See* conduct discourse
Northup, Solomon, 60–61; *Twelve Years a Slave*, 55, 69, 81–83, 106

occupations, male, attitudes toward, 42–43

Paul, Nathaniel, 22, 115
Paul, Susan, 2, 101; on childrearing, 102–3

Paul, Thomas, 101
Payne, Daniel Alexander, 109
Pennington, James W. C., 3, 88; on activism, 59; on enslaved children, 65; on remembering slavery, 68; on self-made men, 55–57; on sexual abuse of enslaved women, 71
Plácido. *See* Gabriél de la Concepción Valdes
prejudice, 16–19, 25–28
Prigg v. Pennsylvania, 68
print culture, 2–4, 12–15
Prosser, Gabriel, 114, 128
Purvis, Robert, 5–6, 52, 115

Ray, Charles B., 52; on women's education, 91
Remond, Charles L., 134
republicanism, 41–46, 75, 87–88
respectability, 1–2, 7–8, 29–30, 34–36; and black nationalism, 5–6
revolutionaries: admiration for, 4, 114–17, 122–24, 129–31; European, 117–21; Haitian, 114, 126. *See also* American Revolution
Rock, John, 130
Ruggles, David, 57, 88; on male morality, 48
rural life. *See* landownership
Russworm, John, 19–20

Salem, Peter, 112
segregation. *See* prejudice
self-improvement, 3, 29–34
self-made men, 40–41, 55–60, 134
Sketches of the Higher Classes of Colored Society in Philadelphia (Willson), 7–8, 18–19
slave narratives: as conduct discourse, 3; on education, 57–58; on enslaved children, 63–66; on family bonds, 66–69, 79–80; on male dependence, 61, 74–78; on marriage, 70–71, 76, 88–89; on self-fashioning, 54–57, 59–60; on sexual abuse, 71–73, 76–78
Smith, James McCune, 109; on family bonds, 69; on self-made men, 55, 59–60; slavery's effects, 76
Stanley, Sara, 123
Steward, Austin, 31; on rural life, 44–45
Stewart, Maria: on childrearing, 103; on divine retribution for slavery, 115; on housewifery, 90; on male morality, 48, 50; on self-improvement, 33
Still, Mary, 99–100
Stowe, Harriet Beecher, *Uncle Tom's Cabin*, 82, 116
suicide, slaves, 121–22

Tappan, Arthur, 25
theater, anxieties about, 49
true womanhood, 47, 98. *See also* female influence
Truth, Sojourner, 31; on remembering slavery, 66–67
Turner, Nat, 80, 114, 124–25, 127–28
Twelve Years a Slave (Northup), 55, 60–61, 69, 81–83, 106

Uncle Tom's Cabin (Stowe), 82, 116
uplift, 1, 6–7, 9

Valdes, Gabriél de la Concepción, 114, 131
Vesey, Denmark, 80, 114, 124, 128
Virginius, 32, 122, 124, 129

Walker, David, 33, 113, 115
Ward, Samuel Ringgold, 2–4, 8, 59, 68–69, 90, 92; *Autobiography of a Fugitive*

Negro, 37–40; on effects of slavery, 78; on prejudice, 27–28; on respectability, 34; on revolutionaries, 120; self-made men, 56–57
Washington, George, 107, 113–14, 125
Washington, Madison, 80, 113–14, 120, 124
Watkins, William, 100
Wheatley, Phillis, 125
Whipper, William, 4–5, 52
Williams, Peter, 25
Willson, Joseph: on prejudice, 18–19; on respectability, 7–8; *Sketches of the Higher Classes of Colored Society in Philadelphia*, 7–8, 18–19
Wilson, William, J., 124–27, 130; "Afric-American Picture Gallery," 124–27
women, enslaved, 95–96, 98; fictional representations of, 128–29
Woodson, Lewis: on education, 91; on male morality, 48, 52
Wright, Theodore S.: on prejudice, 17–18; on racial responsibility, 22

"Zillah." *See* Sarah Mapps Douglass

RACE IN THE ATLANTIC WORLD, 1700–1900

The Hanging of Angélique: The Untold Story of Canadian Slavery and the Burning of Old Montréal
by Afua Cooper

Christian Ritual and the Creation of British Slave Societies, 1650–1780
by Nicholas M. Beasley

African American Life in the Georgia Lowcountry: The Atlantic World and the Gullah Geechee
edited by Philip Morgan

The Horrible Gift of Freedom: Atlantic Slavery and the Representation of Emancipation
by Marcus Wood

The Life and Letters of Philip Quaque, the First African Anglican Missionary
edited by Vincent Carretta and Ty M. Reese

In Search of Brightest Africa: Reimagining the Dark Continent in American Culture, 1884–1936
by Jeannette Eileen Jones

Contentious Liberties: American Abolitionists in Post-Emancipation Jamaica, 1834–1866
by Gale L. Kenny

We Are the Revolutionists: German-Speaking Immigrants and American Abolitionists after 1848
by Mischa Honeck

The American Dreams of John B. Prentis, Slave Trader
by Kari J. Winter

Missing Links: The African and American Worlds of R. L. Garner, Primate Collector
by Jeremy Rich

Almost Free: A Story about Family and Race in Antebellum Virginia
by Eva Sheppard Wolf

To Live an Antislavery Life: Personal Politics and the Antebellum Black Middle Class
by Erica L. Ball

www.ingramcontent.com/pod-product-compliance
Lightning Source LLC
Chambersburg PA
CBHW011743220426
43666CB00017B/2887